Isolation

Over the nineteenth and twentieth centuries, the mad, the infectious, the deviant and the unfit were categorised and confined to a widening range of isolated places and institutions. There they were subjected to treatment that spanned correction, care and control. Through these practices state agencies and expert authorities refined their efforts to classify and coercively segregate people deemed to be un-desirable or dangerous.

This book examines legally sanctioned strategies of exclusion and segregation undertaken over the last two centuries across a range of national and colonial contexts. In addition to offering new perspectives on the continuum of medico-penal sites of isolation, from the asylum to the penitentiary, contributors examine less well-known sites, from 'leper villages' to refugee camps to Native reserves.

Exclusionary practices took on new forms and meanings in the nineteenth and twentieth centuries, and they continue to raise questions about the relationship between coerced isolation and modernity. Why and how did practices of exclusion proliferate over the modern period, precisely when legal and political concepts of 'freedom' were invented? Why has isolation been such a persistent strategy in liberal and non-liberal nations, in colonial and post-colonial states?

Carolyn Strange teaches at the Centre of Criminology, University of Toronto. She has published on the history of imprisonment, as well as capital and corporal punishment in Canada, the U.S. and Australia. She is the editor of *Qualities of Mercy: Justice, Punishment and Discretion* (University of British Columbia Press, 1996). She is the principal investigator on a collaborative project that studies prison history tourism at Alcatraz, Port Arthur and Robben Island.

Alison Bashford is senior lecturer in the Department of History, University of Sydney. She is author of *Purity and Pollution: Gender, Embodiment and Victorian Medicine* (Macmillan, 1998) and *Imperial Hygiene: A Critical History of Colonialism, Nationalism and Public Health* (Palgrave, forthcoming). She is also co-editor with Claire Hooker of *Contagion: historical and cultural studies* (Routledge, 2001).

Routledge Studies in Modern History

1 Isolation
Places and practices of exclusion
Edited by Carolyn Strange and Alison Bashford

Isolation

Places and practices of exclusion

Edited by Carolyn Strange and Alison Bashford

Routledge
Taylor & Francis Group

LONDON AND NEW YORK

First published 2003 by Routledge
11 New Fetter Lane, London EC4P 4EE

Simultaneously published in the USA and Canada
by Routledge
29 West 35th Street, New York, NY 10001

Routledge is an imprint of the Taylor & Francis Group

Typeset in Baskerville by Taylor & Francis Books Ltd, Printed and bound
in Great Britain by TJ International Ltd, Padstow, Cornwall

British Library Cataloguing in Publication Data
A catalogue record for this book is available from the British Library

Library of Congress Cataloging in Publication Data
Isolation: places and practices of exclusion/ edited by Carolyn Strange
and Alison Bashford
p. cm.
Includes bibliography references and index.
1. Social isolation – History. 2. Segregation–History.
3. Imprisonment – History. 4. Exile (Punishment) – History. 5. Insane –
Commitment and detention – History. 6. Isolation (Hospital Care) –
History. 7. Institutional care – History. I. Strange, Carolyn, 1959– II.
Bashford, Alison, 1963–
HM1131 .I86 2003
302.5'45–dc21   2002036908

ISBN 0–415–30980–8 (hbk)

Contents

Illustrations

Figures

Contributors

Clare Anderson is Lecturer in Economic and Social History at the University of Leicester. She has published a number of chapters and articles on issues relating to the transportation of Indian convicts overseas, and the monograph *Convicts in the Indian Ocean: Transportation from South Asia to Mauritius, 1815–53* (Macmillan, 2000). She is currently writing about colonial interventions on Indian convict bodies, and will publish *Legible Bodies: race, criminality and colonialism in South and Southeast Asia* in 2004.

Alison Bashford is Senior Lecturer in the School of Philosophical and Historical Inquiry, University of Sydney. She is the author of *Purity and Pollution: Gender, Embodiment and Victorian Medicine* (Macmillan, 1998); the co-editor with Claire Hooker of *Contagion: Historical and Cultural Studies* (Routledge, 2001). *Imperial Hygiene: A Critical History of Colonialism, Nationalism and Public Health* (Palgrave, forthcoming) is her next monograph.

Ethan Blue is a doctoral candidate in history at the University of Texas at Austin. He is writing a dissertation on the cultures of punishment in Texas and California in the 1930s and 1940s.

Susan L. Burns is a Professor of History and Asian Studies at the University of Chicago. Her recent publications include 'Constructing the National Body: Public Health and the Nation in Meiji Japan', in Timothy Brook and André Schmid (eds), *Nation Work: Asian Elites and National Identities* (University of Michigan Press, 2000). She is currently completing a monograph on public health in nineteenth-century Japan.

Elise Chenier is a postdoctoral fellow in the Department of History at McGill University in Montreal, Québec where she teaches courses in Canadian and women's history. Her current research concerns débutant balls in twentieth-century French and English Canada. The chapter in this volume draws on research undertaken for her doctoral dissertation, 'Stranger in our midst: male sexual "deviance" in postwar Ontario', Queen's University, 2001.

Harriet Deacon has worked extensively on the history of exclusionary institutions like prisons and leprosy or mental hospitals since 1989. Her PhD thesis was on Robben Island's medical institutions (Cambridge, 1994) and she worked at Robben Island Museum between June 1999 and March 2002. Her other interests include the history of nursing, private practice and midwifery at the Cape in the early nineteenth century, technology and history, and heritage in post-apartheid South Africa.

Randa Farah is an Assistant Professor of Anthropology at the University of Western Ontario. She is also an Associate Researcher at the Refugee Studies Centre (RSC) at the University of Oxford, where she co-teaches a course on Palestinian refugees and the Universal Declaration of Human Rights. She has published on the relationship between memory and identity in Palestinian refugee camps. Her current research, initiated and supervised by the RSC, is on the impact of prolonged conflict and displacement on Sahrawi refugee children.

Mark Finnane is Professor of History and Dean, Postgraduate Education at Griffith University, Brisbane. His principal research interests are in criminal justice history and his books include *Punishment in Australian Society* (Oxford University Press, 1997) and *When Police Unionise: the politics of law and order in Australia* (Institute of Criminology, University of Sydney, 2002).

Paloma Gay y Blasco is a British-trained Spanish anthropologist. Her first book, a feminist analysis of Gypsy life in Madrid, came out in 1999. She is currently preparing her second book on Gypsies and a co-authored monograph on 1930s anthropology. She teaches at Queen's University Belfast, Northern Ireland.

Renisa Mawani is an Assistant Professor of Anthropology and Sociology at the University of British Columbia. Her research interests are in the areas of race, racism and law; post-colonial legal studies/critical race theory; and race, space and law. Her current research explores the interface between medical and penal practices of exclusion through D'Arcy Island, a Chinese leper colony that was established off the coast of Vancouver Island and operative between 1891 and 1924.

John Pratt is a Reader in Criminology at Victoria University of Wellington. He has published extensively in the area of the history and sociology of punishment, including *Punishment in a Perfect Society* (Victoria University Press, 1992), *Governing the Dangerous* (Victoria University Press, 1997), and *Punishment and Civilization* (Victoria University Press, 2002).

Kristin Ruggiero is Associate Professor of History and Director of the Center for Latin American and Caribbean Studies at the University of Wisconsin–Milwaukee. Her current work is entitled 'Modernity in the flesh: medicine, law and society in turn-of-the-century Argentina'. Research for this work was supported by the National Endowment for the Humanities and the National Science Foundation.

Carolyn Strange is an historian who teaches at the Centre of Criminology, University of Toronto. She has authored several books and numerous articles in criminal justice history and is the editor of *Qualities of Mercy: Justice, Punishment, and Discretion* (University of British Columbia Press, 1996). She has published several articles on the management, marketing and practice of prison history tourism at Alcatraz, Port Arthur and Robben Island.

Acknowledgements

The editors wish to thank the contributors for their insights, expertise and commitment to the project. It was funded with assistance from the Associated Medical Services, the Connaught Committee (University of Toronto) and the Social Sciences and Humanities Research Council. This support allowed us to bring the contributors together for a public symposium and a workshop at the University of Toronto in June 2001. Our thanks also go to Bryan Hogeveen and Mickey Cirak, who were valuable assistants prior to and during the symposium, and to Allyson Lunny, who provided her copy-editing skills.

In its earliest guise the introduction was delivered to the History Department at the University of Sydney. We extend our thanks to the seminar participants whose questions helped to sharpen our focus. We are especially grateful for the detailed critical comments we received from our friends and colleagues: Catriona Elder, Joanne Finkelstein, Barbara Sullivan and Lorna Weir. The contributors, and Ethan Blue in particular, provided constructive feedback on the introduction after the workshop.

Finally we wish to thank Joe Whiting, Vanessa Winch and Yeliz Ali at Routledge for their assistance in bringing this collection to fruition.

1 Isolation and exclusion in the modern world

An introductory essay

Alison Bashford and Carolyn Strange

From the transportation of convicts to the moral therapy of the insane, the techniques, rationales, targets and sites of exclusionary practices proliferated over the nineteenth and twentieth centuries. Over this period state agencies and expert authorities refined their efforts to classify and coercively segregate people deemed to be undesirable or dangerous. As a critical project of modern government, 'problem populations' (those categorised as the mad, the infectious, the deviant or the unfit) were confined to specific isolated places, and were subjected to and subjectified by treatments that spanned correction, care and control.

Isolation and exclusion are issues that have inspired a rich tradition of scholarship particularly in sociological and anthropological literature, which examines rituals of inclusion and exclusion, as well as the drawing, maintenance and policing of boundaries between the desirable and undesirable. Exclusion is also examined in psychoanalytic, philosophical and literary studies that explore expressions of self/ other, of alterity, difference and identity.[1] This collection of essays draws upon this multi-disciplinary literature but approaches isolation as an historical exercise of state power. First the chapters concentrate on coercive and legally sanctioned exclusionary strategies as well as the official and unofficial tactics of segregation within places of mandated isolation. Second, the essays focus on the ways in which a range of modern states have implemented and justified multiple means of isolation over the last two centuries.

The political and cultural history of this period raises a number of questions about coercive exclusion. Why has spatial isolation been such a persistent strategy for the management of problem populations in liberal and non-liberal nations, in colonial and post-colonial states? Why did practices of exclusion proliferate over the modern period, precisely when legal and political concepts of 'freedom of movement' and 'liberty' were invented and inscribed? What do places of coerced confinement mean for the authorities that build them and fund them, and for the communities in whose name they are maintained? Finally, how have the isolated themselves reconstituted places of exclusion through contestation and resistance? Moving beyond the conventional historiographical approach of studying only one form of coerced isolation, or one jurisdiction or a short span of time, this collection of essays, ranging from early modern Japanese leprosaria to contemporary 'special colonies' for Spanish Gitanos, provides a wider empirically textured canvas of inquiry.

Practices of exclusion emerged well before the modern period, and are far from limited to Western cultures, as historians and anthropologists have documented. As a result, we know a great deal about the exclusion of lepers outside town walls in medieval Europe,[2] as well as Indian spatial and bodily separations, for example.[3] Other forms of isolation, notably the Jewish ghetto, spanned many centuries, the measures of regulation and restriction refining and changing within local legal systems. Nevertheless, the post-Enlightenment era was a watershed. Over the nineteenth and twentieth centuries definitively modern institutions of confinement emerged: the penitentiary, the asylum, the concentration camp, the training institute.[4]

Scholars working from a variety of disciplinary perspectives have acknowledged the architectural, geographical and micro-managerial continuities between these different institutions of isolation: this is Foucault's famous 'carceral archipelago', the modern reconstitution of the 'Great Confinement'.[5] Yet historians tend to study tactics and sites of coercive exclusion discretely, as though they were separate 'islands' for analysis.[6] Moving beyond this generally compartmentalised approach requires the consideration of carceral institutions (the penitentiary, for example), in concert with other forms of coerced segregation that confine without walls or buildings (such as the Native reserve). Furthermore it requires analysing practices meant to punish and segregate, as well as techniques designed to cure and reintegrate in places of isolation. This is what the articles in this collection do: they leave aside questions about the historical origins of confinement to explore instead how modes of enforced isolation operated, proliferated and hybridised in the modern era, not just in Europe and North America but also in the colonial and non-Western world.

This introductory chapter works at two levels. First, it sets out the political and philosophical context in which practices of exclusions operated in modern polities, and liberal democracies in particular. Second, it shows how the essays in this collection instantiate and elaborate this connection. As social theorist Joel Kahn argues, 'the modern must be understood to be embedded in particular cultural and historical circumstances', neither purely nor exclusively Western.[7] Cutting across modernity's pluralities, however, are three key characteristics of enforced isolation in the modern era: the flexibility of rationales for segregation or confinement, which often move seamlessly between punishment, protection and prevention; the careful consideration of isolation's architectural and spatial dimensions; and the subjectification of the isolated, both the official project of modern exclusion and a crucible for the cultivation of selfhood.

Isolation, modernity and liberalism

What separates moderns from their earlier counterparts or postmodern inheritors is not the impulse to classify and order, but the expectation, will and concerted attempt to order everything.[8] That this utopic vision produced the dystopic Stalinist Soviet system and the Nazi Reich, which segregated and annihilated in the name of political and racial purity, casts a shadow over the study of coercive isolation. While the atrocities of totalitarian regimes have rightly commanded historians' attention, the intellectual association between coercive isolation and authoritarian states can sometimes obscure the history of democratic liberal governments' capacity to rationalise and implement exclusionary places and practices. The nineteenth and twentieth centuries produced the Gulag and the concentration camp, but they also gave us the sanatorium and the refugee camp – places dedicated to protecting and curing, yet employing oppressive measures and restricting movement in order to do so. Alongside the codification and expansion of rights and freedoms in the modern period, liberal democratic states funded more and different ways to isolate people considered a danger to themselves or to others.[9] By the twentieth century, an array of legally mandated exclusionary practices classified and contained not only the bad, the sick and the mad but those deemed racially inferior, the intellectually unfit and, importantly, the *potentially* dangerous.

In the post-Enlightenment West new political imaginings of 'freedom' – the invention of 'liberty' as an inalienable right – created the very possibility of its denial as a new form of punishment. Historians of punishment have established that innovations in exclusionary practices and the proliferation of places of isolation occurred in the nation-states where political philosophies of democratic rights and freedoms first emerged.[10] So, for instance, Philadelphia, the city that preserved the famed Liberty Bell, was also the city that established the model for penitentiaries in the midst of the American Revolution.[11] Confinement became not simply exclusion but the deprivation of newly enshrined freedoms – of movement, association, religion, expression and thought.[12] Precious rights, won through revolutionary struggles, could be stripped away if miscreants failed to obey the law. Once confined in 'laboratories of virtue', it was hoped, criminals would transform into law-abiding citizens.[13] Thus, while methods of coerced isolation have long histories in many cultures, exclusionary practices took on new architectural forms and weighty new meanings in countries where ideals of individual freedom were extolled and where they were constitutionally inscribed.

Historiography on the rise of the welfare state in the West recounts the now-familiar story of governing authorities' unprecedented commitment to the management of individuals and groups identified and classified as requiring care, correction and control. As government agencies assumed responsibility over sectors of life such as education and health, previously the responsibility of families, charities or parishes, isolation was not an aberration from liberal governance but central to its internal logic.[14] Over the nineteenth and twentieth centuries public monies were spent on costly building projects, and the staffing and maintenance of institutions dedicated to long-term isolation of populations requiring reform. As schemes of 'normalisation' were implemented, experts in the new human sciences and the emergent disciplines of psychiatry, state medicine and criminology took on authoritative roles on the basis of their professed abilities to distinguish between the normal and the abnormal or the dangerous, and to classify and isolate people according to novel diagnoses of illness, immorality, criminality and deviance. The 'dangerous' became those who did not deserve, or those who could not be trusted with, the freedoms that responsible and healthy citizens enjoyed. In both liberal and totalitarian regimes, experts and government bureaucrats stretched the definition of 'dangerousness' to capture individuals who had not yet committed offences. Everyone from the disease carrier to the 'pre-delinquent' came to be confinable.

While medical and penal historiography rarely intersect, historical practices of correctionalism within prisons and the punitiveness of medical isolation in modern democracies are often difficult to distinguish. Public health, itself a modern enterprise closely tied to governance of populations was, and in certain contexts still is, an inherently spatialised set of practices. From early quarantine to the eighteenth-century 'medical police' to the health regulation of immigrants at national borders over the twentieth century,[15] the medical and the penal have dovetailed as tactics to define and manage problem populations and as spatial strategies, involving precise geographies of isolation, similar imperatives towards internal segregation, and shared histories of the policing of boundaries of exile and enclosure. Geographically and coercively separating the 'clean' from the 'unclean' in pursuit of the greater health of nations was one formative site where emerging liberal states practised their new and sometimes effectively disputed powers of detention. As a result of what Nikolas Rose has called 'the liberal vocation of medicine',[16] the modern liberal subject emerged in part through the contestation of governments' capacity and right to detain and compulsorily treat the infected separately from the community.

Coerced exclusion is intricately connected with modernity, with citizenship, with territory, with biopolitical governance of national, colonial and post-colonial populations.[17] The proliferation of prisons, asylums, isolation hospitals and racially segregated zones over the nineteenth and twentieth centuries bears witness to the modern state's ambition to track, know and manage populations. In liberal polities this socio-political ordering impulse was tied to the differential distribution of rights: restrictions on the freedom of some were justified by the protection of many others.[18] Thus, as a tool for the improvement and management of irresponsible or undesirable populations, state-implemented isolation sits squarely inside classic liberal problematics of rights and obligations, wherein personal liberties and public benefits are constantly calibrated.

How were these governing objectives balanced and implemented, not only in the West but in those parts of the globe that fell under its expansionist desires in the nineteenth and twentieth centuries? Political theorists note that from its origins, liberalism allowed for despotic rule over individuals and sub-populations deemed to be inadequate or irresponsible, thus either wilfully or not, forfeiting the rights of the liberal subject.[19] As Mitchell Dean argues: 'Liberal rule is completely consistent … with authoritarian rule of colonial societies in which populations are yet to attain the maturity required of the liberal subject.'[20] These general features of legally enforced isolation took on distinct characteristics as modern institutional practices of isolation emerged in Europe and North America and spread to their colonial 'possessions'. In colonies that imagined themselves as 'settler societies', such as nineteenth-century Australia and Canada, modern developments in penal, medical and psychiatric institutional design and management were reproduced along metropolitan models. In African, Asian and South American spheres of colonisation, imperial experts and government agents selected outlying posts for the containment of both indigenous and home countries' problem populations.[21] Western techniques and rationales of exclusion were exported throughout the world, encountering, transforming and accommodating different populations, cultures and histories of isolation in the process. Hybrid practices of exclusion evolved in places with their own cultures of punishment and cure and their own histories of isolation techniques.[22]

The explosion of post-colonial studies and critical race scholarship in recent decades has sharpened criticism of liberal democracies' historic tendency to exclude and spatially contain. As David Goldberg puts it, drawing on the work of Bauman, Balibar and others, race is one of the 'central conceptual inventions of modernity'.[23] The liberal paradox here is that as 'modernity commits itself progressively to idealized principles of liberty, equality and fraternity … there is a multiplication of racial identities and the sets of exclusions they prompt and rationalize, enable and sustain'.[24] Access to rights and citizenship status were routinely denied in avowedly democratic states on the ground of race, both in colonial and metropolitan centres.

The Jewish ghetto or the indigenous reservation provide well-known strategies of coercive ordering of 'others' in the modern era.[25] As medical, psychiatric and penal historians have shown, rationales for exclusion in the nineteenth and twentieth centuries also encompassed concepts of mental or physical 'unfitness' and new notions of 'dangerousness'.[26] Eugenically informed social government was embraced by British Fabians, North American liberals and Swedish social democrats enamoured with the rational project of social engineering. The modern fantasy of ultimate perfection, shared by authorities across political divides, was 'necessarily asymmetrical and thereby dichotomising', Peter Beilharz observes.[27] The institutional and geographical isolation of problem populations was a solution that modern totalitarian, socialist and social welfare states implemented in pursuit of that illusory goal.

To connect isolation strategies under liberal and totalitarian regimes is not to deny significant distinctions between authoritarian and democratic rule, between different modes of isolation, and between distinct rationales and objects of exclusion. Indeed, liberal authorities' provision of grounds for the denial of individual liberties and the prominence of a rhetoric of humanitarian protection flags a deep ambivalence about coerced isolation's awkward fit with democracy. Critics of exclusionary practices, including people forced into isolation, have made good use of liberalism's high ideals of 'liberty', 'rights' and 'freedom'. Retaining its revolutionary heritage, liberalism provides a language of protest, understood and accessible to the excluded and their champions. Historical evidence of formal legal appeals, not to mention humble petitions, confirms the capacity of classical liberal language to contest the legitimacy of forced confinement, if not to liberate those confined against their will.

Rationales of isolation

When Uday Mehta proclaimed that the 'inclusionary pretensions of liberal theory and the exclusionary effects of liberal practices needs to be explained' his prescription was meant for critical scholars.[28] But he also reminds us that policy-makers and experts in modern governments felt compelled to provide credible explanations for their exclusionary practices. Protection, punishment, prevention, cure, correction, restoration and purification were rationales that underwrote the invention and elaboration of exclusionary practices in the nineteenth and twentieth centuries.[29] Although *Isolation* is organised to distinguish between distinct objectives, the chapters simultaneously expose the close connections *between* official objectives. The slippage between seemingly contradictory rationales and their practical inseparability – conceptually, architecturally, administratively, historically – largely accounts for the repeated use and re-invention of coerced exclusion and isolation.

With remarkable constancy the rationale of protection has characterised liberal and especially colonial governance. Many different kinds of populations, particularly indigenous people but also 'pre-delinquent' youth, for example, have been aggregated and spatially contained by governments ostensibly offering protection. Yet forced isolation for such purposes was implemented both to protect the confined and to provide protection *from* the confined, because segregated communities – the mad, the racially 'inferior' or sexual other – have often been conceptualised simultaneously as vulnerable and dangerous to the wider community. It is precisely this clustering and often conflation of vulnerability and danger which drew such intense intervention from the paternal state.

While protective rationales were expounded with vigour in the nineteenth and early twentieth centuries, an older rationale – punishment – was refigured according to utilitarian theories and humanitarian principles. While there is no inherent or automatic relation between punishment and incarceration, as penal historians have clearly shown,[30] the prison as a site of punishment was a penal innovation that developed haltingly over the late eighteenth and early nineteenth centuries. It was only with the rise of the disciplinary society, in Foucault's words, that the deprivation of liberty, the imposition of strict rules, and the techniques of surveillance and segregation came to stand for punishment. Beginning in European metropoles, then expanding to colonial centres, the penitentiary became the iconic image of state-imposed exclusion.[31]

If the penitentiary stands symbolically for incarceration-as-punishment, the confinement or exile of the infected is emblematic of the rationale of prevention. Over many cultures and eras, on both religious and medical grounds, people suffering from leprosy were the objects of elaborate rituals of exclusion. In this collection Burns contrasts early modern Japanese segregation of the leper with the more total modern systems imported from Western medicine and public health. In the case of the leper, and indeed for many of the other non-criminal 'problem populations' we discuss in this volume, penal and medical systems of isolation entwined with damning security, as prevention of contagion came to be an increasingly pressing and persuasive justification for exclusion.

Robert Castel has suggested that confinement-as-prevention was a difficult social problem in the nineteenth century, especially once the *potentially* criminal or the *potentially* infected (the new category of the disease 'carrier') circulated as dangers in the community, too numerous to institutionalise. Partly as a result there was a trend by the later twentieth century away from confinement strategies towards population-level risk-based strategies of prevention.[32] As we show here, what he calls 'traditional confinement' flourished especially at the turn of the century, as the preventive–punitive rationale slid into the 'therapeutic' and even into the 'restorative'. Bacteriological techniques for diagnosis led to intensification and innovation in public health isolation practices – in infectious disease hospitals, in quarantine stations or in homes, always 'for the public good'.[33] Bashford's chapter examines the sanatoria for tuberculosis sufferers that were established in Europe, Britain, North America and Australia in the late nineteenth and early twentieth centuries. She shows how, in concert with preventive segregation, public health detention has also involved installing habits and rules of safe and responsible self-governance into the bodies and souls of the 'dangerous'.

Classically elaborated in the historiography of state punishment in the West, there was a shift in the official objectives of many kinds of isolation, from deterrence and retribution prior to the nineteenth century to the rationales of correction, reform and normalisation by the century's end. A parallel transition occurred in regard to the confinement of the mentally ill. The mid nineteenth-century movement in favour of insane asylums turned on a change from a custodial to a therapeutic rationale. As Finnane shows in his chapter, leading nineteenth- and early twentieth-century psychiatrists hoped to rehabilitate the insane to a state of normalcy compatible with their release: to install 'ruly' self-governance. In the case of psychiatric confinement, more than any other, however, the analytic and historical literature turns constantly on the incarceration–decarceration axis, as mid-twentieth-century critical scholarship – not least Foucault's own work on madness and institutions – helped to produce the general trend towards deinstitutionalisation in many countries.[34]

The rationale of normalisation and reform links the history of isolation and incarceration to longer histories of population management for social order. In the early modern period, institutions of confinement were established for those considered disorderly in one way or another in emerging capitalist economies – beggars, vagabonds, so-called 'wild children'. But as segregative institutions, they not infrequently aimed to restore these people to 'usefulness' because they still belonged to the social body. As Giovanna Procacci has put it: 'Procedures of exclusion are in the end a way of including, not through juridical rules but through social scientific norms. Beyond madness and poverty one can see a process of normalization.'[35] Institutions of confinement, then, have long aimed both to clean up the streets, as it were, *and* to rehabilitate and normalise those confined in the interests of a hegemonic social order. Even the populations banished to the most impermeable and separate places of isolation are still imagined as *belonging* in one way or another to the community that isolated them. This is true of most of the modern places of isolation discussed in this book: the asylum, the sanatorium, the house of deposit, the refugee camp, the policed housing zone. Despite Foucault's own constant return to the processes of exclusion, he stressed that exclusionary practices linked, and mutually defined, the isolated and the isolators: 'Between him and society, an implicit system of obligation was established; he had the right to be fed, but he must accept the physical and moral constraint of confinement.'[36] The articles in this volume reveal the complexity and significance of this relation, and the system of obligation inherent between outside and inside, between isolator and isolated.

Attempts at re-education, correction and reform, of course, frequently fail, in part because of conflicting exclusionary rationales. There is always a tension in these places between the classification and treatment of the confined or exiled population as 'different' and the attempt to rehabilitate, integrate and correct, that is, to 'make-the-same' or normalise. The paradox – segregation and isolation on the ground of difference, with the intention of making-the-same – is dealt with from several fresh angles in this volume. Gay y Blasco discusses the forced relocation and concentration of Roma on the ground of ethnic difference, and then their assimilative education in Spanish urban centres. In her chapter on refugee camps, Farah works through the contested integration–separation axis of exiled Palestinians, in which camp internees, the UN and the Jordanian community are differently placed and have very different ambitions with regard to territory, citizenship and community.

Legally mandated segregation in the modern period has also been rationalised and imagined within a discourse of ethnic and racial purification. Jim Crow laws in the US South and Western Australia's 'Leper Line', for example, signal that racialised strategies of exclusions and separations ranged widely over the nineteenth and twentieth centuries. Although distinct in many ways, the practices undertaken in disparate places of isolation shared significant features. One that stands out is the ubiquity of disease metaphors in liberal languages of isolation. In the modern period, 'difference' has been intensely pathologised in discourses of medicine and psychiatry, the pronouncements of which have underwritten political justifications for segregation.[37] This language of hygiene and contagion crosses over constantly from instances of isolation for the actual control of epidemics – compulsory quarantine, for example – to its always-more-than metaphorical use in eugenic political cultures, of which Nazi Germany stands at the extreme end. What lingers into the early twenty-first century, in places such as refugee camps, is a reified language of purity and integrity, contamination, contact and contagion.[38] As Mawani's chapter on the making and unmaking of an urban Aboriginal reservation indicates, several levels of government drew and redrew literal lines between those who did and did not belong in the white settler society of British Columbia, in part through a language of moral and physical hygiene. Just as the penitentiary wall divided the criminal from the law-abiding, just as the isolation hospital marked the difference between the infected and the healthy, so the borders of Native reservations symbolised the modern era's core distinction between European colonisers and indigenous peoples.

Although historians are drawn to trace shifts over time, what often charac-
terises places of isolation is the co-existence and awkward fit of multiple carceral
objectives. Analysing this tendency requires charting rationales synchronically as
well as chronologically. For example, isolation in a quarantine station in the late
nineteenth century was simultaneously preventive, protective and therapeutic.
Or, from the point of view of policy-makers, a reserve for indigenous people in
the early twentieth century was both a racially purifying strategy and a strategy
that ostensibly protected the indigenous community. And, of course, the same
institution or practice has entirely contradictory significance for the communities
who isolate and the communities who are isolated. The refugee camp or the indigenous reserve, for example, might be protective from the perspective of the
government agency, but illegitimately custodial and punitive from the perspective
of those confined. For indigenous people or refugees, it might also be simultaneously a desirable space-of-belonging and an undesirable, entirely unchosen
space-of-punishment and restriction.

Similarly, this collection's treatment of diverse forms of isolation confirms
how multiple kinds of marked populations, not just criminals inside prisons, have
been subjected to punitive strategies of exclusion. Examination of the crossover
between the penal and the medical, between punishment, protection and
prevention, between means, ends and effects, is what drives this book. For
instance, Kristin Ruggiero shows how the Argentinean 'house of deposit' was
not instituted as a place of punishment for women (indeed, women could enter
voluntarily) yet the segregative move itself, as well as various internal institutional
practices, punished troublesome women confined within its walls. People
excluded in places of care or cure might be punished for failing to follow rules,
or for developing 'dangerous' subcultural allegiances within the confined populations. They might also be punished for transgressing internal spatial order. In
such cases, punishment was a means to keep order within the isolating institution, rather than being the governing rationale for exclusion.

The capacity of exclusionary practices to hold several meanings at once has
made isolation a flexible and effective technique for the management of populations over the modern period. While the aim to protect or improve officially
justified coercive exclusion, unspeakable rationales, which cut right across liberal
principles of freedom, also governed institutions and places of isolation. Thus
while the placement of indigenous peoples on reserves protected them from
unscrupulous colonials, for instance, the seizure of commercially valuable ancestral land could not justify their confinement. Similarly, forms of isolation and
forced modes of treatment within liberal political cultures might render incarceration plausible and tolerable for one sub-population, but entirely intolerable for
other sub-populations (for example, distinctions in the placement and treatment
of Aboriginal and white lepers). It is the case, then, that isolation has proven a
flexible technique for modern states to manage all types of dangers and all kinds
of 'undesirable' people. So far-reaching was this ambition that modern nations
reinvented old forms of isolation and sought out new sites and institutions in
order to fulfil it.

Places of exclusion

Institutional and non-institutional practices of isolation derive their meanings from the geography and social use of sites. They involve place-making – the rendering of certain spaces into undesirable zones of exclusion, or into enclosed sites of confinement and incarceration. The spatiality of isolation is a critical theme in this collection. Drawing on work in cultural geography and adding historical specificity to it,[39] this collection examines how sites of isolation derive their meanings from their physical features (such as islands or wastelands), while exclusionary practices impose new meanings on spaces by design. The erection of buildings, compounds and barriers provides visible evidence of exclusion, but within those sites elaborate internal systems of partitioning produce interior forms of segregation.

Natural geographies have always inspired the planning of exclusionary sites. In the modern period isolation experts combined new architectural styles with geographical features in order to reinforce rationales of exclusion. The integration of natural and culturally produced geographies rendered places *as* isolated. Where the rationale of isolation was punitive – convict colonies, for example – state authorities worked to make places harsh and undesirable in order to deter. While this effect was achieved primarily through the deprivation of liberty itself, as the main form of punishment in the modern period, it was compounded by physical and geographical isolation, frequently involving displacement to a world almost unimaginably far away. Places remote from settled populations were always already cultural when selected as sites for the exclusion and concentration of people. Thus, as Anderson argues in her chapter, the British criminal justice system in India chose the Andaman Islands for convict settlements precisely because they were located over 'the black water', an ocean Indians feared to cross, or so colonial rulers believed. As geographer David Sibley has put it, the 'imaginary geographies' of exclusion put people in social peripheries or spatial peripheries, 'like the edge of the world or the edge of the city'.[40] Once marked by exclusionary practices, sites of isolation were further transformed through cultural representations, story-telling and memorialisation of those places over time.

Despite and, ironically, because of their marginality, sites of isolation capture the imagination and retain the capacity to haunt cultural memory long after internees are released. This is especially the case when categories of citizenship are spatialised and, in the context of isolation, racialised. Nineteenth- and twentieth-century civil authorities and colonial powers produced 'boundaries of rule' not only as 'interior frontiers', as Ann Laura Stoler has shown, but also much more crudely as legally mandated, geographic and architectural exclusion.[41] Built structures and locales of exclusion were sometimes hidden, sometimes obscure, but always highly symbolic of ruling strategies. Robben Island in the apartheid era was one such place of exclusion in a nation deeply scarred by segregations and unfreedoms. Thus, as Deacon shows, it acquired a core role in South Africa's history, lending it a prominent place in the imagining of national identity and security.

The banishment of the undesirable in wastelands is only one means of separating them from the healthy or the law-abiding. Douglas' compelling argument that rituals of purity and danger focus attention on boundaries and on points of contact and separation can be put to work here.[42] If we begin with walls, for example, we appreciate that designers of isolation sites devoted considerable effort to their structure, refinement, functionality and representation. Consider the ha-ha wall, used in mental asylum design. Originally a landscape architecture feature introduced in eighteenth-century aristocratic gardens, it involved erecting a retaining wall at the base of a slope of land, thereby affording the master an unob-structed (visually un-walled) view of his estate. In the nineteenth-century asylum it simultaneously symbolised and concretised the objectives of 'moral therapy' and conveyed the dual meaning of 'asylum'. Imposingly visible from the outside, it was entirely invisible to insiders, for whom the illusion of freedom and space was considered vital to their cure. Indeed the self-concealing ha-ha wall stands for many of our thematic concerns in this book, much in the way that Bentham's Panopticon represented a new mode of power for Foucault. It offered both protec-tion *of* and protection *from* certain populations; it expressed different objectives simultaneously, depending on one's position relative to it, as heterotopic carceral and segregative practices always do.[43]

As the essays in this collection confirm, the nature of barriers and of their policing suggests much about the intention of authorities and how experts imag-ined the confined populations. The object of the penitentiary wall, in contrast to its ha-ha counterpart, was to remind both outsiders and *insiders* that this was a place of coerced isolation, of enforced deprivation of liberty and punishment. Pratt's chapter traces the shifting architectures and changing forms of enclosure of the criminal over the last two centuries. In the eighteenth century, prisons were temporary holding places, more or less indistinguishable from other buildings. Once deprivation of liberty became the standard course of punishment by the mid nineteenth century, escape-deterring walls were erected and grand gates (literal thresholds) were constructed, symbolically attesting to the passage from 'normal' life to a life (up to a life-term) of imprisonment. But even the most rigidly policed and architecturally separate exclusionary places are not impermeable. For instance, maximum-security prisons are open to all kinds of traffic, sanctioned and unsanc-tioned. As Ethan Blue's chapter shows, African-American inmates' prison hip-hop music leaps over and beyond the prison walls, demanding to be heard.

Legally enforced segregation always involves setting borders between insiders and outsiders, but the management of institutions and inmates' own exclusionary principles simultaneously entails the establishment of internal lines of isolation. In modern places of confinement, state authorities separated men, women and children and subdivided captives on the basis of expert diagnoses and legal desig-nations as well as cultural identifications. Nineteenth-century penal institutions, for example, categorised and spatially demarcated inmates according to offence profile but also in regard to habits, such as intemperance. By the twentieth century, finer distinctions were made: paedophiles and other sex offenders were typically kept out of general populations; more recently persons with hepatitis, tuberculosis or AIDS have been subjected to heightened exclusionary regimes. Chenier's chapter discusses the historical practice of 'fairy segregation' in North American prisons over the twentieth century in response to prison administrators' concerns that same-sex prisons engendered homosexuality. In this way, practices of isolation – especially penal and medical isolation – involved the arrangement of bodies-in-space and the regulation of contact between them. The placement of differently gendered, sexualised and racialised embodied individuals *vis-à-vis* each other became a policy obsession in the modern era.

Because places of isolation are also places of concentration, managers and experts have worried constantly, and not unwarrantedly, about the possibility that exclusionary practices might unintentionally increase undesirable behaviours and breed new and unforeseen dangers. Foucault wrote of this with respect to the contagion that was generated by the new institutions of confinement of the early modern period, and which, more easily than the inmates, slipped through the walls and contaminated those outside. His description of what he calls the 'Great Fear' of disease captures not only this literal spread of disease as a result of confine-ment, but also invokes the sense in which metaphors of contagion have been used repeatedly to describe the reproduction of undesirable or dangerous qualities, acts, symptoms, identities and practices in enclosed spaces and institutions of confine-ment. For example, critics of the asylum argued that confining the mad with the mad aggravated insanity rather than cured it. In reformatories and prisons, un-desirable practices like masturbation were reportedly 'caught' and passed on from one inmate to another. In this way, separation and segregation solved some prob-lems (of disease, of crime, of the roving and raving mad) but concentration in space also produced *new* problems specific to the techniques of isolation itself.

Subjectivities

People forced into isolation are rendered objects through exclusionary practices, yet they remain subjects, who claim and remake spaces through patterns of accommodation and resistance. In this dynamic process their identities, and those of their warders, are constituted. Places of isolation take shape in stone and concrete, but they are also built up through relations between individuals and groups.[44] As a growing body of scholarship contends, the relationship between place and identity is reflexive.[45] Cultural geographers and anthropologists in particular have argued that subjectivities are literally grounded but polysemous.[46] All exclusionary practices put individuals and collectivities 'out of place', but modern forms of exclusion aimed further to put people *in* their place in order to protect, cure or reform. The constant spatial and temporal surveillance in places of isolation, combined with intervention over the minutest aspects of daily life, has been driven by the objective to produce desirable subjectivities.

While premodern practices of isolation were concerned primarily with efforts to confine, modern forms have been characterised by a deep investment to remake the excluded into new and improved kinds of selves. The prisoner by the mid nineteenth century had to be incarcerated for decades, not only as a penal substitute for techniques of torture and execution but also to provide sufficient time to correct his criminal tendencies and to render him penitent. Indeed, the stated objective of augmenting individuals' prospects for productive and law-abiding citizenship was critical to allay concerns about the deprivation of individual liberty in liberal democracies.

The confinement of people deemed to be dangerous or undesirable provided governable spaces in which to shape captives' subjectivities. Individuals placed in reformatories or asylums and given new identities, such as 'pre-delinquent' or 'psychiatric case', were there to be worked on. As Foucault noted, modern carceral institutions deployed the 'disciplinary technique', the ultimate product of which was 'a "soul" to be known and a subjection to be maintained'.[47] While not all of the essays here develop Foucauldian literature, his insights inform this collection in two senses. Initially his project was specific enclosure of space, the continuum of modern institutions of confinement, famously, as we have noted, the asylum, the prison, the 'plague town' and the hospital. Subsequently, he turned to the 'self' and its cultivation. But while the latter emerged as a problematic of the former, Foucault's projects never quite folded into one another substantively. That is to say, the techniques of the self he wrote about were not in the main those of the lunatic, the convict or the leper.[48] This is the challenge this collection pursues. Ranging across different national and colonial cultures and across differently rationalised segregations, the essays analyse both the constitution of identity through the exclusion of 'the other', and the cultivation of isolated selves – the subjectification of those within the modern carceral archipelago.

Modern experts certainly imagined that they could shape and monitor the identities of those whom they segregated, but empirical studies based on institutional records and memoires expose the limits on those ambitions. Exclusion produces submission but it also provokes non-compliance at the very least, and organised rebellion at the extreme. The literature of confinement, an artistic form that flourished with the Enlightenment, bears consideration here, for it explores the oppressiveness of isolation in concert with the individual's search for freedom. While fictional works, such as Dickens' *Little Dorrit* (1857), typically treat isolation metaphorically, captives' memoires, such as Oscar Wilde's *De Profundis* (1905), explore the individual's capacity to resist, to defy, to transcend in the grimmest of circumstances.[49] Several of the essays in this volume follow these themes. Even the most alienating forms of isolation have forged disruptive bonds between prisoners, solidified ethnic solidarity and inspired critiques of treatment techniques. Within confined spaces, isolated individuals' subjectivities are as much a product of interaction with fellow confinees as they are a reaction to regimes of control and correction.

Documenting the interior lives of people forced into exclusion is challenging as the historical record privileges authority and expertise. Nevertheless, the contributors to this volume have worked to highlight the subjectivity of people forced into exclusion, as well as those who consented to their isolation (for example, those self-admitted to asylums, sanatoria and houses of deposit). For example, Chenier makes excellent use of confiscated notes sent between male prisoners. These letters revealed more than homosexual desire: they express a capacity to turn their captivity into an opportunity for love: 'You said that you liked what you saw, do you like it well enough to … determine whether you would like to spend the rest of your life, and energy, to help me create a world for you and I?' The essays on current practices of exclusion go even further towards an analysis of subjectivities. Through ethnographic research and oral histories, Farah and Gay y Blasco have listened intently to Palestinians and Gitanos respectively, peoples caught in political struggles and battling attempts to confine them to territories not of their own choosing. Their diasporic identities have become rooted in these new places of exile and exclusion.[50] In these policed places, community identity, expressed in music and dress fashions, for instance, has taken on powerful political meanings for people whose citizen status is unstable and whose legal channels for protest are limited. When these expressions are politicised, as they are in post-colonial struggles for self-determination, or when they are commercialised, as is the case with hip-hop music, they call attention to the subjectivities of people otherwise placed out of sight, out of earshot and out of mind. And they offer a powerful reminder that spaces of isolation are not simply made from above, by legislators, architects, doctors and overseers: they are constantly reshaped by those whom they aim to reform, cure or expel.

A further element of isolation beyond the control of authorities is the distinction the excluded make, not only between themselves and outsiders but among themselves. Institutions of total internal isolation, such as Bentham imagined, were actually rarities, in large measure due to the extraordinary costs associated with solitary confinement. In the modern period internal segregations in places of isolation were officially designated for specific wards or barracks; however, unofficial demarcations of space, produced through captives' alliances and conflicts, also develop, especially in places where people are confined for years on end. In most modern institutions of isolation, hierarchies follow external, culturally inscribed identities, and maintaining boundaries has led to brutal violence. As Chenier documents, prison guards stood by when homophobic male prisoners assaulted and raped men whom they despised as 'fairies'. Thus the authorities are not the only agents who isolate: captives and exiles also impose exclusionary practices on their own self-governing terms.

While some of the excluded, notably Native peoples and lepers, are isolated in perpetuity, if in varying degrees of totality, most populations subjected to confinement experience their seclusion as a passage of time, to be reflected upon after release. Sociological and anthropological work on the history of memory and trauma draws attention to the production of post-isolation consciousness in individuals and groups.[51] Collective identity, solidified through the shared experience of isolation, can challenge disciplinary regimes, but it can also form slowly, reappearing generations after exclusionary places are abandoned. The forced exclusion of indigenous people and racial minorities under imperial rule has been especially productive of politicised post-colonial identities. For instance, *Kala Pani*, a 1958 film about the British practice of transporting Indian prisoners to the Andaman Islands, sparked a transformation in their 'imagined geography' as the symbolic birthplace of resistance to British rule, according to Clare Anderson. More recently, citizens excluded through their own nation's rationales of public health preservation have joined indigenous peoples in seeking redress. In Japan, as Burns discusses, a significant strand of human rights cases in the late twentieth century has been the complaint that the exclusion of Japanese lepers from public life was unjustified.

Securing the legitimacy of exclusionary places is thus a matter both of controlling potentially rebellious inmates and of managing public impressions. State authorities may fail to anticipate how exclusionary practices will later be commemorated or condemned, however they invariably attempt to deflect dissent and curry support while imposing practices of isolation. Each governing authority has its own ways of presenting the public face of exclusion, but some general historical patterns are apparent. For example, the penitentiary replaced the 'spectacle of the scaffold' as democratic governments devised a different way to teach criminals a lesson. Imprisonment registered a new configuration of power throughout the social body (and removed the potential for public displays of disapproval at unpopular executions). Lunatics were unshackled and protected from public view because alienists thought that they could heal them. At the same time, expounding theories of cure proclaimed the important message that therapeutic practices of isolation were the marks of a civilised society. Exclusion is rationalised in legislation and politicians' speeches but it is also legitimated through appeals to public fears and sentiments concerning suffering.[52]

When the non-incarcerated identify with individuals or groups subjected to exclusionary practices, state-imposed and especially non-criminal isolation becomes difficult to justify or maintain. Yet even repressive regimes have been eroded through criticism generated by external human rights groups attempting to universalise democratic ideals. It is difficult to imagine the dismantling of apartheid in South Africa, for example, without the chorus of international calls to release high-profile political prisoners on Robben Island. Occasionally, public protest, as well as political activity and theorising from the site of confinement itself, has successfully exposed practices that taint governments as inhumane and unjust, even as illegitimate by those whom they seek to govern. Liberalism and the idea of democratic rule – most recently through the language of human rights – problematises arbitrary detention, the incarceration of non-criminals and of political prisoners. Thus individual and collective appeals for freedom, justice and equality have sometimes turned sites of isolation inside out.

The collection

In the foregoing discussion we have oriented our study of legally mandated exclusionary practices by examining the diverse historical and theoretical literature on the subject and by charting isolation's rationales and geographies, as well as the subjectivities produced and desired in isolation. While this analytical template might well be applied to any number of historical and contemporary contexts, forced exclusion in the modern period, particularly in liberal regimes, presented peculiar problems of justification and possibilities for resistance. By tracing the intentions and effects of state-mandated isolation in a broad range of Western and colonial contexts, the essays in this collection do the important work of historicising these wider themes.

The chapters move thematically from the most coercive and apparently impermeable places of isolation, to closed institutions designed for care and cure, to more porous forms of exclusion. Essays in the first section analyse the punitive strategies, the changing architectural forms and the geographical placement of prisons, now the archetypal institutions of confinement. In the second section, chapters examine institutions which imposed tight restrictions and elaborate rules but which were governed, ostensibly, according to therapeutic and preventive rationales. The lunatic asylum, the leprosarium, the sanatorium, the 'house of deposit' for unruly women: all were in some senses both refuge and gaol. In the final section, 'Banishment, exile and exclusion', contributors consider non-institutional manifestations of isolation, which were nevertheless legally mandated and highly policed: the refugee camp, the Native reserve, the ethnically segregated housing zone. The chapters in this last section underline the capacity for forced confinement to engender national, racial and community identity and difference, in both desired and unchosen forms.

Notes

1 For example, L. Hagendoorn, 'Ethnic categorization and outgroup exclusion: cultural values and social stereotypes in the construction of ethnic hierarchies', *Ethnic and Racial Studies*, 1993, vol. 16, no. 1, pp. 26–51; R.D. Wilton, 'The constitution of difference: space and psyche in landscapes of exclusion', *Geoforum*, 1998, vol. 29, no. 2, pp. 173–5; E. Grosz, 'Judaism and exile: the ethics of Otherness', in Erica Carter, James Donald and Judith Squires (eds) *Space and Place: Theories of Identity and Location*, London, Lawrence and Wishart, 1993; G. Lee and R. Loveridge (eds) *The Manufacture of Disadvantage: Stigma and Social Closure*, Philadelphia, Open University Press, 1987.

2 F. Bériac, *Histoire des lépreux au Moyen Age: une société d'exclus*, Paris, Éditions Imago, 1988.

3 S. Bayly, *Caste, Society and Politics in India from the Eighteenth Century to the Modern Age*, Cambridge, Cambridge University Press, 1999; On other forms of separation see M. Douglas, *Purity and Danger: An Analysis of Concepts of Pollution and Taboo*, Routledge, London and New York, 1994 [1966]; also M. Douglas, 'Witchcraft and leprosy: two strategies of exclusion', *Man*, 1991, vol. 22, pp. 723–36.

4 On the origins of modern forms of legally enforced confinement, see P. Spierenburg, *The Prison Experience: Disciplinary Institutions and their Inmates in Early Modern Europe*, New Brunswick, Rutgers University Press, 1991; A.T. Scull, *The Most Solitary of Afflictions: Madness and Society in Britain, 1700–1900*, New Haven, Yale University Press, 1993; R. Castel, *The Regulation of Madness: Origins of Incarceration in France*, trans. W.D. Halls, Cambridge, Polity Press, 1988.

5 M. Foucault, *Discipline and Punish: The Birth of the Prison*, trans. A. Sheridan, 2nd edn, New York, Vintage, 1995 [1975]; M. Foucault, *Madness and Civilization: A History of Insanity in the Age of Reason*, New York, Vintage, 1984; A. Still and I. Velody (eds) *Rewriting the History of Madness: Studies in Foucault's Histoire de la folie*, London, Routledge, 1992. For a critical response to the thesis see J.F. Harrington, 'Escape from the Great Confinement: the genealogy of a German workhouse', *Journal of Modern History*, 1999, vol. 71, pp. 308–435.

6 Exceptions include N. Frinzsch and R. Jutte (eds) *Institutions of Confinement: Hospitals, Asylums, and Prisons in Western Europe and North America, 1500–1950*, Cambridge, Cambridge University Press, 1996; and P. Spierenburg, *The Emergence of Carceral Institutions: Prisons, Galleys and Lunatic Asylums, 1550–1900*, Rotterdam, Erasmus Universiteit, 1984.

7 J.S. Kahn, *Modernity and Exclusion*, London, Sage, 2001, pp. 8, 15.

8 Z. Bauman, *Modernity and Ambivalence*, Oxford, Polity, 1991, p. 7.

9 D. Rothman, *Conscience and Convenience: The Asylum and its Alternatives in Progressive America*, Boston, Little, Brown, 1980.

10 N. Morris and D.J. Rothman (eds) *The Oxford History of the Prison: The Practice of Punishment in Western Society*, New York, Oxford, 1997.

11 D.J. Rothman, *The Discovery of the Asylum: Social Order and Disorder in the New Republic*, Boston, Little, Brown, 1990.

12 The timing and culturally specific political forms of liberalism varied widely in the West. See, for example, I. Shapiro, *The Evolution of Rights in Liberal Theory*, Cambridge, Cambridge University Press, 1986; S.F. Englehart and J.A. Moore, Jr, *Three Beginnings: Revolution, Rights, and the Liberal State: Comparative Perspectives on the English, American, and French Revolutions*, New York, P. Lang, 1994; R. Bellamy (ed.) *Victorian Liberalism: Nineteenth-century Political Thought and Practice*, London, Routledge, 1990.

13 M. Meranze, *Laboratories of Virtue: Punishment, Revolution, and Authority in Philadelphia, 1760–1835*, Chapel Hill, University of North Carolina Press, 1996.

14 R.R. Friedmann, N. Gilbert and M. Sherer (eds) *Modern Welfare States: A Comparative View of Trends and Prospects*, New York, New York University Press, 1987.

15 A.M. Stern, 'Buildings, boundaries and blood: medicalization and nation-building on the US–Mexico border, 1910–1930', *Hispanic American Historical Review*, 1999, vol. 79, no. 1, pp. 41–81; A. Bashford, *Imperial Hygiene: A Critical History of Colonialism, Nationalism and Public Health*, London, Palgrave, 2003.

16 N. Rose, 'Medicine, history and the present', in C. Jones and R. Porter (eds) *Reassessing Foucault: Power, Medicine and the Body*, London, Routledge, 1994, p. 65.

17 On the biopolitical, see M. Foucault, *The History of Sexuality: An Introduction*, New York, Penguin, 1987, p. 135ff. On biopolitics and its relations to exclusion, see G. Agamben, *Homo Sacer: Sovereign Power and Bare Life*, Stanford, Stanford University Press, 1998, part 3.

18 J.C. Scott, *Seeing Like a State: How Certain Schemes to Improve the Human Condition Have Failed*, New Haven, Yale University Press 1998.

19 M. Valverde, ' "Despotism" and ethical governance', *Economy and Society*, 1996, vol. 25, no. 2, pp. 357–72.

20 M. Dean, 'Authoritarian governmentality', in *Governmentality*, London, Sage, 1999, p. 133. For a development of this argument, see Dean, 'Liberal government and authoritarianism', *Economy and Society*, 2002, vol. 31, no. 1, pp. 37–61.

21 S. Sen, *Disciplining Punishment: Colonialism and Convict Society in the Andaman Islands*, Oxford, Oxford University Press, 2000; I. Duffield, 'From slave colonies to penal colonies: the West Indians transported to Australia', *Slavery and Abolition*, 1987, vol. 7, no. 1, pp. 24–45. Imperial authorities also imposed racial *cordons sanitaires* between colonial settlers and indigenous people. See B. Bush, *Imperialism, Race, and Resistance: Africa and Britain, 1919–1945*, New York, Routledge, 1999.

22 S. Watts (ed.) *Epidemics and History: Disease, Power, and Imperialism*, New Haven, Yale University Press, 1997.

23 D.T. Goldberg, *Racist Culture: Philosophy and the Politics of Meaning*, Cambridge, Mass., Blackwell, 1993, p. 3.

24 *Ibid.*, p. 6.

25 J. Jervis, *Transgressing the Modern: Explorations in the Western Experience of Otherness*, Oxford, Blackwell, 1999.

26 J. Pratt, 'Dangerousness and modern society', in Mark Brown and John Pratt (eds) *Dangerous Offenders: Punishment and Social Order*, London, Routledge, 2000, pp. 35–48.

27 P. Beilharz, *Zygmunt Bauman, Dialectic of Modernity*, Thousand Oaks, Sage 2000, p. 109.
28 U.S. Mehta, 'Liberal strategies of exclusion', *Politics and Society*, 1990, vol. 18, no. 4, pp. 427–54, p. 427.
29 E. Goffman, *Asylum: Essays on the Social Situation of Mental Patients and Other Inmates*, Harmondsworth, Penguin, 1961. Goffman theorised five distinct isolated populations: harmless people considered incapable of self-care; people unable to care for themselves but who posed unintended threats; people who posed intentional dangers or threats; people in need of training to improve efficiency; and finally people seeking retreat from the world.
30 D. Garland, *Punishment and Welfare: A History of Penal Strategies*, Aldershot, Gower, 1985; M. Feeley and J. Simon, 'The "New Penology": notes on the emerging strategy of corrections and its implications', *Criminology*, 1992, vol. 30, pp. 449–74.
31 Morris and Rothman (eds) *The Oxford History of the Prison*, 'Introduction', p. ix.
32 R. Castel, 'From dangerousness to risk' in G. Burchell, C. Gordon and P. Miller (eds) *The Foucault Effect: Studies in Governmentality*, Chicago, University of Chicago Press, 1991, pp. 283–7.
33 J. Walzer Leavitt, *Typhoid Mary: Captive to the Public's Health*, Boston, Beacon Press, 1996. To the extent that the infected remain subject to forcible confinement in the twentieth century, their isolation is notably in response to fears about 'sexual' diseases in 'dangerous' populations or the confluence of immigration and infectious disease control. See B. McSherry, '"Dangerousness" and public health', *Alternative Law*, 1998, no. 57, pp. 276–80; G.S. Meyer, 'Criminal punishment for the transmission of sexually transmitted diseases: lessons from syphilis', *Bulletin of the History of Medicine*, 1991, vol. 65, pp. 549–64.
34 The historiography and professional literature on psychiatry revolves around the incarceration–decarceration as well as the custodial–therapeutic axis. See, for example, R. Kosky, 'From morality to madness: a reappraisal of the asylum movement in psychiatry, 1800–1940', *Australian and New Zealand Journal of Psychiatry*, 1986, vol. 20, no. 2, pp. 180–7; L.D. Smith, 'Close confinement in a mighty prison: Thomas Blakewell and his campaign against public asylums, 1810–1830', *History of Psychiatry*, 1994, vol. 5, pp. 191–214.
35 G. Procacci, 'Governing poverty: sources of the social question in nineteenth-century France' in J. Goldstein (ed.) *Foucault and the Writing of History*, Oxford and Cambridge, Mass., Blackwell, 1994, p. 212.
36 Foucault, *Madness and Civilization*, p. 48.
37 S. Gilman, *Difference and Pathology: Stereotypes of Sexuality, Race and Madness*, Ithaca, Cornell University Press, 1985.
38 U.S. Mehta, *Liberalism and Empire: A Study in Nineteenth-Century British Liberal Thought*, Chicago, University of Chicago Press, 1999.
39 For studies of this nature see E. Soja, *Postmodern Geographies: The Reassertion of Space in Social Theory*, London, Verso, 1994; and the special edition of *Geoforum* on 'exclusion', edited by D. Sibley, *Geoforum*, 1998, vol. 29, no. 2.
40 D. Sibley, *Geographies of Exclusion: Society and Difference in the West*, London, Routledge, 1995, p. 49.
41 A.L. Stoler, 'Sexual affronts and racial frontiers: European identities and the cultural politics of exclusion in colonial Southeast Asia', *Comparative Studies in Society and History*, 1992, vol. 34, no. 3, pp. 514–51.
42 Douglas, *Purity and Danger*. See also D. Armstrong, 'Public health spaces and the fabrication of identity', *Sociology*, 1993, vol. 27, pp. 393–410.
43 M. Foucault, 'Of other spaces', *Diacritics*, 1986, vol. 16, no. 1, pp. 22–7.
44 Soja, *Postmodern Geographies*, p. 120.
45 Important contributions to this growing field include E. Carter, J. Donal and J. Squires (eds) *Space and Place: Theories of Identity and Location*, London, Lawrence and Wishart, 1993; M. Keith and S. Pile (eds) *Place and the Politics of Identity*, New York, Routledge, 1993; S. Feld and K.H. Blasco, *Senses of Place*, Sante Fe, School of American Research Press, 1996.

46 P. Shurmer-Smith and K. Hannam, *Worlds of Desire, Realms of Power: A Cultural Geography*, New York, Routledge, Chapman and Hall, 1994, p. 16.

47 Foucault, *Discipline and Punish*, p. 295.

48 Indeed, these subjects were always 'others' for him. He put it thus:

> through studying madness and psychiatry, crime and punishment, I have tried to show how we have indirectly constituted ourselves through the exclusion of some others: criminals, mad people, and so on. And now my present work deals with the question: How did we directly constitute our identity through certain ethical techniques of the self?

> > (M. Foucault, 'The political technology of individuals', in J.D. Faubion (ed.) *Michel Foucault: Power*, New York, The New Press, 1994, pp. 402–4)

49 W.B. Carnochan, 'The Literature of Confinement', in Morris and Rothman (eds) *The Oxford History of the Prison*, pp. 427–56.

50 S. Lavie and T. Swedenburg (eds) *Displacement, Diaspora, and Geographies of Identity*, Durham, Duke University Press, 1996.

51 P. Antze and M. Lambek (eds) *Tense Past: Cultural Essays in Trauma and Memory*, New York, Routledge, 1996; M. K Matsuda, *The Memory of the Modern*, London, Oxford University Press, 1996.

52 P. Spierenburg, *The Spectacle of Suffering: Executions and the Evolution of Repressions, from a Preindustrial Metropolis to the European Experience*, Cambridge, Cambridge University Press, 1984.

Part I

Punitive isolation

Geographies and subjectivities

2 The disappearance of the prison

An episode in the 'civilising process'

John Pratt

The prison is well known as one of the most exclusionary, secretive and impenetrable sites in modern society. One aspect of this relates to its physical exclusion and remoteness. The history of prison architecture and location in modern society, in effect, is a history of the prison's own 'disappearance'. From its entrance in the modern world in the early nineteenth century – some of the largest, most expensive and most technologically advanced buildings then in existence – we find, a hundred years later, that its grandeur had been scaled down and its presence was becoming more remote; then, by the 1960s this trend to have the prison removed from public view had become so pronounced that it had come to be camouflaged, anonymised, hidden away in remote, outlying areas of the modern world.[1]

How do we explain these changes in the physicality of the prison? What I want to suggest, by examining prison architecture and siting from the early nineteenth century up to the 1970s, is that this disappearance constitutes a discrete episode in a much longer-running saga – what Norbert Elias[2] referred to as 'the civilising process'. Here, what we understand as 'the civilised world', with all its teleological assumptions about advancement, development and progression, is not some natural innate quality of essentially Western societies. Instead, it is understood as the contingent outcome of long-term socio-cultural and psychic change from the Middle Ages onwards (primarily in Europe) that brought with it two major consequences. First, the modern state began to assume much more centralised control over the lives of its citizens, to the point where it came to have a monopoly regarding the use of force and the imposition of legal sanctions to bring redress to disputes. Second, citizens in modern societies came to internalise restraints, controls and inhibitions on their conduct, as their values and actions came to be framed around increased sensibility to the suffering of others and the privatisation of disturbing events, such as executions.[3] In this way, the threshold of sensitivity and embarrassment was gradually raised. Over the course of several centuries, we find, on the one hand, changing attitudes to the sufferings of animals, children, the physically and mentally impaired and so on. On the other, various aspects of common scenes from everyday life – in fact, central to the functioning of everyday life – were turned into 'disturbing events', from the performance of bodily functions to the killing of animals for food, and were increasingly placed behind the scenes in the modern world. They effectively became the property of experts and specialists, in some cases, and thereby hidden from the general public.

At the same time, it is important to acknowledge that Elias' use of the term 'civilised' is much broader than commonsensical understandings of kindness or politeness. Instead, it can involve those strategies for defining and dealing with those scenes or groups of people who have become unwanted or undesirable. Again, the civilising process does not bring with it a programmatic effect. It does not lend itself to greater sympathy for the suffering of all: in the nineteenth century, while there was indeed much greater awareness and intolerance of the suffering of animals, those humans with physical deformities or unusual character-istics might be shown off to the public as circus freaks, like the Elephant Man. Furthermore, not only might the civilising process enhance the need for the effi-cient removal from society for some groups or events, so distasteful had their presence become, but at the same time the modern refinement of sensibilities might only heighten awareness of the 'otherness' of these deviant groups and intensify pressure to have them removed. Again, responsibility for this task was increasingly placed on the central state and its bureaucratic organs of government, such as public health departments and prison services. Indeed, the very emphasis on rationality and efficiency in the civilised world helped to establish processes of removal that provided the least disturbance to predominant sensitivities.[4]

Although Elias himself said next to nothing about punishment in his *magnum opus*, his argument suggests that the cultural values of the civilising process must also have imprinted the way and the places in which this task is performed in modern society. The presence of prisons and their architectural form became another of those disturbing, distasteful features of modern society that the general public would prefer to have hidden from view. Yet this sensitivity did not necessarily extend itself to prisoners: indeed, the lack of sensitivity to them, particularly when judged against more worthy groups (such as the honest poor or workhouse residents) was a significant factor in restricting extravagance in prison design and any suggestion of luxuries contained within them. Prisoners had become the most threatening, most obvious outsider group,[5] for whom the general lack of empathy on the part of the public necessitated that they should be subjected to the most spartan conditions. But again, this was not a constant or universal factor. With the growth of central state responsibilities, expert knowledge, more neutral and objective than public senti-ment, gained prescience and attempted to ameliorate the appearance of the prison – refining it to the point where it did indeed become bland and unnoticeable. What these competing but ultimately converging forces point to is a familiar theme in Elias' work: the contingent nature of social development and the way in which this is the product of localised 'configurations of power'.[6]

Prison architecture in the early nineteenth century

A large new building walled all round, with a long series of madhouse-like windows, showing above the tall bricken boundary. In front of this, upon the raised bank beside the roadway, stands a remarkable portcullis-like gateway jutting, like a huge square porch or palatial archway, from the main entrance of the building, and with a little square clock-tower just peeping up behind. This is Pentonville Prison.[7]

The opening of Pentonville model prison in London in 1842 represented a major step in the 'civilising' of modern punishment (see Figure 2.1). Imprisonment in this manner would come to replace, on the one hand, the raucous, carnivalesque public spectacle of punishment,[8] which was now seen as highly repugnant by significant groups of middle- and upper-class élites. And, on the other, the totally haphazard prison development of premodernity, at the discretion of local rather than central state authorities.[9]

Now, as the main site of punishment, the prison would take on a recognisably modern form: the high walls, the gatehouse, the slatted windows, imposing size and so on – and behind all this, punishment would be administered away from

PORTCULLIS GATEWAY OF PENTONVILLE PRISON.
(*Designed by Sir Charles Barry.*)

Figure 2.1 Pentonville's 'palatial' entrance

Source: Mayhew and Binny, *The Criminal Prisons of London*, 1862

public view. At the same time, as products of growing state power and responsibilities, these new buildings were regarded with pride – emblematic features of 'the organisation of a civilised social life'.[10] They attracted the interest of leading architects, for whom such designs generated considerable prestige, and they were shown off to admiring foreign dignitaries, potentates and local worthies.[11] As the model prison, Pentonville represented a distinctive break from the old prison forms, and it was to be influential in the swift building of new prisons and the regeneration of old ones that then took place. However, at that time, its design was only one of three competing architectural influences at work on prison construction.

The other two were, first, neo-classicism. In England, Winchester Prison, opened in 1788, had been one of the first to be built in this style, drawing on architectural forms associated with Ancient Greece and Rome. Thus:

> the prison is enclosed on three sides by a low fence-wall, ten feet high. This is rendered very conspicuous by a noble and spacious gate, of the Tuscan order, constructed from a design of Vignola, at the Firnese gardens' gate or entrance into Campo Vaccini: and adorned with rustick columns and pilasters, supporting a handsome entablature. The spaces between the advanced structures are ornamented with niches, finished in a style of chaste simplicity, and the arcades are embossed with rustick quoins: over the niches are moulded square compartments, which give a simple and easy relief to the space between the crowning of the niche and the beautiful Dorick cornice; which is a grand and striking object, imitated from the theatre of Marcellus at Rome.[12]

The exteriority of the prison itself, sometimes embellished with gargoyles or other forms of penal representation, meant that the public would now be able to 'read off' from them appropriate messages about its interior, as the new prison designs effectively screened from public scrutiny what was talking place behind their walls. In contrast, the second influence was Gothic revivalism. This invoked medieval associations of penal confinement in dungeons and towers, with spires, flying buttresses, battlements, gables, perpendicular windows, three-cornered towers, turrets and extravagant gargoyles. It was exemplified at Reading (1844) (see Figure 2.2):

> every traveller by the Great Western Railway is familiar with [its] exterior splendours … the palace-prison as it is styled. After the regal residence at Windsor, it is the most imposing structure seen from the line of view between Paddington and Bath; it is beyond all question, the handsomest building – [Windsor] castle alone excepted – in the county of Berkshire.[13]

Notwithstanding the differing effects that these contrasting neo-classical and Gothic styles had produced in the early nineteenth century, what unites both are the imposing size of their prisons and the impression of luxury and extravagance

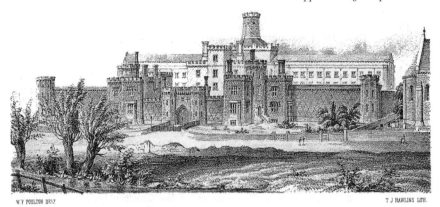

W. F POULTON DEL.?   T J RAWLINS LITH.

Figure 2.2 The 'exterior splendours' of Berkshire County Gaol, Reading
Source: John Field, *Prison Discipline*, 1848

they conveyed. In these ways, the idea of imprisonment could break free from its associations of squalor and disorder which had been exposed initially by John Howard[14] and which were later condemned with vehement disgust in Charles Dickens' prisons novels of the 1830s and 1840s.[15] Thus the journalist and barrister Hepworth Dixon[16] described the neo-classical Manchester New Gaol as making 'a striking addition to the architectural beauties of the city'. In these respects, these two designs were able to demonstrate the different economy of scale that now ordered imprisonment, while at the same time, in either style, the prison was a site for the ostentatious, dramatic, communicative penality associated with early modern society.[17] This could be done in the form of the *architecture parlante* of neo-classicism, or in the form of Gothic *architecture terrible*.[18] Hepworth Dixon, again writing on Newgate, rebuilt after fire in the 1770s:

> once seen, it is not a place very likely to be forgotten. Inside and outside it is equally striking: massive, dark and solemn, it arrests the eye and holds it. A stranger to the capital would fix upon it at a glance; for it is one of the half dozen buildings in this wilderness of bricks and mortar which have a character … who can pass by it unmoved? … is there one who heedlessly goes by, without bestowing on it a glance of curiosity, a shudder, a sign? It is doubtful.[19]

Whether it was the neo-classical or Gothic prison, however, the very grandeur of such buildings quickly came to be seen as offensive and distasteful. By following such designs, it was as if prisons had been turned into buildings of magnificence and triumph, thereby rewarding and honouring crime. Instead, in modern society, the infliction of punishment was something to be regretted, to be carefully measured out and then dispensed frugally, so that all the penal excesses and extravagances from previous eras could be avoided. Now, just as the sight of punishment in the public domain had become offensive and distasteful to the sensitivities of a range of élite groups – reformers, essayists, novelists, philosophers and so on – so too was the way in which the ostentatious new prisons seemed to turn punishment into an elaborate and expensive drama, providing those who broke the law with some kind of privileged existence, over and above the squalor and delapidation of the surrounding communities; why reward those who only endangered society, while ignoring those who tried to maintain an honest existence but without any assistance from the state to improve their circumstances? Such concerns had been registered, often from those same sectors which had also expressed revulsion at the old public punishments, from Howard onwards, who himself had complained that 'the new gaols, having pompous fronts, appear like palaces to the lower class of people and many persons are against them on this account'.[20] Similarly, the Society for the Improvement of Prison Discipline wrote:

> it has indeed been the aim of some architects to rank prisons among the most splendid buildings in the city or town where they have been erected, by a lavish and improvident expenditure of the public money in external decoration, and frequently at the sacrifice of internal convenience. Some prisons, injudiciously constructed, present a large extent of elevation next the public road or street: an opportunity was then afforded for the architect to display his talent, in the style and embellishment of the exterior.[21]

As the effects of industrialisation in Britain and the acute levels of poverty and immiseration it had created in honest working-class communities became more apparent, so too did the 'palace prisons' and the like seem all the more incongruous and unjustifiable. One trade paper wrote that

> the sums hitherto expended on prison buildings have in some cases been enormous. The cost is seldom less than £100 or £150 per prisoner (a sum sufficient for building 2 or 3 neat cottages, each able to contain a whole family) and in some instances it has been much more. A portion only (the newest) of the county prison at York, capable of accommodating only 160 prisoners, cost £200,000, which is more than £1,200 per prisoner; enough, if it had been desired, to build for each prisoner a separate mansion with stable and coach house.[22]

Among the more influential élite groups, Dickens articulates these concerns in the description of a visit to a new prison in *David Copperfield*:

> an immense and solid building, erected at a vast expense. I could not help thinking, as we approached the gate, what an uproar would have been made in the country, if any deluded man had proposed to spend one half of the money it had cost on the erection of an industrial school for the young, or a house of refuge for the deserving old.[23]

Similarly Hepworth Dixon, who singled out the grandeur and 'palatial character' of Wakefield New Gaol for particular criticism:

> ask some of the miserable creatures – miserable but honest – who live under the shadow of the new Wakefield Gaol, and who feel its grandeur insult their wretchedness – and they will tell you how it courts their attention, occupies their thoughts, and tempts them with its seductions.[24]

In other words, not only did these prisons seem to elevate criminals unfairly above the status of the honest poor – thereby disregarding the social distance that now existed between them and the rest of society – but, by ostentatiously advertising their extravagance, they gave encouragement to lawbreakers; the state and its bureaucrats would provide for this group, but would do nothing to assist those who obeyed the law.

However, in contrast to the excesses of prisons reflecting these neo-classical and Gothic designs, Pentonville seemed to have been constructed around principles of functional austerity, with an almost complete abandonment of exterior decoration in its architecture: although neo-classical themes were in evidence around the gatehouse, the point of entry to the prison, they were missing elsewhere. Indeed, given the drama of prison that was now associated with entry to it, it was perhaps appropriate that the gatehouse, through its architectural form, should highlight the importance of this point of departure from 'normal' life to the very different world that now lay behind the prison walls. But in other respects, the 'cheerless blank' of the rest of its exterior gave a more appropriate message to onlookers about what was now contained within the prison – the monotonous deprivation its regime imposed on its inhabitants, rather than any semblance of ostentatious extravagance implicit in the other contemporary designs. In contrast to the other two modern prison styles, Pentonville had given expression to a kind of *architecture faisante* (see Figure 2.3).[25]

It was now recognised that the very starkness of the prison exterior itself would be sufficient to inspire trepidation rather than wonder, reticence rather than terror. Punishment in the modern world was designed to strike no chord of affection with its citizens through majestic display, [nor] awe-inspiring terror through its flamboyant representations: instead, the deliberate austerity of its architecture would convey the appropriate sense of loss and deprivation now associated with the act of punishment. Reaction to Pentonville, with its impressions of solemnity, frugality and restraint, was more favourable than it had been to its rival designs. Thus Hepworth Dixon noted that

> there is perfect order, perfect silence. The stillness of the grave reigns in every part. To a person accustomed to see only such gaols as Giltspur-street and Horsemonger Lane – with all their noise filth and disorder – the change is striking in the extreme. The observer feels as if he had come upon a new and different world ... a model prison: an example of the efficiency and economy of the country at large.[26]

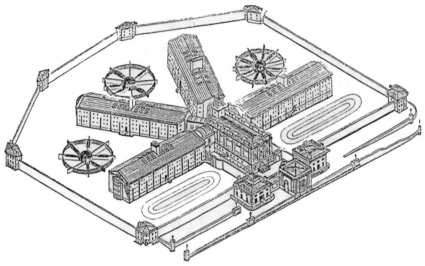

BIRD'S-EYE VIEW OF PENTONVILLE PRISON.
(From a Drawing in the Report of the Surveyor-General of Prisons.)

Figure 2.3 An overview of Pentonville Prison, illustrating the architecture of exclusion and internal segregation

Source: Mayhew and Binny, *The Criminal Prisons of London*, 1862

Its appearance **seemed** able to demonstrate that here at least imprisonment was neither excessively extravagant nor wastefully profligate, but was instead something that could be purposeful and productive.

It was for these reasons that the Pentonville austerity in prison design gains precedence over its competitors – Pentonville did indeed become 'the model'. From the mid nineteenth century, elaborate castellation and decoration would be stripped down and concentrated only around the entrance: here, now, was the defining moment of contemporary punishment, as one left the free world and entered the prison.

Prison location

Where, though, should these new prisons be built? Up to the early nineteenth century, there were no obvious hostilities to them being placed in the centre of towns and cities: the site would be determined by local tradition and convenience. Thus the philanthropist James Neild, in a duplication of Howard's 1777 prison survey, commented that 'Leicester county gaol looks as it should do. It has a prison like appearance. The noble stone face of the building extends 120 feet in front of the street, and near to it is the free school'.[27] What clearly was of no concern to Neild was the proximity of the gaol to the school, nor the fact that this building, like any other public building, bordered the main city thoroughfare – there was no dividing wall between the prison and the public. Even so, it is now possible to discern a clear pattern emerging in relation to the positioning of prisons: old prisons were likely to be found in the centre of their communities, new ones were more likely to be built on outlying, elevated sites. In contrast to Leicester, Neild noted that 'Bury St Edmunds New Gaol (1805) is situate at the east-end of the South Gate, nearly a mile from the centre of town. The buildings are enclosed by a boundary wall, 20 feet high, built in an ir-regular octagon form'.[28] Indeed, by now we find criticisms of prison buildings which were not located in outlying areas: Winchester was criticised by its Visiting Justices in 1817 as follows: 'the present gaol has been most injudiciously built nearly in the centre of the city of Winchester, surrounded by buildings, which not only impede the free circulation of air, but are in many other respects of great inconvenience'.[29]

Public health issues seem to have been the main reason for the siting of the new prisons, as Howard explained:

> every prison should be built on a spot that is airy and, if possible, near a river or brook ... an eminence should be chosen; for as the walls round a prison must be so high as greatly to obstruct a free circulation of air, this inconve-nience should be lessened by a rising ground. And the prison should not be surrounded by other buildings; nor built in the middle of a town or city.[30]

Similarly, the Society for the Improvement of Prison Discipline:

> the situation must be healthy, open and calculated to secure a free circula-tion of good air ... it is highly objectionable for a prison to be surrounded with buildings, or asked to have any, contiguous to its boundaries. It ought never to be placed in the midst of a city or town.[31]

In these respects, the humanitarian concerns of the authorities and reform-minded individuals and organisations embedded these principles of elevation, isolation and perimeter-defining boundary wall (they were not unaware of the se-curity implications of these new buildings) into subsequent prison construction.[32] Thus in Leeds, 'a large new prison [Armley] has been erected ... in a high and healthy situation, about a mile and a half from the town. It is constructed on the same general plan as the prison at Pentonville.'[33] And Pentonville itself had been built 'in the country'.

The combined effect of these trends in architectural design and location was to transform the prison, both from its place as unremarkable object of everyday life, often indistinguishable from any other public building, and from its place as a kind of extravagant theatre of punishment, to a place where it would be set back from and elevated above modern society: looming over it, but at the same time closed off from it, with its windowless high walls and secure gate; its size made it unmistak-able, and the austerity of its design provided a chilling sombre threat, as we see in another description of Pentonville: 'at night [the] prison is nothing but a dark, shapeless structure, the hugeness of which is made more apparent by the bright yellow specks which shine from the easements. The Thames then rolls by like a flood of ink'.[34]

There had been no one plan, no one individual behind this transformation of the prison, but instead a series of contingent alliances between influential organisations and individuals, often based around contrasting sensitivities: revulsion at squalor, disorder and chaos, and an equal revulsion of extravagance and flamboyance; humanitarian concerns for the health of prisoners, juxtaposed against a recognition that they had become one of modern society's most unwanted groups. Their confluence had produced an institution that at this juncture hid the administration of punishment from view, but which would become hidden from view itself; despite its physical disappearance, the prison's early representations would remain in the public's imagination, with the power to haunt the *weltanschauung* of modern society.

Hiding the prison

For a good part of the nineteenth century, the modern prison continued to represent, for the prison authorities, an illustration of advanced social development; modern prisons were institutions appropriate to a civilised society – as the imposing structure and technology embodied in such buildings confirmed. Sir Edmund Du Cane, head of the English Prison Commissioners, claimed that

> the creation of this prison system and the general improvement in all matters relating to the treatment of criminals or the prevention of crime has placed England in the foremost rank in this important social reformation. Our prison establishments, particularly those in which penal servitude is carried out, are visited by foreigners from all countries ... They are spoken of with the highest encomiums, and are the envy of most foreign prison reformers.[35]

Notwithstanding the pride of the prison bureaucracy in its own institutions, it is also possible, at this point in the late nineteenth century, to discern a growing sentiment that the 'prison look' of Pentonville and its successors was something that should be avoided in subsequent designs, as if that austerity and implicit deprivation had now become too threatening and unpleasant – at least for the more reform-minded elements of the penal system. These sensitivities seem to have been first manifested in the design of Wormwood Scrubs Prison in London, opened in 1884. As subsequent visitors confirmed, it was a prison whose surroundings had been beautified – now the architect's task was not to design turrets, terrifying gargoyles and battlements but, instead, landscaped gardens, fountains and flower beds:

> a visitor might, for a moment, imagine he had arrived at a school or university college ... At the background stands a fine chapel built in grey stone in

the Norman style. To the right and left of the chapel run graceful arches like cloisters and reminiscent of a monastery.[36]

Later, the Report of the Gladstone Committee noted that 'we see no reason why prison yards should not be made less ugly by the cultivation of flowers and shrubs'.[37] The development of Camp Hill Prison, in the Isle of Wight, represented a further step away from the 'cheerless blank' of the earlier prison monoliths: 'what may be called a "garden village" is being built.'[38]

In such ways, the penal authorities were attempting to draw a more attractive veil across what they now thought to be the unnecessarily spartan exterior of their own institutions. The increasing duty on the central state to provide for the well-being of all its citizens, alongside a growing commitment to reform practices based around scientific principles, was narrowing the social distance between prisoners and the penal authorities. In these respects, the remorseless severity of the appearance of its prisons no longer fitted what it was trying to achieve within them, nor the relationship that now existed between prisoners and the state authorities. Just as the interiors of prisons were beginning to be redecorated with 'soft' colours and photographic montages of rivers, forests and the like on its interior walls,[39] so the exterior appearance could be similarly ameliorated.

In the early twentieth century, the borstal, built so that it had 'nothing of the prison about it',[40] became the new model institution, rather than Pentonville:

> our object will be to provide institutions with opportunities for healthy outdoor work and exercise as far as possible. [Prisoners] will be housed in small groups in separate pavilions or houses which will allow of better classification and greater individualization than is now possible.[41]

Indeed, the term 'modern' was now applied to borstals precisely because they neither looked nor were positioned like prisons. The very qualities which had erstwhile provided the prison with an identification with modernity now only indicated how outdated such institutions had become, in the sense that they no longer reflected the combination of humanitarian intentions and scientific objectivity which (formally at least) now guided the authorities' governance of these institutions:

> for many years the Commissioners have drawn attention to the unsuitability for the development of reforms on modern lines ... the old prisons will always represent a monument to the ideas of repression and uniformity which dominated penal theory in nineteenth century society.[42]

Now, for the authorities, from being originally regarded as a source of pride, the prisons they had inherited were seen as obstacles to more progressive, therapeutic models of penal rehabilitation that their experts wanted to pursue, more suited to psychiatric clinics than prisons. For this reason, they were increasingly prepared to experiment with designs that abandoned the previous nineteenth-century conceptions of prison building altogether. For example, in contrast to the earlier (and much criticised) grandeur of Wakefield New Gaol, at Wakefield Open Prison, established in 1934, 'there were no walls, not even a boundary fence – the men sleeping in wooden huts, and the boundaries designated, if at all, by whitewash marks on the trees'.[43] Here, the defining features of the modern prison had simply vanished. By the same token, architects had long since lost what interest they originally had in this field – as if any involvement would tarnish them as well as the prisoners.[44]

Removing the prison

However, such ameliorative attempts by the authorities were insufficient to allay growing public distaste at any evidence of the presence of prisons. During the nineteenth and early twentieth centuries, modern urban development had eroded much of the distance that had originally existed between the early modern prison and city outskirts. New estates were taking the general public right up to the edges of those prominences on which the prisons had been located; or alternatively, proposals for new prisons now threatened the increasingly precious 'greenbelt' areas of the modern urban environment. One of the first such occasions in England when such issues were raised took place in 1875, over the plans to build Wormwood Scrubs itself:

> are we prepared for the infusion of a convict element in our population at Notting Hill? There is an establishment rising like Aladdin's Palace on the once pleasant site of Wormwood Scrubs ... Why should Notting Hill submit to a penal establishment being quartered upon it? We want Wormwood Scrubs as a breathing space for our growing population; and object to its being made a country residence for the Claimant and his friends.[45]

Notwithstanding the changing sensitivities of the authorities towards prisons and prisoners, for the general public it was as if the very idea of the prison had become indelibly tainted with ugliness and morbidity, in terms of both what its design represented and that outcast population that was known to be hidden behind its walls: indeed, it was as if the very remoteness and exclusion of the prison and its inmate population only made them more undesirable – sights that were intolerable in the modern world. At the turn of the century, pressures grew to have the disfigurement that the prison represented for local citizens removed from view altogether, and the land put to more tasteful use for the respectable members of the community. Thus, the Report of the Prison Commissioners refers to 'a new prison ... near Nottingham, to take the place of one in the centre of town, which has been condemned on account of the unsatisfactory nature of its site'.[46]

For the general public, the prison, on the basis of what it now represented in their imagination, had become the least desirable of landmarks, as if its brooding presence on the nineteenth-century skyline was still physically visible.

Aside from the dangers of the population housed within it, any plans to build one would immediately threaten local land values, so unwanted a neighbour had it become.[47] In the post-war period, the authorities encountered strong opposition, with their plans for new prisons vehemently rejected by any community in which they planned to situate them:

> the difficulty is that while it may be generally agreed that the Commissioners ought to acquire adequate accommodation for the prisoners, any specific attempt to do so almost invariably meets with a firm local conviction that they should do it somewhere else.[48]

They were thus reduced to converting sites that had otherwise lost their original purpose or no longer had a role to play: disused army camps and airfields, on the one hand; and on the other, country homes in their surrounding estates[49] which belonged to a class structure and economic order itself in the process of disappearing. If these remote, redundant sites were the only ones available for prison building, they further assisted in their camouflage and disguise, their exclusion and secrecy.

The invisible prison

The subsequent building programmes of the post-war period took this process a stage further, introducing designs that would make prisons completely anonymous – invisible even to those members of the public who happened to come across them in the remote outlying areas of the modern world where they were to be built. Thus, the Home Office reported as follows on the first major prison-building programme in Britain in the twentieth century:

> the design, elevations and methods of construction and finishing are intended to get away as far as possible from the traditional appearance of a prison … *this type of construction gives a pleasanter and quieter effect*, with better lighting, heating and ventilating.[50]

Similarly, the plans for the new Blundeston Prison: 'There will be no high wall, but privacy will be maintained by an eight foot concrete wall, within which there will be a twelve foot chain link fence topped with barbed wire for security purposes.'[51] In effect, prison security, to avoid otherwise distasteful sights, was being maintained by means of a *trompe l'oeil*. The offensive, exterior high wall, which might also give away the identity of the prison, was scaled down, to be less obtrusive: but behind it, of course, lay a more discreet series of fencing. Again, the dramatic effect of the prison entrance was now something that only prisoners need experience. Visitors would now be spared such shameful, distasteful associations in the prison construction. And as Sparks *et al.* later noted,[52] these new prisons had become hidden, anonymous, largely unrecognisable buildings. The prison had now, as it were, disappeared.

This did not mean, however, that prisons were *completely* removed from view. The above specifications for architecture and location referred to the *new* prison-building programme. Many of the nineteenth-century prisons remained in use, but now projected an appearance and a set of images that set them, and the localities in which they were situated, adrift from the modern civilised world. The grandeur and elegance that had initially placed them in the advance guard of civilisation had largely turned to unsightly squalor and decay. In 1960, the formerly 'healthy situation' of Armley Gaol, Leeds, was described:

> a walk from the railway station to Armley Road takes you through descending levels of civic blight. In the winter murk you pass ancient warehouses, untidy shops, and the unmaintained flats consigned to the very poor. Finally, you reach the sooty decrepitude of HM Prison at Leeds. This is the bottom. In all England, I saw no comparably resounding statement of man's persisting determination to render evil for evil.[53]

Indeed, it was as if such prisons had themselves become imprisoned: trapped within their original locations which had been engulfed by urban development: but which were now denied any investment because of the proximity of the prison to them. These areas had come to represent a hidden symbiosis of decay – the fate of the prison and its immediate locality linked together, as the rest of the civilised world carefully avoided any intrusion on this degenerating micro-world. Such prisons were still needed, despite periodic plans for their closure, but they could neither expand nor modernise through rebuilding because of lack of space, and there was opposition to any suggestion to move them elsewhere. In this way, they could only advertise urban blight and the kinds of sights the civilised world preferred to have hidden away and forgotten – and make the prison still more of an undesirable, unwanted neighbour.

Because, for many citizens of the modern world, the prison now did have a physical invisibility (hidden away in the rural hinterland or left to decay in such inner-city ghettos), it could now only exist as a spectral memory based around representations in popular culture of the gaunt, austere, menacing institutions of the nineteenth century. From these obscure locations, the prison still had a role to play in the civilised world: as a hidden receptacle for those whose crimes indicated that they too no longer had a place within it. By the same token, any perceived departures from what had become the cultural expectations of prison design would provoke outrage; the legacy of the nineteenth-century prison and its look of chilling austerity had been able to provide a lasting public memory about what prison should look like, if at the same time the cultural sensitivities of this world also insisted that such buildings be camouflaged and hidden from view. And for the penal authorities themselves, the nineteenth-century institutions were also unwanted, representing as they did the unnecessarily repressive remnants of the penal past, and out of place with the scientific, treatment-oriented ethos to which they had now become committed.

Against such extensive distaste, it is hardly surprising that over the course of the modern period, prison became an increasingly exclusionary and prohibited site, even for those who broke the law, as more and more barriers were placed in front of it to keep them out. It was seen as too dramatic a penalty for an increasingly wide range of offenders – juveniles initially, but then the mentally ill, the elderly and destitute, first offenders, young adults – even, by the 1970s, some groups of persistent offenders. By this juncture, in much of official penal discourse, the prison had become a 'last resort' option. It still had its removal function to perform, of course, but it would now do this on the unobtrusive margins of the modern civilised world, which had taken such an objection to any more visible presence than this.

What we can see from these trends is how deeply embedded the penal bureaucracies and the anonymous, disguised, exclusive prisons they preside over have become in modern society. To make the prison visible again, to make it accessible once more to the general public, would require more than just a dramatic reversal of public attitudes and sensibilities. It would require a major interruption to the civilising process itself.

Acknowledgements

I would like to thank the editors for helpful comments on earlier drafts of this chapter.

Notes

1 R. Sparks, A.E. Bottoms and W. Hay, *Prisons and the Problem of Order*, Oxford, Clarendon Press, 1996, p. 101.
2 N. Elias, *The Civilizing Process*, Oxford, Blackwell, 1984 [1939].
3 D. Garland, *Punishment and Modern Society*, Oxford, Oxford University Press, 1990; P. Spierenburg, *The Spectacle of Suffering*, Cambridge, Cambridge University Press, 1984.
4 Z. Bauman, *Modernity and the Holocaust*, Cambridge, Polity Press, 1989.
5 N. Elias and J. Scotson, *The Established and Outsiders*, London, Sage, 1965.
6 It also needs to be recognised that the fragility of these contingencies can be interrupted at any time by war, catastrophe, dramatic social change and the like, bringing an end, or at least a temporary cessation, to particular episodes of the civilising process, and the beginning of a new script that marks this realignment of the social and cultural forces implicit in it. Under such circumstances, the civilising process would be 'put into reverse' and decivilising forces would then begin to shape social and individual development, making possible a re-emergence of conduct and values more appropriate to previous eras. Indeed, at the present time there are some signs that a new cultural tolerance of the prison is emerging, reflective of a greater readiness to view these previously distasteful sights. Their recent visibility in some locations (particularly the United States) may thus be reflective of much broader social changes and serve as an indicator that the foundations of the civilising process are undergoing some 'unravelling.'
7 H. Mayhew and J. Binny, *The Criminal Prisons of London*, London, Frank Cass, 1862, p. 113.
8 T. Laqueur, 'Crowds, carnival and the state of English executions 1604–1868', in A. Beir, D. Cannadine and J. Rosenheim (eds) *Modern Society – Essays in English History in Honour of Lawrence Stone*, Cambridge, Cambridge University Press, 1989, pp 305–55.

9 See A. Brodie, J. Croom and J. Davies, *The Prison Experience*, Swindon, English Heritage, 1999.

10 L. Woodward, *The Age of Reform*, Oxford, Oxford University Press, 1938.

11 M. Ignatieff, *A Just Measure of Pain*, London, Macmillan, 1978.

12 J. Neild, *The State of Prisons in England, Scotland and Wales*, London, John Nichols and Son, 1812, p. 381.

13 J. Field, *Prison Discipline*, London, Longmans, 1848, p. 73.

14 J. Howard, *The State of the Prisons*, London, Dent, [1777] 1929.

15 See C. Dickens, *The Pickwick Papers*, London, Oxford University Press, 1969 [1836]; *David Copperfield*, London, Thames Publishing, 1959 [1850]; *Barnaby Rudge*, London, Thames Publishing, 1959 [1841]; *Nicholas Nickleby*, London, Thames Publishing, 1959 [1837].

16 W.H. Dixon, *The London Prisons*, London, Jackson and Walford, 1850, p. 303.

17 M. Foucault, *Discipline and Punish*, London, Allen Lane, 1978.

18 J. Bender, *Imagining the Penitentiary*, Chicago, University of Chicago Press, 1987; Garland, *Punishment and Modern Society*.

19 Dixon, *The London Prisons*, pp. 191–2.

20 Howard, *The State of the Prisons*, p. 44.

21 Society for the Improvement of Prison Discipline, *Remarks on the Form and Construction of Prisons: with Appropriate Designs*, London, SIPD, 1826.

22 *The Builder* 1849, p. 519.

23 Dickens, *David Copperfield*, p. 714.

24 Dixon, *The London Prisons*, p. 368.

25 Bender, *Imagining the Penitentiary*; Garland, *Punishment and Modern Society*.

26 Dixon, *The London Prisons*, p. 157.

27 J. Neild, *The State of the Prisons in England, Scotland and Wales*, p. 334.

28 J. Neild, *The State of the Prisons in England, Scotland and Wales*, p. 84.

29 Society for the Improvement of Prison Discipline, *Remarks on the Form and Construction of Prisons*, p. 9.

30 Howard, *The State of the Prisons*, p. 20.

31 Society for the Improvement of Prison Discipline, *Remarks on the Form and Construction of Prisons*, p. 36.

32 See *Report of the Inspectors of Prisons of the Home District*, London, PP XXXII, 1837.

33 *Report of the Inspectors of Prisons (Northern District)*, London, PP XXV, 1848, p. 54.

34 Mayhew and Binny, *The Criminal Prisons of London*, p. 119

35 *Report of a Committee Appointed to Consider Certain Questions Relating to the Employment of Convicts in the United Kingdom*, London, PP XXXIV, 1882, p. 656.

36 S. Hobhouse and F. Brockway, *The English Prison System*, London, Macmillan, 1923, p. 78.

37 *Report of the Gladstone Committee*, London, PP LVII, 1895, p. 23.

38 *Report of the Prison Commissioners*, 1908–9, London, PP cd 4847, 1909, p. 28.

39 See *Report of the Prison Commissioners*, 1935, London, PP XV cmd 5430, 1936/7.

40 W. Healy and B. Alper, *Criminal Youth and the Borstal Systems*, New York, Commonwealth Fund, 1941.

41 *Report of the Prison Commissioners*, 1936, London, PP cmd 5430, 1937/8, p. 2.

42 *Report of the Prison Commissioners*, 1937, London: PP cmd. 4308, 1937/8, p. 30.

43 H. Jones and P. Cornes, *Open Prisons*, London, Routledge, 1973, p. 5.

44 See R. Davison, 'Prison architecture', *Architectural Record*, vol. 67, no. 30, pp. 69–100.45.

45 *Kensington News*, 12 June 1875, p. 3.

46 *Report of the Prison Commissioners*, 1889, London, PP (1889) XLI, p. 4.

47 A. Hopkins, *Prisons and Prison Building*, New York, Architectural Book Publishing, 1930, p. 12.

48 *Report of the Prison Commissioners*, 1947, London, PP cmd. 7475, 1947/8, p. 11.

49 See *Report of the Prison Commissioners*, 1949, London, PP cmd. 8080, 1950/1, p. 28.

50 Home Office, *Penal Practice in a Changing Society*, London, HMSO, 1959, p. 92, my italics.

51 Home Office, *Penal Practice in a Changing Society*, p. 117.
52 Sparks *et al.*, *Prisons and the Problem of Order*.
53 *The Guardian* 15 May 1960, p. 18.

3 The politics of convict space

Indian penal settlements and the Andaman Islands[1]

Clare Anderson

From the late eighteenth century, as the British made incursions into India, they established a series of penal settlements for the reception of South Asian convicts. Bencoolen (Sumatra) was the first destination, from 1773. It was later joined and eventually replaced during the first half of the nineteenth century by convict settlements in Prince of Wales' Island (Penang), Singapore, Malacca, the Tenasserim and Martaban Provinces (Burma), Mauritius and Aden. In the wake of the 1857 Uprising, the British further settled the Andaman Islands as a penal colony, situated in the Bay of Bengal, 900 miles east of continental India. Within ten years the Islands had become the sole destination for Indian transportees. Transportation was a punishment that removed offenders from society, isolated them in distant settlements overseas (islands or mainland areas often surrounded by hostile landscapes and populations) and put them to work. At the same time, during the early years of transportation, colonial officials believed that the journey across the ocean ('black water', or *kala pani*) threatened convicts with loss of caste and hence social exclusion. This created a powerful colonial representation of transportation as a punishment Indians feared as much as death.

This chapter begins by analysing the contradictions between colonial discourses and convicts' perceptions of the *kala pani*. South Asian convicts were often afraid of transportation but they did not always register the prospect of their exclusion in relation to loss of caste. During the nineteenth century, it became increasingly clear that transportation was not the general focus of terror that administrators had expected and hoped for. Colonial administrators gradually had to acknowledge and accommodate convicts' differing views and desires about the punishment. In the 1890s, the Government of India tried to reconfigure transportation as a focus of terror, by constructing the Cellular Jail at Port Blair in the Andamans. During the first decades of the twentieth century, the British used this large institution of secondary confinement to incarcerate nationalist agitators, as well as ordinary transportation convicts. The chapter concludes by looking at how the imprisonment of political offenders in the Andaman Islands has led to their post-colonial representation as a symbolic space of anti-colonial struggle. Paradoxically, this representation has resurrected colonial discourses of the power of the *kala pani*.

The construction of the Cellular Jail followed a history of secondary exclusion in Indian penal settlements. The authorities usually tried to separate male and female convicts from each other, for instance. In some sites, they also segregated convicts on a regional basis. The Mauritius government separated convicts transported from Ceylon from those from Bengal and Bombay.[2] In all the penal settlements there was also the thorny problem of how further to punish and isolate convicts who breached discipline or committed further crimes. The settlements always employed further zones of isolation for this purpose, and usually chose islands for these exclusive penal spaces. During the early nineteenth century, Rat Island was used for this purpose in Bencoolen.[3] Viper Island in the Andamans served the same function until 1908, when most inmates were transferred to the Cellular Jail.[4]

There was an extensive interplay between penal colonies and other spaces of confinement in the treatment of convicts. The Mauritius government, for example, imprisoned some convicts in Port Louis Jail,[5] and retransported more serious secondary offenders to Robben Island (South Africa) and the penal colony at Van Diemen's Land (Tasmania).[6] Other convicts were further removed to leper colonies. Diego Garcia and Ile Curieuse in the Seychelles were both used for this purpose by the colonial government of Mauritius.[7] During the second half of the nineteenth century, a prohibition was placed on the shipment of lunatics sentenced to transportation to the Andamans. Convicts who were believed to be insane were initially shipped back to mainland asylums, though this ended in 1876 over fears that the policy encouraged convicts to feign madness.[8]

Caste, place and punishment: transportation, isolation and the *kala pani*

By the late eighteenth century, the British were beginning to formulate ideas about caste as one of the most important determinants of Indian social and economic life.[9] They believed that the significance of caste to Indians made transportation a hugely effective punishment. The threat of caste defilement, associated with the crossing of the *kala pani* which made convicts social outcasts, gave it special potency.[10] Of the thirty-five magistrates questioned during a Bengal judicial enquiry of 1801–2, for example, twenty-nine agreed that transportation was a huge deterrent to crime.[11] As late as 1838, and despite growing evidence to the contrary, the Committee on Prison Discipline similarly wrote of transportation's 'indescribable horror' to Indians. It was, they reported, 'a weapon of tremendous power … little short of the effect of a sentence of death'. The effect of transportation on the wider community was believed to be even greater than capital punishment.[12]

Given their reliance on the social observations of high-caste Brahmins in understanding the Indian subcontinent, the origins of this discourse can be located in official acceptance of a *varna*-based model of caste as central to social organisation. The meaning of caste to Hindus was inevitably more complex than the simple model presented by British administrators, with social position also connected to factors such as community, kinship, gender and occupation. Of course, these factors also shaped convict attitudes to transportation. Yet, from the late eighteenth century, the British imagined the meaning of transportation as a punishment to Indians within what we might term an orientalist discourse.[13]

For some convicts, transportation certainly induced the caste fears colonial penologists articulated. Fragments of convict voices emerge through the colonial archive, with individuals expressing anxiety about the loss of caste they faced. In August 1846, for example, two days before his ship was due to sail for Singapore, convict Shreekristna Wassoodewjee petitioned the government. Wassoodewjee was a clerk who could read and write English, and wrote the petition himself. He claimed that he was a 'high class of Hindu', and desired 'separate warter [sic] and Diet as required by his religion that he may preserve it unsullied and retain his Caste'. His relations would, he added, pay any additional expense.[14] There is other evidence that high-caste Bengali convicts refused to eat communally prepared food on board ships to Singapore.[15] Here, convicts were attempting to carve out their own cultural spaces of inclusion and exclusion within the practice of transportation. In theory, caste was not to impact upon colonial prison discipline. In practice, it did.[16]

Convicts made further attempts to maintain such cultural boundaries on arrival in the penal settlements. During the early period, common messing had not been introduced in many settlements and convicts cooked their own rations. In 1835, a policeman in Mauritius reported how a convict had refused to allow him to light his pipe from his fire. The convict told the officer 'he could not take the fire outside while cooking, it being against his religion'.[17] As common messing was introduced in Southeast Asia, it undoubtedly impacted on some convicts' cultural practices. A convict of some means, Goherdone Babboo, was transported to the Tenasserim Provinces at the beginning of 1835. He was sent to Moarny Island and later that year petitioned the Bengal Supreme Court about the loss of caste he faced:

> The head man of the aforesaid jail made himself a Regulation amongst the prisoners that one of the prisoners should boil and prepare victuals for 40 prisoners whether a Hindoo or moreman [Muslim] and this way many of the Hindoo prisoners by the force of the Head man of the jail became moreman.

Not only was he forbidden from preparing his own rations, he protested, but also he had been made to clean the convict latrines, that most polluting of labour.[18]

Even though the experience of transportation impacted on the cultural practices of exclusion and isolation of these convicts, these were exceptional cases. During the first half of the nineteenth century, a very large proportion of transportation convicts completely lacked caste, at least as the British understood it. Many were Muslims or from tribal (*adivasi*) communities. Only half of the convicts transported to Mauritius in the period 1815–37, for instance, were Hindu. Of those Hindus from the Bengal Presidency, just 7 per cent were high-caste Brahmins. By far the largest proportion of Hindu convicts were low-caste, peasants or *dalits* ('untouchables') who had quite a different relationship to caste from higher-status communities.[19] The politics of social exclusion were not equivalent in these cases, as an analysis of other convicts' attitudes reveals.

After 1828 all those sentenced to life imprisonment in Calcutta's Alipur Jail were given the right to petition for the commutation of their sentence to life transportation.[20] This was in response to prisoners' demands. There are few surviving caste lists of convict petitioners; the records of just seventy-six convict petitioners transported to Burma in 1847 survive. Yet almost all of the convicts in this small sample (sixty-six) were Hindus, including a handful of Brahmins.[21] This challenges colonial discourses of the significance of caste. On the other hand, the number of prison inmates applying for commutation of sentence to transportation remained at just 5–6 per cent annually over the course of the next decade, evidence used by the 1838 Prison Discipline Committee to confirm Indians' terror of transportation.[22] Yet transportation was an attractive alternative punishment for some prisoners, even those of high caste. It is worth noting that a number of the 1847 petitioners had been convicted of the same offences. This suggests that the promise of continuing companionship influenced their decision. Did its lack of appeal to most others relate to issues of caste, as the Prison Discipline Committee believed? Increasingly, according to the colonial administration, it did not. They recognised that what the vast majority of prisoners were afraid of was the prospect of back-breaking labour in unknown places.

The Southeast Asian and Mauritian penal settlements were developed in unfamiliar sites, distant from the Indian mainland. Care was taken to ensure that convicts were not transported to places known to them, nor close to their native place. The Commissioner of Arakan (Burma), for instance, asked that convicts from East Bengal be transported elsewhere.[23] This maximised their sense of geo-cultural displacement – and reduced the risk of successful escape. The basis of the transportation system was, of course, the supply of cheap labour to fuel colonial expansion. When penal settlements were first established, convicts were engaged in exhausting and often dangerous infrastructural hard labour such as land clearance and road construction. It was inevitable that as these settlements grew there was less need for such labour. At the same time, they became further interlocked with the regional economy. As convict and other migratory streams to these spaces increased, they gradually came out of isolation. Further, as convict spaces became more familiar in India (or at least to Indian inmates), convicts were not as frightened of transportation as they had once been. Convicts (or paid scribes) wrote letters to relatives and friends; others escaped; many more returned home at the expiration of their sentence. Convicts were accepted back into their communities after serving their time; they were not outcast. Knowledge about the location of and penal regime in the settlements spread. At the same time, Indian fears receded.

The colonial authorities recognised this as early as 1804.[24] There were several cases of prisoners assuming the identity of convicts destined for transportation in order to be sent to Penang. In 1805, for example, the prisoner Gunnah Pyke took the name of prisoner Gungaram Dome, who had died in Alipur Jail, and was shipped to the settlement to serve out his sentence.[25] By 1824, officials acknowledged that convicts no longer feared the prospect of transportation to the island.[26] Ten years later, officials in the Madras Presidency expressed concerns that transportation to the Straits Settlements (Singapore, Penang and Malacca) no longer entailed hard labour. They described 'a system which when more generally known will deprive the punishment of transportation of all its terrors'.[27] In 1836, all Madras Presidency convicts in the Straits were transferred to the Tenasserim Provinces instead.[28]

With the colonisation of new areas like the Tenasserim Provinces (1828), new zones of isolation came into being, about which nothing was known and where convicts were engaged in infrastructural construction. Convicts disfavoured what was an ideal site of punishment in the opinion of the Madras authorities. Prisoner petitioners simply refused to go there. When the Superintendent of Alipur Jail asked for volunteers for transportation in 1828, 116 life prisoners initially put their names forward.[29] When they learnt that their destination was the Tenasserim Provinces, they all withdrew their applications.[30] The same group of jail inmates was equally sceptical when the call was made two years later.[31] Their fears had less to do with caste and more to do with shipment to a newly established, unknown penal space. This was by no means unique to India. British convicts' attitudes to transportation to the Australian colonies during the late eighteenth and early nineteenth centuries reflected the same anxieties and followed the same pattern.[32]

The Andaman Islands were established as a penal colony after the 1857 uprisings swept across North India. The British urgently needed a place to which rebels could be removed from India. An earlier attempt at establishing a penal settlement in the Islands in 1794 had ended in disaster. Many settlers and convicts had died. Between 1800 and 1801, the surviving convicts were transferred to Prince of Wales' Island, and the settlement abandoned.[33] Of course, it was these harsh, isolated conditions that made the Islands ideal as a penal settlement. This was a place about which little was known; a place of unmapped topography, of thick, impenetrable jungle. Moreover, various indigenous tribal (*adivasi*) groups inhabited the Islands, and sometimes responded to foreign settlers with violence. Most nineteenth-century European visitors to the Andamans were more interested in these reclusive and often hostile populations than the penal settlement itself. During the second half of the nineteenth century, a series of anthropologists encountered, enumerated, photographed and measured what they viewed as the most primitive of the so-called dying races: the Onge, the Sentinelese and the Jarawa.[34] As Satadru Sen argues in his groundbreaking account of the Andamans in the nineteenth century, the indigenous Andamanese were central to how the British conceptualised the Islands.[35] When the settlement was first established in 1858, the British saw the sea, the jungle and its inhabitants as natural convict guards. If convicts were foolish enough to attempt to escape, they faced recapture or certain death. One official wrote that it was not even technically correct to speak of 'escape', as convicts had no overseers.[36] They were guarded by the landscape alone.

As we have seen, by the mid nineteenth century it was evident that convict attitudes to transportation were based on knowledge about particular penal settlements rather than fears about caste. Going overseas did not necessarily affect caste, as the colonial authorities tacitly acknowledged. From the 1860s, for instance, they promoted a convict family emigration scheme to the Andamans.[37] However, I would not go as far as Sen, who argues that there was no culturally ingrained dread of crossing the *kala pani* at all.[38] In relation to the family emigration scheme, there is evidence that some relatives refused to undertake the voyage when they discovered they had to travel by ship.[39] Nevertheless, like early nineteenth-century transportees, Andaman convicts were primarily drawn from low-caste Hindu, tribal or Muslim communities.[40]

Although transportation was supposed to exclude convicts from their former social and kin networks, it did not. Transported convicts and their scribes were prodigious letter-writers.[41] The detailed knowledge that many Indians had about their convict relatives is astonishing. In addition, many convicts returned to their communities at the expiration of their sentence. If ex-convicts wished to go back to India, they could only do so if their relatives agreed to support them. It was unusual for them to refuse.[42] There is even evidence that during the later period some convicts received visitors from the mainland, much to the consternation of the Government of India who feared an investigative journalist might slip in.[43]

The spread of subaltern knowledge about the Andamans impacted on colonial policy there. In 1877, the Prison Conference urged the abolition of transportation on the grounds that its deterrent effect had been lost due to the return of ex-convicts to India: 'Port Blair is now a haven where prisoners would be.'[44] The 1888 Jail Management Committee made a similar point.[45] At the same time that the Islands emerged from isolation, there had been a great deal of land clearance, and relations with their indigenous peoples had improved. The cultural landscape could no longer be imagined or feared as a natural prison. In 1890, two years after the Jail Management Committee had met, C.J. Lyall and A.S. Lethbridge's *Report on the Andamans* was published. It also argued that convicts now viewed transportation to the Andamans as preferable to imprisonment in Indian jails. It recommended that in order to intensify transportation discipline, a 'penal stage' should be introduced, with convicts subjected to a harsh regime on arrival.[46] This was the spur to the construction of the Cellular Jail, a place of exclusion and isolation within a more broadly constituted remote penal space (see Figure 3.1).

Work began in 1896, and the jail was completed in 1906. It was an imposing Benthamite structure consisting of a central panoptican watchtower overlooking seven wings, each with three storeys. There were 698 cells, each thirteen feet by nine. The jail rivalled anything built in Britain at the time.[47] As convict ships arrived, it loomed on the horizon in Aberdeen. It was a bold architectural representation of the changing politics of convict space, for its purpose was to fulfil the penal role that the topography and people of the Islands had once played. Yet not all colonial observers were satisfied that it would. Two years before the jail was completed, Superintendent of Convicts W.R.H. Merk wrote that by their very nature, transmarine penal settlements could only exist in the short term. Eventually, 'the terrors of distance and of the unknown disappear' and transportation loses its effect. This, he predicted, would be as true for the Andamans as it had been in Australia, Singapore and New Caledonia.[48]

Figure 3.1 Model of the Cellular Jail, Cellular Jail Museum, Andaman Islands

Source: Author's photo

Note: This panoptican – comprising a central watchtower and seven
wings – was completed in 1906

Isolation, imagination and the Andaman Islands

Although the Andaman Islands were chosen and deployed as a geographically
bounded place of isolation, they must also be understood as an imagined space on
to which the complexities of colonial/post-colonial relationships have now been
mapped. With the demise of the grand narrative and the emergence of postmodernism, cultural geographers, anthropologists, social theorists and historians have
begun to consider the multiple ways in which the histories of people and events are
constituted. Doreen Massey, in a nuanced consideration of 'Places and their pasts',
argues:

> The identity of places is very much bound up with the histories which are
> told of them, how those histories are told, and which history turns out to be
> dominant ... it may be useful to think of places, not as areas on maps, but as
> constantly shifting articulations of social relations through time.[49]

This point is well illustrated in Wendy Singer's recent examination of contemporary oral accounts of the Freedom Fighter movement in South Asia. Singer
shows how story-telling has become central to the creation of written histories of
anti-colonial agitation in the state of Bihar (north India). In this way, 'mythic and
material pasts' have become intertwined in revealing and reflecting aspects of
contemporary politics.[50] Singer is right to stress this close relationship between the
past and its present articulation. To take a further Indian example, in considering
the significance of the contemporary in framing national memories and identities,

Tim Edensor discusses the contesting narratives that have been used to interpret the meaning of the most famous image of India, the Taj Mahal. He argues that the Taj has now become integrated into India's 'imagined geographies'. As a symbolic site, it reflects fears about the country's national integrity.[51]

While the British established penal settlements throughout the Empire during the colonial period, since decolonisation few have been culturally configured in the same way as the Andamans. Relatively little has been written about early penal settlements in Southeast Asia. The contemporary silence about convict settlement in these regions perhaps reflects historians' reluctance to engage critically with the fact that colonial expansion was predicated on the extensive use of forced labour, long after the abolition of the slave trade in 1807. At the same time, the insertion of a specifically Indian 'convict stain' into the history of multi-ethnic communities in modern Southeast Asia is problematic and potentially socially destabilising. Perhaps most significantly, these regions were not colonised as penal settlements, but as territories to which convicts were sent. It is thus relatively easy to remove convicts from narratives of colonisation.[52] Even the most recent study of the making of the urban built environment of Singapore does not acknowledge the crucial role of convict labour in early nineteenth-century public works programmes, though it tackles colonial power relations during the later period head on.[53]

In contrast, convicts make a brief appearance in the historiography of Mauritius. They are (mis)represented either as high-caste Hindus transported for rebelling against colonial rule or *sepoys* (soldiers) transported for minor military offences.[54] This kind of nationalist discourse is also visible in contemporary articulations of the Andaman Islands. However, unlike Mauritius, representations of the Islands' convict history have become important to how British rule, and the struggle against it, is imagined in post-colonial India. The Andamans were of course colonised as a penal settlement, rather than as a colony to which convicts were later sent. The forced migration of convict transportees to the Islands is thus impossible to ignore. It is in this context that, as a state of independent India, the Islands and their convict history have become firmly embedded in the process of post-colonial nation-building. Parallels might be drawn here with the relationship between the representation of convict history and nation-building in Australia and, more dramatically still, the central place Robben Island now occupies in post-apartheid South Africa.[55] Both Robben Island and convict heritage sites in Australia draw tens of thousands of visitors each year. Yet the post-colonial cultural mapping of the Andaman Islands focuses narrowly on a limited aspect of Indian convict transportation: the reception and treatment of anti-colonial agitators.

From the turn of the twentieth century, nationalist prisoners were removed from India and transported to the Islands. These prisoners were educated middle-class men, convicted of conspiracies or sedition against the British state.[56] After shipment to the Islands, they were isolated from the mass of ordinary offenders in the Cellular Jail and made subject to different treatment. Most significantly, they never passed through the jail's 'penal stage'. For them, the Cellular Jail was a permanent site of isolated incarceration within a site of exclusion. It was not long after their transportation before details of the Freedom Fighters' plight began to leak out. Reports appeared in the Indian press, including *The Bengalee* and *Lahore Tribune*.[57]

After release, a number of nationalists published memoirs detailing their experiences. These are tales of British cruelty and inhumanity, degradation and fear, in which the Cellular Jail is central. Prisoners described the kind of work they were expected to perform, notably oil-pressing and rope-making, and the abuse suffered at the hands of convict warders, together with hunger strikes and other indignities.[58] These men had little sympathy with the mass of convicts, whom they viewed in much as the same way as the British did. As Sen reminds us, Indian élites shared and even supplied the colonial state's vision of 'native' criminality.[59] The most famous inmate of the Cellular Jail, V.D. Savarkar, transported to the Andamans for his part in the Nasik Conspiracy Case at the end of 1910, wrote of his first impression of a convict chain gang thus: 'How hideous to behold! There was in it a type of every kind. One looked very fierce, another ... an incarnation of terror.'[60] Another prominent nationalist, Bhai Parmanand, wrote of 'murderers and ruffians' employed as warders. The ordinary convicts were, he said, 'the very worst badmashes' (bad characters).[61]

It is not surprising, then, that the Islands have become prominent symbols of colonial oppression and the fight against it. In the 1960s Indira Gandhi wrote of the Islands as 'a nursery for our great revolutionaries'.[62] Contemporary nationalist historiography has reiterated the Islands' place in the twentieth-century struggle against British rule. L.P. Mathur writes: 'It is rather surprising and painful to note that civilised government like the British perpetrated barbaric punishments and showered unimaginable indignities on people who had sacrificed all for their motherland.'[63] Mathur splits the convicts into two distinct categories – criminal convicts and political prisoners. Only the political prisoners are named or discussed; the so-called criminal convicts are barely referred to, and never in terms of either their historical agency or massive socio-economic contribution to the settlement.

It was, of course, during the period in which the Cellular Jail was built that nationalist ideas of emancipation were starting to threaten the basis of colonial power. If liberty can only be denied to those who are already free, it is a deep irony indeed that it could also be taken away from the very people who were fighting for freedom. It is perhaps this paradox which best explains the powerful symbolism both the Islands generally and the jail more specifically have now taken on as sites of unified anti-colonial struggle. Indeed, the jail is marked as 'the Indian Bastille'. Correspondingly, historians have rewritten the history of many other convicts transported during the nineteenth century, turning them from local activists to agitators with a proto-nationalist agenda. In 1957, a hundredth anniversary memorial honouring the 1857 'martyrs' was erected in the Andaman Islands' capital, Port Blair (see Figure 3.2). An example of the symbolic power of the Cellular Jail, which was not in fact constructed by then, it reads: 'In hallowed memory of those heroes who participated in the National Revolution of 1857 from different states of India and were incarcerated in the Cellular Jail, Port Blair, by an alien Government.' S.N. Aggarwal writes of those convicts transported after

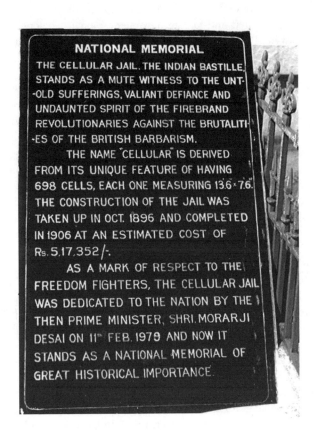

Figure 3.2 Hundredth anniversary memorial, Cellular Jail, Andaman Islands

Source: Author's photo

Note: The memorial maps the cultural significance of the history of the Cellular Jail thus: 'In
hallowed memory of those heroes who participated in the National Revolution of 1857 from
different states of India and were incarcerated in the Cellular Jail, Port Blair, by an alien
Government.'

the 1857 uprising as 'heroic sons of India', and refers to the uprising as the First
War of Independence. The Andaman Islands are 'sanctified by the dust of
Martyrs' feet and their sweat and blood'.[64] Yet the character of the uprising is still
subject to enormous controversy. That it was a unified national movement is
doubtful.[65] Aggarwal goes on to argue that very few ordinary convicts were transported; and in a curious logic states that even they can be described as Freedom
Fighters, 'because they were in the Andamans when mostly Freedom Fighters were
transported to the Andamans'.[66]

Historians have given undue prominence to other localised movements who
made up just a tiny handful of the total number of transportees. These include the

Wahabi convicts transported from Eastern Bengal in the 1860s, after the British led a crackdown on their anti-foreign movement. Convicts belonging to the Kuka Movement that in 1871 led a pre-Gandhi non-cooperation and economic boycott campaign against the British have also been cited. The Moplahs, too, transported from the Malabar coast in the early 1920s after skirmishes with the British, are seen as nationalist offenders.[67] They are clearly distinguished from other 'hardened criminals'[68] who, until the publication of Sen's *Disciplining Punishment*, were almost completely removed from the history of transportation to the Islands. The result of this is that the history of the Andaman Islands is now primarily conceived in terms of its place in the anti-British struggle. As Sen writes: 'It is no exaggeration to say that the Andamans have been thoroughly colonised by the hegemonic memory of Indian nationalism.'[69] Yet, of the tens of thousands of Indian convicts transported to the Andaman Islands after 1857, the Freedom Fighters shipped to the islands between 1906 and the Second World War numbered no more than 500.[70] This figure does not increase greatly even if we include nineteenth-century offenders. The multiple histories of ordinary convicts – who numbered at least 50,000 – have been all but forgotten.

In 1997 India commemorated the fiftieth anniversary of Independence. In the same year, the Cellular Jail Museum in Port Blair underwent extensive renovation. Although transported convicts were liberated from the Cellular Jail during the Second World War and two of the building's wings were destroyed either during the war or when a devastating earthquake hit the Islands in 1941, the site had remained a local prison until 1979. It was then closed, and reopened as the Freedom Fighter Museum. The inauguration ceremony was conducted by no less than the Indian Prime Minister, Moraji Desai.[71] In 1994, the museum expanded into the jail's original Administrative Headquarters, and was renamed the Cellular Jail Museum. During the fiftieth anniversary of Independence celebrations, a new building, exhibiting a series of photographs of the penal settlement, was opened. A series of publications was commissioned at the same time, focusing on those 'Indian patriots' incarcerated in the Cellular Jail.[72] The museum houses a series of plaques, naming the twentieth-century Freedom Fighters incarcerated on the Island. A handful of these Freedom Fighters are still alive. A few members of their Political Prisoners' Fraternity Association, based in Calcutta, make a highly publicised visit (*Mukti Tirtha*, or 'Pilgrimage of Salvation')[73] to the Islands each year.

One of the main attractions in the Cellular Jail Museum is the V.D. Savarkar Cell, which is openly acknowledged as no more than a symbolic site. To prevent communication between prisoners, inmates were constantly shifted from cell to cell. Other convicts – notably the 1857 mutineers and the Moplahs – are cast as heroes fighting British oppression. Life-size models of convicts in fetters, at work and on the flogging triangle are all represented on the site. The gallows have also been restored. Yet for all its symbolism as a place of colonial oppression and nationalist struggle, the museum only attracts about a hundred visitors a day.[74] This, of course, is directly related to its isolation from the mainland. The Islands are a two-hour flight, or three-day boat trip, from Chennai (Madras) or Calcutta. This physical distance creates a post-colonial gaze that has much in common with what colonial eyes saw. The Islands are seen as an isolated place of wild natural beauty. They have been recast as a honeymoon paradise, a stunningly beautiful place, with white sand and crystal clear sea, far away from the mainland and as yet relatively untouched by the ravages of tourism. Underlying tensions between Indian settlers and the tribal Jarawa, which sometimes lead to violent skirmishes, add a slight edge to any visit.

As we have seen, the nationalist prisoners shipped to the Andamans in the early twentieth century were middle-class men. In addition, they were frequently drawn from high-caste communities. It was perhaps inevitable that the discourse of the *kala pani* would re-emerge in contemporary representations of experiences of transportation. Clearly, middle-class prisoners were unfamiliar with many aspects of prison life, including common messing and communal bathing. These and other sufferings also related to their community status. V.D. Savarkar, for instance, wrote of the jail administrators' deliberate use of Muslim and low-convict warders to oversee high-caste Hindus.[75] As a result, nationalist historiography is filled with references to the indignities of crossing the *kala pani*, and as such closely echoes early nineteenth-century colonial discourses of transportation. S.N. Aggarwal writes in one such publication, *The Heroes of Cellular Jail*:

> A sentence to '*Kala Pani*' meant a warrant for throwing the prisoner in the living hell to face heard or unheard trials and tribulations and to lead the life like a beast or even worse than that. Transportation to '*Kala Pani*' for life was worse than [the] death penalty.[76]

Post-colonial readings of convict transportation to the Andamans such as these have thus strengthened the colonial discourse of caste.

Notes

1 This article has emerged from material collected during several years' research in the British Library, India Office Library, London (IOL), Mauritius Archives (MA), National Archives of India, New Delhi (NAI), National Library of Scotland and Tamil Nadu State Archives, Chennai (TNSA). I thank the British Academy, the British Academy Southeast Asia Committee, the Carnegie Trust for the Universities of Scotland and the Faculty of Social Sciences, University of Leicester, for their generous support. Fieldwork in the Andaman Islands was conducted in Spring 2001; I am again grateful to the British Academy for the award of a research grant to fund this trip. In addition, I am indebted to Swapnesh Choudhury, Curator of the Port Blair Cellular Jail Museum, and his staff, for all their help. Mukeshwar Lal generously shared his wide knowledge of the Islands with me. The editors, other authors and Ian Duffield commented extensively on earlier drafts.

2 C. Anderson, *Convicts in the Indian Ocean: Transportation from South Asia to Mauritius, 1815–53*, London, Macmillan, 2000, p. 44.

3 IOL P/134/48: Regulation for the Better Management of the Bengal Convicts, 5 October 1820; IOL MSS Eur D.742/46: A Regulation for the better order and management of the Convicts at Bencoolen, under sentence of transportation from Bengal and Madras, 1 January 1824.

4 NAI Home (Port Blair) A Proceedings, June 1907, nos. 10–16.

5   Anderson, *Convicts in the Indian Ocean*, pp. 101–2.

6   Anderson, *Convicts in the Indian Ocean*, pp. 79 and 106.

7   Anderson, *Convicts in the Indian Ocean*, p. 42. The government also sent leprous slaves there.

8   NAI Home (Port Blair) A Proceedings, January 1874, no. 1017 and September 1876, nos. 2–6.

9   There is a burgeoning literature on caste in India. For a recent overview, see S. Bayly, *Caste, Society and Politics in India from the Eighteenth Century to the Modern Age*, Cambridge, Cambridge University Press, 1999.

10   Anderson, *Convicts in the Indian Ocean*, pp. 15–18. The relationship between caste and imprisonment is discussed by D. Arnold, 'The colonial prison: power, knowledge, and penology in 19th-century India', in D. Arnold and D. Hardiman (eds) *Subaltern Studies VIII; Essays in Honour of Ranajit Guha*, New Delhi, Oxford University Press, 1994, pp. 148–87.

11   J. Fisch, *Cheap Lives and Dear Limbs: The British Transformation of the Bengal Criminal Law, 1769–1817*, Wiesbaden, Franz Steiner Verlag, 1983, pp. 59–62.

12   *Report of the Committee on Prison Discipline, 8 January 1838*, Calcutta, Baptist Mission Press, 1838, pp. 86 and 97.

13   I refer here to E.W. Said, *Orientalism: Western Conceptions of the Orient*, London, Pantheon, 1978. On orientalist constructions of India, see R. Inden, *Imagining India*, London, Blackwell, 1990.

14   IOL P/404/3: Petition of Shreekristna Wassoodewjee, 1 August 1846; List of Convicts in Bombay County Jail Under Sentence of Transportation to Singapore, 27 July 1846.

15   NAI Home (Judicial) A proceedings, 3 June 1859, nos. 7–13.

16   On caste in Indian jails, see Arnold, 'The Colonial Prison', pp. 170–5.

17   MA Z2A83: Police report, Savanne, 22 August 1835. For further discussion of convict attempts to maintain caste distinctions in the Mauritian settlement, and their manipulation of colonial beliefs about caste, see Anderson, *Convicts in the Indian Ocean*, pp. 93–6.

18   IOL P/140/70: A. Holroyd, Clerk of the Crown, to R.D. Mangles, Secretary to Government Bengal Judicial Department, enclosing Abstract Translation of the Bengal Letter of Goherdhone Babboo and Petition of the Defendant above named and now a prisoner of the Jail of Moarny Island [Tenasserim Provinces], 15 August 1835.

19   Anderson, *Convicts in the Indian Ocean*, appendices B6 and C2. Of the known origins of 986 convicts sentenced in the Bengal Presidency and transported to Mauritius, 55 per cent were Hindu, 32 per cent Muslim and 14 per cent *adivasi* (figures rounded up to nearest 1 per cent).

20   Parliamentary Papers 1830 XXVIII: A Regulation for empowering the Governor-General to commute Sentences of Imprisonment for Life in the Allypore Gaol, to Transportation for Life to any of the British Settlements in Asia, in certain cases, 10 April 1828 (Regulation I 1828).

21   IOL P/142/60: List of nine convict petitioners to Moulmein per *Enterprize*, 10 January 1847; IOL P/142/61: List of twelve convict petitioners to Moulmein per *Enterprize*, 10 January 1847; IOL P/143/3: List of thirty-seven convict petitioners to Moulmein per *Enterprize*, 10 June 1847; IOL P/143/4: List of eight convict petitioners to Kyouk Phyoo per *Tenasserim*, 10 July 1847; and, IOL P/143/5: List of ten convict petitioners to Kyouk Phyoo per *Tenasserim*, 10 August 1847.

22   *Report of the Committee on Prison Discipline*, p. 86 (figures for the period 1827–37).

23   IOL P/142/8: A. Bogle, Commissioner of Arakan, to F.J. Halliday, Secretary to Government Bengal, 7 November 1843.

24   IOL P/129/6: S.M. Threipland, East India Company Counsel, to J.A. Grant, Secretary to Government Bombay Judicial Department, 4 May 1804.

25 IOL P/129/36: E. Thornton, Magistrate Twenty-four Parganas District, to G. Dowdeswell, Secretary to Government Bengal Judicial Department, 18 November 1805.

26 IOL P/136/31: Minute of W.E. Phillips, Prince of Wales' Island Government, 15 April 1824.

27 TNSA Madras Judicial Proceedings (henceforth MJP) vol. 291: J.F. Thomas, Register Foujdaree Udalut, to F.R. Wheatley, Chief Secretary to Government Madras Judicial Department, 22 August 1835; TNSA MJP vol. 306A: W. Douglas, Register Foujdaree Udalut, to H. Chamier, Chief Secretary to Government Madras, 25 April 1836.

28 TSNA MJP vol. 310: H. Chamier to W.H. Macnaughten, Secretary to Government of India, 12 July 1836.

29 IOL P/138/59: J. Master, Superintendent Alipur Jail, to H. Shakespear, Secretary to Government Bengal Judicial Department, 23 February 1828.

30 IOL P/139/1: Master to Shakespear, 22 August 1828.

31 IOL P/139/66: Master to Shakespear, 29 December 1830.

32 On the fear of transportation in Britain, see: R. Hughes, *The Fatal Shore: A History of the Transportation of Convicts to Australia, 1787–1868*, London, Harvill, 1987, ch. 3; and D. Meredith, 'Full circle? Contemporary views on transportation', in S. Nicholas (ed.) *Convict Workers: Reinterpreting Australia's Past*, Cambridge, Cambridge University Press, 1988, pp. 14–27.

33 IOL P/128/54: Return of the Bengal convicts brought to Prince of Wales' Island from the Andamans, 1 November 1800 to 31 January 1801. There were 234 surviving men.

34 For a critical analysis of nineteenth-century Andamans ethnography, see E. Edwards, 'Science visualized: E.H. Man in the Andaman Islands', in E. Edwards (ed.) *Anthropology and Photography, 1860–1920*, London, Yale University Press, 1992, pp. 108–21.

35 S. Sen, *Disciplining Punishment: Colonialism and Convict Society in the Andaman Islands*, New Delhi, Oxford University Press, 2000, p. 28.

36 NAI Home (Judicial) A Proceedings, 28 May 1858, nos. 12–17: Minute of H. Ricketts, 16 July 1858.

37 On family emigration, see S. Sen, 'Rationing sex: female convicts in the Andamans', *South Asia*, 1999, vol. 30, no. 1, pp. 29–59.

38 Sen, *Disciplining Punishment*, p. v.

39 The father and wife of Rughonath Singh turned back from Calcutta when the realisation dawned: NAI Home (Judicial) A Proceedings, 30 July 1870, nos. 11–13.

40 Although detailed caste lists of the kind compiled for convicts shipped to Mauritius and Southeast Asia do not survive, census data still exists. For the first census, see NAI Home (Port Blair) A Proceedings, October 1873, nos. 49–59: Census of the Andaman Islands, December 1871.

41 NAI Home (Port Blair) A Proceedings, February 1876, nos. 53–5: Note of C.A. Barwell, 18 November 1875.

42 Extensive correspondence relating to the return of ex-convicts to India (and family knowledge about their transportation experiences) can be found in the TNSA Judicial Proceedings series, from the 1880s onwards.

43 NAI Home (Port Blair) A Proceedings, October 1904, nos. 60–1: W.R.H. Merk to H.H. Risley, 2 July 1904; Risley to Merk, 27 October 1904.

44 NAI Home (Judicial) A Proceedings, September 1877, nos. 68–88: Report of the Prison Conference (1877).

45 NAI Home (Jails) A Proceedings, December 1889, nos. 1–47: Report of the Committee on Jail Management in India (1888).

46 NAI Home (Port Blair) A Proceedings, June 1890, nos. 74–8: Report on the Andamans by Mr C.J. Lyall and Surgeon-Major A.S. Lethbridge.

47 For an excellent overview of British penal policy during the same period, see M.J. Wiener, *Reconstructing the Criminal: Culture, Law and Policy in England, 1830–1914*, Cambridge, Cambridge University Press, 1990.

48 NAI Home (Port Blair) A Proceedings, July 1906, nos 38–40: W.R.H. Merk, 'Note on the Andamans', 15 September 1904.

49 D. Massey, 'Places and their pasts', *History Workshop Journal*, 1995, vol. 39, pp. 186–8.

50 W. Singer, *Creating Histories: Oral Narratives and the Politics of History Making*, New Delhi, Oxford University Press, 1997.

51 T. Edensor, *Tourists at the Taj: Performance and Meaning at a Symbolic Site*, London, Routledge, 1998.

52 The main exceptions to this are K.S. Sandu, 'Tamil and other Indian convicts in the Straits Settlements, AD 1790–1873', *Proceedings of the First International Tamil Conference Seminar of Tamil Studies*, vol. I, Kuala Lumpur, International Association of Tamil Research, 1968, pp. 197–208; and C.M. Turnbull, 'Convicts in the Straits Settlements, 1826–67', *Journal of the Malay Branch of the Royal Asiatic Society*, 1970, vol. 43, no. 1, pp. 87–103.

53 B. Yeoh, *Contesting Space: Power Relations and the Urban Built Environment in Colonial Singapore*, Singapore, Oxford University Press, 1996.

54 B. Bissoondoyal, *The Truth About Mauritius*, Bombay, Bharatiya Vidya Bhavan, 1987, pp. 19–23; M. Emrith, *History of the Muslims in Mauritius*, Mauritius, Editions le Printemps, 1994, pp. 20–2; K. Hazareesingh, *History of Indians in Mauritius*, London, Macmillan, 1977, p. 20; A.R. Mannick, *Mauritius: The Development of a Plural Society*, Nottingham, Spokesman, 1979, p. 39; M.N. Varma, *Indian Immigrants and their Descendants in Mauritius*, Mauritius, published by the author, 1973, pp. 16–17. The exception to this is my own *Convicts in the Indian Ocean*. For a breakdown of the offences for which the convicts were transported, see appendices B1 and B2.

55 H. Deacon, 'Introduction', in H. Deacon (ed.), *The Island: A History of Robben Island 1488–1990*, Cape Town, David Philip, 1996, p. 5.

56 U. Kumar Singh, *Political Prisoners in India*, New Delhi, Oxford University Press, 1998, pp. 50–9.

57 Sen, *Disciplining Punishment*, p. 268; L.P. Mathur, *Kala Pani: History of Andaman and Nicobar Islands with a Study of India's Freedom Struggle*, New Delhi, Eastern Book Company, 1992, p. 82.

58 B.K. Ghose, *The Tale of My Exile*, Pondicherry, Arya Office, 1922; B. Parmanand, *The Story of My Life*, New Delhi, S. Chand, 1982; V.D. Savarkar, *The Story of My Transportation for Life*, Bombay, Sadbhakti Publications, 1950; B. Kumar Sinha, *In Andamans, the Indian Bastille*, New Delhi, People's Publishing House, 1988 (1st edn 1939).

59 Sen, *Disciplining Punishment*, p. 47.

60 For a full description, see Savarkar, *The Story*, pp. 34–7.

61 Parmanand, *The Story*, pp. 106 and 111.

62 B.L. Chak, *Green Islands in the Sea*, New Delhi, Publications Division, Ministry of Information and Broadcasting, Government of India, 1967 (Preface by Indira Gandhi).

63 Mathur, *Kala Pani*, n.p. (Preface).

64 S.N. Aggarwal, *The Heroes of Cellular Jail*, Patalia, Publication Bureau, Punjabi University, 1995, pp. 20–6.

65 For an historiographical overview, see C.A. Bayly, *Indian Society and the Making of the British Empire*, Cambridge, Cambridge University Press, 1987, ch. 6.

66 Aggarwal, *The Heroes*, p. 26.

67 Aggarwal, *The Heroes*, pp. 32–7; and N. Iqbal Singh, *The Andaman Story*, New Delhi, Vikas, 1978, pp. 176–88; Mathur, *Kala Pani*, pp. 73–6.

68 R.C. Majumdar, *Penal Settlement in Andamans*, New Delhi, Government of India, Publications Division, 1975. p. 125.

69 Sen, *Disciplining Punishment*, p. v.
70 Sen, *Disciplining Punishment*, pp. 264–72. See also Singh, *Political Prisoners in India*, pp. 50–9.
71 The traveller Gavin Young describes a trip to the Museum in the late 1970s: *Slow Boats to China*, London, Picador, 1995 [1981], pp. 424–5.
72 Published lists of Freedom Fighters imprisoned in the Cellular Jail include R. Iqbal, *Unsung Heroes of Freedom Struggle in Andamans*, Port Blair, Directorate of Youth Affairs, Sports and Culture, Andaman and Nicobar Administration, 1998; G.S. Pandey, *Patriots of Andaman in Freedom Struggle Movement 1942–45*, Port Blair, Sangeeta, 2000; P. Roy and S. Choudhury, *Cellular Jail: Cells beyond Cells*, New Delhi, Farsight, 2000.
73 Aggarwal, *The Heroes*, p. 22.
74 In contrast, approximately 200,000 tourists per year visit Port Arthur; C. Strange, 'The Port Arthur massacre; tragedy and public memory in Australia', *Studies in Law, Politics and Society*, 2000, vol. 20, pp. 158–82.
75 Savarkar, *The Story*, p. 125. Sen writes of this as an extraordinary social experience for warders and convicts: *Disciplining Punishment*, p. 267.
76 Aggarwal, *The Heroes*, p. 18. For a similar reading, see also Iqbal Singh, *The Andaman Story*, p. 183.

4 Beating the system

Prison music and the politics of penal space

Ethan Blue

This essay begins in the 1940s in a backwoods Texas prison camp. It ends on a compact disc, navigating the channels of the global economy. From prison work-songs to hip-hop, this essay tracks the insurgent culture of prisoners' music in the United States over the second half of the twentieth century as it ruptures the isolations of incarceration. Inside prison walls, inmates' music re-territorialises the space–time of exile in a grounded politics of community against the grain of unfreedom; the polyrhythms inflect a temporality that pays little allegiance to the linear metric of time-as-punishment. Through sound, prisoners craft an oppositional milieu that is functional (songs can pace work), expressive (of desire, fear, pain) and resistant (surveillance is inverted as prisoners constitute knowledge of their keepers). Prisoners' music refashions community in this overtly male domain, operating within and expressing the conflicted masculinities of penal worlds.

As advanced capitalism in the United States spawns a prison-industrial complex, prisoners and the racialised urban communities from which they disproportionately come create a powerful oppositional culture, undermining the isolations of a hostile criminal justice system in ways that worksongs never could. Participants in hip-hop culture perform a global oppositional public sphere, forging territories, communities and subjectivities resistant to the practices and alienations of mass incarceration. At the same time, domains of punishment circulate outside prison walls, as chain gangs re-emerge in spectacles of state power.

Prison music is more than aesthetic production, more than a rare and important source for locating prisoners' voices. It is a vital force in the production of life, meaning and subjectivity. For better or for worse, music is always steeped in power, and power – particularly in the experience of space and time – is always embedded in music. Music constitutes a force of deterritorialisation – of challenging and reformulating conflicted environments and reterritorialising new ones. From the early years of the twentieth century into the twenty-first, sounds joined with architecture and violence in the production of prison life, each of which merged in the complex determination of identity, experience and opposition to domination in penal contexts.

In the century following the Civil War, the law was a crucial domain of racial and economic domination of poor blacks across the US South.[1] Racial hierarchies sustained prison systems, just as they structured Southern society overall, contributing the ideological and violent force of law to the processes of racial formation in the US South. Seasonal and daily farming imperatives still set the timing of prisoners' days, farming food and cash crops from 'can see till can't', so that prisons could function at low cost. Notions of penal reform prevalent in other regions were noticeably absent for Southern, and especially African American, prisoners, whose forced labour subsidised prisons, built roads and, due to their visibility, bolstered the authority of the state itself.

Not only did segregation and the racial state produce racial identities, so too did the music that Southern prisoners sang.[2] According to folklorist Bruce Jackson, worksongs performed numerous functions for black prisoners labouring in fields and road crews so reminiscent of slavery. Songs set the timing and pace of agricultural prison labour and, importantly, allowed for a covert challenge to guards' authority. Along with these crucial insights, Jackson also made a tentative suggestion that worksongs helped to make the labour that prisoners performed their own, to wrest control of their incarceration from their keepers.[3] Building upon Jackson's critical analysis, this chapter explores how music performed these functions, and how, through sound, prisoners claimed space, time and authority.[4]

Recent theorists have argued that spaces have no pre-existing character, they must be actively held together to cohere, 'like a fist clenched around sand'.[5] Of course, architecture is part of spatial contests of power, but so too is sound. According to Gilles Deleuze and Félix Guattari's analytical insight, music can organise spatial and temporal elements into what they term a *milieu* and what Nigel Thrift calls *context*.[6] In the process of singing or listening to music, alternative spatial and temporal milieux can be claimed while other, competing, forces are kept at bay. In the case of prison worksongs, the conflicting elements were guard violence, an unbearable pace of labour, the geography of penal farms, and intra-prisoner fighting. Music enabled prisoners to create a 'wall of sound, or at least, a wall with some sonic bricks in it', crafting a space and protecting themselves from these multiple destructive forces.[7] And though recent analysts have studied the power implicit and contested in spaces, relatively few have questioned how time, too, is a contested domain. Prison worksongs operated in these inseparable fields to reconfigure punitive carceral milieux.[8]

Prisoners' worksongs voiced suffering through beautiful sound. Most of the songs expressed longing, want and distance from loved ones, as prisoners lamented the duration of their imprisonment. Multiple cadences based the timing of the axe or hammer; harmonies and intonations, calls and responses all set prisoners' bodies in motion to the time of music. Their rhythms communicated pace for work, so that they laboured in unison and cooperation, rather than under the suspicions and antagonisms that prisons so often yield, and despite numerous differences between prisoners themselves.[9]

Music also formed a negotiation over the conditions of labour with guards known for racism and brutality. Singing assured a steady pace of work throughout the day without taxing prisoners beyond possible physical endurance or drawing a guard's attention and subsequent punishment. Many died nonetheless. In his recollections as a prisoner on Texas's notorious Retrieve Farm, Albert Race Sample described how the temporality of music drew guards on to a terrain that prisoners set through harmonies and rhythms: 'Every axe hitting in rhythm. Boss Dead Eye sat on his horse contented, "When them ol' nigguhs is sangin, ever thang's awright." With a shotgun laid across his arm, he listened as we sang and sang.'[10] A Mississippi prisoner named Bama said that the most important quality of a good leader was his knowledge of *timing*. 'That's what it takes, the time, that's all it is.'[11] The ability to set the pace of labour, and of seizing moments for rest, was a crucial way that prisoners crafted new penal contexts *within*, but also *exceeding*, Southern penal domains.

One of the primary activities in which prisoners sang worksongs was for chopping down trees. These songs functioned so that men standing in a circle around a tree, each of whom was swinging an axe, would time their strokes so that no blade would fly out of control and maim another. Thus beyond setting a manageable pace of labour, music was a functional part of the productive process, ensuring prisoners' safety and allowing some escape and pleasure from their toil. Through rhythmic modulations and communal participation, leaders and background singers created a sonorous envelope that contested the orientations of penal time with alternative timings. These were timings for memory, and alternative histories, as prisoners folded a different milieu into the context of penal farms, replacing punishment with memories of family or home.[12] As Deleuze and Guattari suggest how places are formed and contested through music, they describe how new territories could be made: 'One opens the circle' – in this case a circle of prisoners felling a tree – 'not on the side where the old forces of chaos press against it but in another region, one created by the circle itself.'[13] Indeed, according to one visitor to Mississippi's Parchman Farm, the sound of the music 'could almost take you off of your feet'.[14]

These new invocations conjured visions of mobility, through sounds and rhythms, and called other places into being. Prisoners sang about places they had visited or wanted to go, but would be unable to see save for these imagined trips to Hot Springs, Arkansas, or to Memphis, Tennessee, places with symbolic importance for these immobilised Southerners.[15] Rivers and riverboats were recurrent motifs of worksongs, and Jackson asserts that these signified both freedom and mobility for prisoners. Numerous songs refer to 'standing on the levee', both a worksite and the bank of the river. And the river was often one of the borders of their incarceration, a symbol of freedom and escape.[16]

Yet still within the very material context of prison farms, worksongs allowed for prisoners to circulate knowledge of guards' habits, weakness and indulgences, as 'an informational site for the transmission of oppositional strategies and popular wisdom about survival'.[17] This was a counter-knowledge to official record-keeping – a reconnaissance, as it were, of enemy territory.[18] One prisoner told Jackson, 'Long time ago when the penitentiary was kind of rough they used to sing songs about the bosses, sergeants, lieutenants, whatever they think about them, that's what they'd sing about them'.[19]

References to guards were often coded in complex ways. Texas Guard Carl Luther McAdams was sometimes called 'Beartracks' by prisoners, for the size of his feet as well as for his ferocity. He was reputed to be able to beat just about anyone in a fight with his bare hands – he wasn't dependent on a shotgun or badge for violent authority. Though despised, prisoners also positioned McAdams as a masculine anti-hero of near-mythic proportion, much like Stacker Lee, an uncontrollable bad man who celebrated nihilistic defiance of black and white norms of behaviour.[20] In one version of the song 'Grizzly Bear', listeners were warned 'Oh don't let that Bear catch you, man, GRIZZLY BEAR … /Well he will catch you and he'll kill you that GRIZZLY BEAR'.

But in another version the singer follows the grizzly bear down to the Brazos River, the river that irrigated huge stretches of Texas penal farmland. 'You know I ain't scared a no bear GRIZZLY BEAR /Because the workin' squad they killed him there, GRIZZLY BEAR.'[21] In this version, the working squad kills the bear, signifying their communal overpowering of the guard. Unlike other versions of this song, and unlike the trickster Brer Rabbit stories, this is the group's – rather than an individual character representing the group's – revenge.

As prisoners claimed spaces away from their keepers, they did so in gendered ways, as a crucial modality through which power was expressed.[22] The spaces that most worksongs claimed were definitively male. In a location where every act and their very lives were controlled by others, performance of masculinity became a crucial component of self-identification. Worksongs allowed for expressions of men's physical potency, and these, it seems, were fulfilling for male prisoners in a situation that attempted to render them powerless, and thus feminised. In versions of 'Let Your Hammer Ring', the leader says that his hammer is on fire because it is so powerful. The axe (seemingly a phallic symbol, and variously called a hammer or a diamond – possibly from its shape when viewed from above) often took on supernatural powers in songs.[23] It is on fire as it bites into the tree he is felling, as a result of his skill and strength. The singer takes it to the Brazos River (again, symbolic of freedom), but it still won't be cooled. In the song 'Alberta', the hammer 'rings like silver and it SHINES LIKE GOLD/Price a my hammer, boys, AIN'T NEVER BEEN TOLD'. The workers claimed value in their labour, and enunciated their pride in their physical strength using tropes of diamonds, precious metals and highly valued goods, valorising the tools they were forced to use.[24]

Singers found common currency in discussing the absence of women and of missing their partners. Big Louisiana hoped that his hammer was loud enough to call his partner to him, and in one song he called out to her because he saw her in a dream the night before. Thus songs and dreams were locations of escape, of sexual and familial contact. Yet many prisoners were guilty of violence against women prior to their arrests, and they sometimes sang such violence into their songs, especially when sexual partners were thought to be unfaithful. Jackson also recorded a number of 'toasts' by Texas prisoners, who boasted of their own sexual prowess by denigrating women and symbolically performing as pimps – owners of women's bodies and sexual labour. Hypermasculine performances operated within the matrices of power and difference exacerbated by penal worlds. And though worksongs sometimes voiced misogynist themes, they also expressed genuine longing for loved ones, and served as a language for the performance of heterosexual masculinity as an inclusive identity. Though worksongs operated as a politics of inclusion for male prisoners vis-à-vis their keepers, they simultaneously performed an exclusion of women, children and 'effeminate' males. The 'wall of sound ... with some sonic bricks' kept these 'others' outside, while gendering those within the worksong's milieu in particular masculinist ways.[25] More complex still, worksongs also allowed for nurturing and supportive male voices in penal farms, ones that may not have otherwise been permitted within codes of masculinity that scorned weakness. Prisoners showed genuine concern for each other, despite the alienations of this punitive world. One leader sang, 'Watch my buddy, buddy he start to fall, Help that boy, won't you make it long'.[26]

Imagine the beat of the hammer blows, of the polyrhythms, of the refrains and endless variations, the freedom to improvise and express yourself. Think of the ability of a group of prisoners to take a tree and, in one prisoner's words, to 'sing it down ... sing it down in harmony'.[27] Think of the ability to ridicule guards under their own noses. Think of the sheer beauty of the music, of remembering other times and places and transposing them, through memory and music, into penal contexts. Contrast the harmony and memories with the linear time of the prison system – calculated, supposedly rational, and structured around forced labour. The ground shifted when prisoners almost couldn't hear the guards shouting, when the crack of the whip was nearly drowned out. As prisoners made gains and incremental increases in privilege (or decreases in work), they gained ground in the battle for control of their lives. They were operating from a position of relative weakness, for their music was but one element among many that converged in penal contexts, but they continually pressed for others. Neither set of sounds – music, nor the guard whip's crack – could entirely eclipse the other, but between the countervailing forces of prisoner music and state violence emerged the culture of Southern punishment: local, violent, backwoods, everyday.

By the late 1960s few were singing worksongs any more, and new penal systems and cultural forms were on the horizon. As prison populations skyrocketed for minor drug crimes, black and Latino/a youth in urban centres experimented with turntables, breakbeats and rhymes that shared much with Southern prison toasts. Each transformation took place in the turbulent years that David Harvey identified as pivoting between a Fordist–Keynesian mode of production and that of flexible accumulation.[28] These political economic shifts could also be seen in inmates' labour: today's prisoners are as likely to work for a private firm straightening the legs on microchips as they are to press license plates, make furniture or chop cotton in this advanced capitalist combination of multiple productive systems.

The wars on drugs and crime have been central elements of recent social control strategies in the United States, maintaining flexible labour markets and scapegoating racial others in new racial formations that are both more subtle and more pervasive than those of the Jim Crow South's apartheid regime. In this post-Civil Rights era, the principal tactic has been the criminalisation of urban public space and the widespread disappearing of the poor and non-white behind prison walls. Through processes of racial, spatial and criminal formations, immigrants and the non-white are increasingly criminalised in their neighbourhoods, to be isolated and immobilised in prisons and immigrant detention centres.[29]

Hip-hop is undeniably allied to and identifies with prisoners of the criminal justice system. Much like the worksongs of an earlier era, hip-hop operates on multiple, overlapping levels against the practice of incarceration. But today's prison music crosses borders and travels across the globe, circulating alternative perspectives and alternative histories from those of mainstream media. Like a needle on a record, it scratches back and forth between groups of people, creating new social and political identities. Hip-hop follows the contours of late capitalism; it is undeniably a part of the global economic system that incarcerates over two million Americans who are disproportionately poor and disproportionately of colour. But hip-hop surpasses the boundaries of economics. Riding along the commodity channels of capital, it carries struggle and forms communities, countering the ideologies of fear and retribution that riddle the evening news. Musicians and listeners circulate music in a mass mediascape opposed to state controls: bridging divisions in space, linking sites of pleasure and moving them through postindustrial city streets and around the world.[30]

Chuck D, front man for Public Enemy, often says that rap music is the CNN for black America, and Heavy D called rap a 'satellite communication system' for black people.[31] But rap works as more than just a form of news distribution within a consumer model of media effects. Hip-hop, especially through its political messages, has the ability to form discursive communities upon the terrain of mass-distributed music, functioning as print media once did to create and maintain nationalist identities. Music is a crucial force in today's processes of identity formation; fences and guard towers pose little barrier to this kind of mobility.[32]

Hip-hop culture combines elements of music, clothing, graffiti and breakdancing, valorising the perspectives and experiences of youth of colour. It emerged (principally, though not solely) from the confluence of global immigrant and capital flows in New York City in the 1970s.[33] Although hip-hop is widely and correctly associated with African Americans and the transatlantic African diaspora, it would be a mistake to silence the roots and continued presence of multiple Latino/a, Native American, Asian American and European American elements. Accelerated globalisation of large cities prompts new cultural and aesthetic mixes, and hip-hop's flexible expressions proliferate in expanding mediascapes, in hybrids of home-grown and imported musical genres.[34]

Terminator X, DJ for Public Enemy, is widely known for mixing in the literal sounds of the streets into Public Enemy's music. According to Puerto Rican hip-hop progenitor Charlie Chase, rap music is 'a street thing. I liked it because it came from the street and I'm from the street … [R]ap is us.'[35] These are the same streets where polyracial youth meet – sometimes violently, over scarce resources or turf battles, but often peaceably, at concerts and music festivals.[36] But the streets are where many young people confront and are confronted by the police. Increasingly, musicians add the sounds of the prison to those of the streets: collect phone call operators, cell doors slamming, guards' commands, and the sonic chaos and unceasing noise in today's prisons.[37]

Rap utilises electronic media and sampling techniques, and re-invents vinyl records as musical instruments in a postmodern mode of production.[38] Old records are re-used in novel ways; samples from old records make allusion to older styles of music and bring different temporal realms into dialogue on the turntables. Houston A. Baker, Jr, notes that through these multiple, non-authoritative sonic references, 'linearity and progress yield to a dizzying synchronicity'.[39] Multiple temporal references in hip-hop samples pay homage to earlier musicians and movements – especially Black Power and Civil Rights – synchronising multiple times and politically salient references in music. Like jazz musicians playing jazz standards, hip-hop 'makes the past literally audible in the present'.[40]

But more than calling other times into listeners' presence, hip-hop conjures new spaces of communication for hip-hop fans. In a compilation album entitled *No More Prisons*, rappers in B.K.N.Y. call out to prisoners throughout the country, locked up because they couldn't live on minimum wages and had to hustle to feed their families: 'All my people up in Attica … All my people up in Sing Sing … All my people in San Quentin, Where ya at?' The call to prisoners in diverse locations brings them together, names and valorises the locations of their unfreedom, bringing free-world listeners into their discursive presence, and vice versa. Tricia Rose cites numerous rap artists who give shout outs to other places and artists, to friends and crews in their neighbourhoods. Claiming pride in home and valorising emplacement in ghettos is a widespread feature of hip-hop music.[41]

Following the lead of these musicians, theorist Jody Berland argues that musical communication creates a 'third space', a non-contiguous location mediated through technological dissemination. Listening is thus a much more powerful, and productive, process, than simply consuming sound; it is a profoundly spatial practice.[42] The third spaces of music are parts of larger networks, but they are always known in intensely local ways – a cell in Folsom, a subway under Manhattan, a neighbourhood in southwest Atlanta. Subjectivities are produced in association with the networks they inhabit and, though known in specific locations, exist in far broader collectivities, as a link in chains of connectivity, or a grounded knot in discursive networks of communicative emplacement.[43] Playing and listening to hip-hop claims places for youth presence, and inflects subjects with new authority. As with work-songs in Southern prisons, hip-hop's urban territories collide with locked-down police zones, as sirens and music beats each struggle to silence the other.[44]

In addition to bridging communities from California to Cape Town, hip-hop travels through prison walls. California rapper X-Raided has recorded four albums (at the time of this writing) from behind bars, and he's one of a growing number of rappers to do so.[45] While the first albums were grainy and the vocals were recorded over the prison telephone in an expensive series of collect calls, his recent album *Vengeance is Mine* has very clear vocals. Prison authorities are at a loss as to how he was able to smuggle a recording device into his cell and record the album, though one guard has since been fired for helping X-Raided project his voice beyond the prison walls. This moment itself demonstrates guard complicity in subaltern prison traffic and economy, and also belies the monolithic nature of the state in daily and covert practice. Nevertheless, the resulting album demonstrates one more way that music is able to move across the prison walls and, through its commodification, draw listeners into communication with prisoners.

X-Raided's rhythms are complex and his rhymes are tight, but they aren't always pretty. They embody many of the themes prevalent in hardcore rap, of personal strength and violence in a violent world. He records the discursive and material violence in California's postindustrial streets and crystallised in its prisons: 'I just write what I see, I might not like what I see, but whether it's wrong or right … the song's my life … it's not just songs, it's life.' Addressing the critics who decry the violence in his music, X-Raided asks: 'What the hell am I supposed to write, how can I compose nice, when I'm sittin in this cell at night?'[46] And a part of both life and music is violence, between gangs and between prisoners, and visited by police on each. Violence results from the competitive drug economies that some poor youth have exploited in an acquisitive street entrepreneurism, but also from police and guard provocation of gang feuds to keep prisoners divided among themselves.[47] Yet we might follow rapper Talib Kweli's lyrical lamentation and theorisation of situations where the downtrodden fight among themselves. Under these conditions, prevalent in much of postindustrial urban America, 'people fight for what's left and not what's right'.[48]

X-Raided's music is situated within systems of dominated and dominating life, of re-creating and communicating 'thug life' to his listeners in celebration of lyrical prowess. His lyrics closely parallel the worksongs and toasts that claim masculine prestige in a disempowered situation. Though he doesn't espouse any concerted political programme to undermine prison authorities (as do articles in the prisoner-authored newspaper *Prison Legal News*), X-Raided's music is a performance of just such a subversion. The lack of 'politics' in his lyrics seems less a weakness in a rebellious identity than sidestepping confrontation with officials who wield so much control over his and other prisoners' lives. Nevertheless, his celebration and intro-spection of thug life – certainly a form of oppositional culture – can and have been turned on him to justify police repression. Lyrics from an album released before he was imprisoned were used against him in court, cited by prosecutors as an admis-sion of guilt rather than artistic expression or a performance of music.[49]

Particularly relevant in any analysis of rap music is its regressive gender politics. But first note that hip-hop is not monolithic; it is not entirely sexist. To paraphrase Rose, rap has been wrongly characterised as homogenously sexist but rightly criti-cised for its sexism.[50] If we stop at the rather obvious point of rap's misogyny, we only demonise rappers instead of understanding why these dominating gendered narratives grew in such force and popularity in late 1980s and 1990s. Without excusing the misogyny that it entails, I would venture a partial answer: the economic and personal insecurities accelerated in the Reagan years and sustained through the 1990s prompted reformulation of gendered identities for those young men suffering from increased poverty, police scrutiny, and aggression. With the criminalisation of public space in recent years, the same technologies and forced insecurities heightening misogyny in worksongs expanded in both prisons and streets. The revitalisation of hypermasculine imagery and misogynistic narratives is a reaction to perceived threats to men's self-images under police control and invasive street searches, heightened by economic insecurity in flexible labour markets.[51]

The group dead prez joins numerous other groups in challenging the current state of incarceration in the United States. They link prisoners' rights movements and carceral complexes with American imperialism in a new socialist, black nationalist movement. They criticise forms of ideological and material control of communities of colour, blurring the boundaries between imprisonment and everyday policing for the urban poor in the US 'Police State' (the name of a song on their album). And though explicitly anti-capitalist, they are equally explicit in using commercial elements of hip-hop as a medium for their message. They embody the most critical elements of a tradition of prison music, locating sources of dominance in racism and political economics, but they invigorate these critiques with expressly political Black Panther ideology that worksongs lacked. Indeed, challenging the lockup of political dissidents in COINTELPRO set-ups animates much of dead prez's lyrics. Their politics make explicit many of the criticisms implicit in worksongs, and gain momentum in today's prison-building hysteria. They challenge not just forces of exploitation and police repression, but also take aim at the corporate dominated aspects of hip-hop that stress materialism. It is little accident that they are not as widely played on MTV or the radio as are less political, more money- and party-oriented musicians. They rap:

> I'm sick of that fake thug R and B rap scenario, all day on the radio,
> Same scenes in the video, monotonous material ...
> Would you rather have a Lexus or Justice, a dream or some substance,
> A Beamer [BMW], a necklace, or freedom? ...
> See, a nigga like me don't playa-hate, I just stay awake
> It's *Real* Hip-Hop
> And it don't stop till we get the po-po [police] off the block.[52]

dead prez claim the place of *real* hip-hop as that which is politically oriented and motivated against domination. They also recognise that their music, as distributed by CD, appropriates the commodity channels of capitalism. Stic says: 'What we trying to do in those songs and our albums in general is use the commercial, which just means the medium of the hip-hop business, to promote revolutionary ideas and revolutionary change and honest expression.'[53] Stic and M1, the artists of dead prez, expressly use the distribution networks and reproductive capacities of the recording industries to spread their revolutionary message against the rising tide of incarceration, and locate themselves in the revolutionary tradition of the Black Panthers, one of whose messages remains prison abolitionism and championing the downtrodden and the wrongly imprisoned.

Worksongs and hip-hop operate within contested political economies and state formations structured around racial domination and mobilised through spatial controls, but neither form of music has been contained by the formations of which they are a part. Nevertheless, a vital distinction between worksongs and hip-hop comes in the threat that each genre made, or makes, to the state, either real or feared. Though worksongs reoriented the milieux of Southern punishment, they nevertheless served as a motivation for labour within this overwhelmingly violent penal regime. Significantly, folklorists like John Lomax saw worksongs as a residue from slavery that would disappear in a narrative of progressive reform. Hip-hop was first laughed at as a fad, but has since been demonised as music out of control, and blamed for everything from gang violence to attacks on police and sustained sexism, when multiracial middle-class critics seize the most extreme elements of hardcore rap as if it were the only kind in existence, and as if mainstream cultures were not thoroughly sexist. Young people's music has been blamed as a cause, rather than a symptom, of the panoply of social ills facing poor, urban, non-white youth today.[54] But musicians have been best at turning the tables, with turntables, on such reductionism: 'They blame it on a song when someone kills a cop, What music did they listen to when they bombed Iraq?' asks Spearhead's Michael Franti.[55]

The hip-hop community offers a potentially new cultural formation that may produce new political subjectivities, as hip-hop culture is re-formed by youth of all colours across the planet. Like any imagined community, it is internally diffracted and its edges are porous; it maintains asymmetries of power, forced silences and new regimes of inequality, amplifying corporate influences only interested in profits, and silencing the voices and presence of women. But this is contested, too, by women musicians, graffiti writers, and male artists like dead prez. If historian George Lipsitz is correct in his assessment that 'realities not yet possible in political life may appear first within popular culture', we may be witnessing a redefinition of racial and political formations via hip-hop's territorialisations, and in its invoca- tions of a community critical of mass incarceration.[56] This happens not just in lyrics, but also in streets, clubs and cars. When people listen to hip-hop in public, they challenge the criminalisation of public space and their erasure from city streets, part of a highly profitable culture industry but also part of an expanding critical resistance.[57]

Hip-hop accelerates the challenges implicit in prison worksongs: community formation, the circulation of struggle and communication of critical messages, and contesting the repressive militarisation of space. As the volume is cranked up, reaching hip-hop's ever-expanding audience, it still meets new walls and forms of sexism and racism, class exploitation and domination. Like worksongs, hip-hop expresses numerous contradictory effects, and the cultural movements it both expresses and sustains may fall prey to containment by state forces, or as privileged white youth find vicarious pleasures but little desire for divestment from foundations of racial, economic or suburban status.[58] There are no guarantees that the expanded communication and communities of hip-hop listeners will lead to egali- tarian lives, just as beyond the milieu of worksongs, prisoners still fought over meagre resources and inmate trusties still bolstered guards' authority. Nevertheless, as fields of conflict change within and around criminal justice systems, prisoners and their allies keep pace with the changes and contribute their own. Struggles to control the milieux of city spaces and penal times are multi-directional and ongoing, and prisoners shackled to one another in chain gangs in postmodern shaming rituals can find pleasure and momentary solidarity as cars drive by booming beats they know. Prisoners invest and invigorate space and time on the new terrains that capital and politicians impose, while conjuring alternative milieux of their own. Just as prisoners' culture contains contradictions that allow for divisions and new dominations, so too are state discourses and milieux cracked and contradictory. Prisoners continue to exploit, exacerbate and navigate those contradictions.

Through music, prisoners and allies challenge today's criminal justice systems, whose heritage is as much a Mississippi plantation as it is in Bentham's panopticon. In rhythms and words, prisoners refuse the gags that silence and the walls that surround them, in the constant battle for their lives; so doing, they destabilise the regimes that ensnare them and patrol city streets. Hip-hop's new subjects may tear down prison walls, or force reactionary governments to build yet more.

Acknowledgements

I would like to thank Carolyn Strange, Alison Bashford and the other participants in the Isolation Symposium for their suggestions on this paper. Luis Alvarez's insightful comments on an early draft vitally shaped the form it has since taken, and Neil Foley, Shae Garwood and Rebecca Montes offered important criticism.

Notes

1 See, for example, E. Ayers, *Vengeance and Justice: Crime and Punishment in the 19th-Century South*, New York, Oxford University Press, 1984; A. Lichtenstein, *Twice the Work of Free Labor: The Political Economy of Convict Labor in the New South*, New York, Verso, 1996; M. Mancini, *One Dies, Get Another: Convict Leasing in the American South*, Columbia, University of South Carolina Press, 1996; D.M. Oshinsky, *Worse than Slavery: Parchman Farm and the Ordeal of Jim Crow Justice*, New York, Simon and Schuster, 1997.

2 M. Omi and H. Winant, *Racial Formation in the United States: From the 1960s to the 1990s*, 2nd edn, New York, Routledge, 1994. According to B. Jackson's *Wake Up Dead Man: Afro-American Worksongs from Texas Prisons*, Cambridge, Mass., Harvard University Press, 1972, only black prisoners sang these metrically functional worksongs – the body of music under consideration here. Greater work is required for the cultural travel and effects of more prisoners' music (country-western, conjunto and border ballads) but this is beyond the scope of this paper.

3 Jackson, *Dead Man*, esp. pp. 30–1. Readers familiar with Jackson's book will recognise my debt to his work.

4 G. Deleuze and F. Guattari, *A Thousand Plateaus: Capitalism and Schizophrenia*, trans. B. Massumi, Minneapolis and London, University of Minnesota Press, 1987; H. Lefebvre, *The Production of Space*, trans. D. Nicholson-Smith, Oxford, Blackwell, 1991; G. Lipsitz, *Dangerous Crossroads: Popular Music, Postmodernism, and the Poetics of Place*, New York, Verso, 1994; N. Thrift, *Spatial Formations*, London, Sage Publications, 1996; and Yi-Fu Tuan, *Space and Place: The Perspective of Experience*, Minneapolis, University of Minnesota Press, 1977.

5 Lefebvre, *The Production of Space*, p. 320.

6 Deleuze and Guattari, *A Thousand Plateaus*, pp. 271–350, esp. 311, 312. Thrift writes:

> in each of these parcels of time-space 'subjects' and 'objects' are aligned in particular ways which provide particular orientations to action … and particular resources for action … In other words, contexts are not passive; they are productive time-spaces which have to be produced.
>
> (*Spatial Formations*, pp. 41–7, esp. 43)

I will use the terms 'context' and 'milieu' in this essay, in addition to the more cumbersome 'space–time'.

7 Deleuze and Guattari, *A Thousand Plateaus*, pp. 311, 312.

8 D. Chakrabarty critiques notions of time as a universal equivalent, everywhere and always the same. J. Bender and D.E. Wellbery argue that time must be understood as complex, contested and heterogeneous, more of a problem to be explored than a constant to be assumed. Chakrabarty, 'The time of history and the times of gods', in L. Lowe and D. Lloyd (eds) *The Politics of Culture in the Shadow of Capital*, Durham, Duke University Press, 1997, pp. 35–60; and J. Bender and D.E. Wellbery, 'Introduction', in their edited volume *Chronotypes: The Construction of Time*, Stanford, CA, Stanford University Press, 1991, p. 15. Conversely, let me stress that there is no essential difference in time-reckoning, and certainly no racial difference in knowledge of time, as M.M. Smith risks in *Mastered by the Clock: Time, Slavery, and Freedom in the American South*, Chapel Hill, University of North Carolina Press, 1997. Below, I attempt to walk a line between a notion of time that is everywhere and always the same, and an equally problematic time that is essentially different for different peoples, most troublingly between moderns and their 'others'. See Johannes Fabian, *Time and the Other: How Anthropology Makes its Object*, New York, Columbia University Press, 1983. The problem in each lies in understanding time as homogeneous and static, rather than as diffracted, variable and an element of conflict. In addition, consider M. Hanchard, 'Afro-Modernity: Temporality, Politics, and the African Diaspora', in D.P. Gaonkar (ed.) *Alternative Modernities*, Durham and London, Duke University Press, 2001, pp. 273–98.

9 Jackson, *Dead Man*, pp. xv–xxii, 29–44.

10 Note that Sample inverted the representation of racial dialect that folklorists often used to transcribe (and mark) black voices, but used it to represent the accent of the poor white guard. Albert Race Sample, *Racehoss: Big Emma's Boy*, Austin, TX, Eakin Press, 1984, p. 165. Cited in the liner notes to the Alan Lomax Collection CD *Prison Songs, Historical Recordings from Parchman Farm, 1947–1948, Volume One: Murderous Home*, Rounder Records, 1997.

11 Bama, 'What Makes a Work Song Leader?' Lomax Collection, *Volume One: Murderous Home*, Rounder Records, 1997.

12 J.M. Wise, 'Home: territory and identity', *Cultural Studies*, 2000, vol. 14, no. 2, pp. 295–310.

13 Deleuze and Guattari, *A Thousand Plateaus*, p. 311.

14 Cited by Oshinsky, *Worse than Slavery*, p. 145.

15 P. Wilson and group, 'I'm Goin' to Memphis', Lomax Collection, *Volume Two: Murderous Home*, Rounder Records, 1997; also M. Barton's corresponding liner notes. Jackson, *Dead Man*, p. 37.

16 For example, see Joseph 'Chinaman'; Johnson's reference to the Brazos River in 'Drop 'Em Down'; Jackson, *Dead Man*, p. 252.

17 L. Lowe, 'Interview with Angela Davis: reflections on race, class, and gender in the USA', in Lowe and Lloyd (eds) *The Politics of Culture in the Shadow of Capital*, p. 311.

18 Lefebvre cites Foucault's distinction between *savoir*, as dominating knowledge, and *connaissance*, as resistant knowledge. *The Production of Space*, pp. 10–11, n. 16.

19 Jackson, *Dead Man*, p. 18.

20 Oshinsky, *Worse than Slavery*, pp. 217–22.

21 Jackson, *Dead Man*, pp. 184–92.

22 See Elise Chernier, this volume.

23 See versions A–G in Jackson, *Dead Man*, pp. 194–200.

24 Conversely, Jackson cites singer J.B. Smith's diminution of guards' firearms – also phallic symbols. Prisoners would sing a shotgun into a 'derringer': a very small pistol. 'That's what we call "down talkin' " it, makin' it small'; *Dead Man*, p. 151.

25 Deleuze and Guattari, *A Thousand Plateaus*, p. 311.

26 J. Butler and Gang, 'Early in the Mornin' ', *Prison Worksongs: Recorded at Louisiana State Penitentiary at Angola, LA, 1959*, Arhoolie Records, 1997.

27 Jackson, *Dead Man*, p. 26.

28 D. Harvey, *The Condition of Postmodernity: An Enquiry into the Origins of Social Change*, Cambridge, Mass., and Oxford, UK, Blackwell, 1990.

29 This truncated history of the racial–spatial nexus of criminal justice controls builds upon D.T. Goldberg, ' "Polluting the body politic": racist discourse and urban location,' in M. Keith and M. Cross (eds) *Racism, the City, and the State*, New York, Routledge, 1993, pp. 45–60; M. Davis, *City of Quartz: Excavating the Future in Los Angeles*, New York, Vintage Books, 1992; M. Keith, 'From punishment to discipline? Racism, racialization, and the policing of social control', in Keith and Cross (eds) *Racism, the City, and the State*, pp. 193–209; C. Parenti, *Lockdown America: Police and Prisons in the Age of Crisis*, New York, Verso, 1999; Lefebvre, *The Production of Space*. See also P. Gilroy, *'There Ain't No Black in the Union Jack': The Cultural Politics of Race and Nation*, Chicago, University of Chicago Press, 1987, p. 98.

30 A. Appadurai, 'Global ethnoscapes: notes and queries for a transnational anthropology', in R.G. Fox (ed.) *Recapturing Anthropology: Working in the Present*, Santa Fe, NM: School of American Research, 1991, pp. 191–210.

31 Cited in S. Best and D. Kellner, 'Rap, black rage, and racial difference', *Enculturation*, Spring 1999, vol. 2, no. 2, http://www.uta.edu/huma/enculturation/2_2/best-kellner.html.

32 Unlike newspapers and novels of an earlier era, hip-hop is only tangentially related to nation-states and the tactics of spatial containment. J. Urla, 'Outlaw language: creating alternative public spheres in Basque Free Radio', in Lowe and Lloyd (eds) *The Politics of Culture in the Shadow of Capital*, pp. 280–300, esp. 294; B. Anderson, *Imagined Communities: Reflections on the Origin and Spread of Nationalism*, London and New York, Verso, 1991.

33 Rose, *Black Noise*, pp. 1–61.

34 J. Flores, *From Bomba to Hip-Hop: Puerto Rican Culture and Latino Identity*, New York, Columbia University Press, 2000; G. Lipsitz, 'World cities and world beat: low wage labor and transnational culture', *Pacific Historical Review*, 2000, pp. 228–9; M. Davis, *Magical Urbanism: Latinos Reinvent the US City*, London, Verso, 2000.

35 C. Chase, quoted by Flores, *From Bomba to Hip-Hop*, pp. 128, 129.

36 Gilroy, *'Ain't No Black in the Union Jack'*, pp. 153–222; L. Back, 'X amount of Sat Siri Akal! Apache Indian reggae music and intermezzo culture', in A. Ålund and R. Grandqvist (eds) *Negotiating Identities: Essays on Immigration and Culture in Present Day Europe*, Amsterdam, Holland, and Atlanta, Ga., Rodopi, 1995, pp. 139–66.

37 Consider Ice Cube's sample from the film *American Me* in which a group of new inmates are strip-searched as they enter a prison. 'The First Day of School (Intro)', *The Predator*, Priority Records, 1992. See also N. Morris, 'The contemporary prison,

1965–present', in N. Morris and D.J. Rothman (eds) *The Oxford History of the Prison*, Oxford, Oxford University Press, 1995, pp. 228–36.

38 Rose, *Black Noise*, pp. 1–61; S.H. Fernando, Jr, *The New Beats: Exploring the Music, Culture, and Attitudes of Hip-hop*, New York, Anchor Books, 1994, p. ix. I do not use the term 'postmodern' to refer to any free play of signifiers or to undermine the political messages of hip-hop culture. In this paper, postmodernity reflects an important shift in global economics and changes in applications of power via the prison-industrial complex, which, while not reducible to the realm of economics, is crucially impacted by political economy and capitalist crisis, as well as changing modes of power through racial, gendered and other forms of marking and difference – especially that of criminality.

39 H.A. Baker, Jr, 'Hybridity, the rap race, and pedagogy for the 1990s', *Black Music Research Journal*, 1991, pp. 217–28, esp. 220.

40 Gilroy, *'Ain't No Black in the Union Jack'*, p. 209.

41 Rose discusses the valorisation of musicians' neighbourhoods, ghettos and barrios throughout *Black Noise*; B.K.N.Y., 'Where Ya At', *No More Prisons*, Raptivism Records, 1999.

42 J. Berland, 'Locating listening: technological space, popular music, and Canadian mediations', in A. Leyshon, D. Matless and G. Revill (eds) *The Place of Music*, New York and London, Guilford Press, 1998, pp. 129–50; Urla, 'Outlaw language', in Lowe and Lloyd (eds) *The Politics of Culture in the Shadow of Capital*; and Rose, pp. 59, 60.

43 Thrift, *Spatial Formations*, pp. 23–8.

44 A. Herman, T. Swiss and J. Sloop, 'Mapping the beat: spaces of noise and places of music', in T. Swiss, J. Sloop and A. Herman (eds) *Mapping the Beat: Popular Music and Contemporary Theory*, London, Blackwell, 1998, pp. 3–29.

45 Davey D, 'X-Raided causing more drama', *Manhunt*, 15 January 2000, http://manhunt.com/news/stories/8258.html.

46 X-Raided, 'Write What I See', *Vengeance is Mine*, Black Market Records, 2000.

47 Davis, *City of Quartz*, esp. pp. 267–322; Parenti, *Lockdown America*, pp. 182–210.

48 T. Kweli, Lord Jamar and Kool G Rap, 'Oz Theme 2000', *OZ: The Soundtrack*, Avatar Records, 2000. Kweli's performance is itself an act to ameliorate divisions and create political unity.

49 J. Caramanica, 'Jailhouse rap', *Seattle Weekly*, 1–7 February 2001, http://www.seattle-weekly.com/features/0105/slanguistics-caramanica.shtml.

50 Rose, *Black Noise*, p. 15.

51 R.D.G. Kelley, 'Kickin' reality, kickin' ballistics: gansta rap and postindustrial Los Angeles', in W.E. Perkins (ed.) *Droppin' Science: Critical Essays on Rap Music and Hip Hop Culture*, Philadelphia, Temple University Press, 1996, pp. 117–58, p. 142; Rose, pp. 15, 24, 146–82; Lipsitz, 'World cities, world beat', pp. 217, 222–31. Because rap music is a male-dominated medium, and because prisons disproportionately incarcerate young men (though women of colour are the fastest growing population in American prisons), I focus on reformulations of masculinity here. New evocations of gender and womanhood in hip-hop culture – against police control and rappers' misogyny – remain beyond the scope of this paper. However, see Rose for more.

52 dead prez, 'Hip Hop', *Let's Get Free*, LOUD Records, 2000.

53 Stic, interviewed by Russell Shoatz III, *BLU Magazine* no. 8; http://blumag.com/archives/articles/deadprez.htm.

54 Kelley, 'Kickin' reality, kickin' ballistics', p. 148.

55 Spearhead, *Home*, 'Crime to be Broke in America', Capitol Records, 1994. Saul Williams plays with the phrase 'turning the tables with turntables' on the CD *Global Guerrillas, BLU Magazine* no. 10.

56 Lipsitz, 'World cities and world beat', p. 217.

57 Herman *et al.*, 'Mapping the beat'. See also K. Negus, 'The music business and rap: between the street and the executive suite', *Cultural Studies*, July 1999, vol. 13, no. 3, pp. 488–508. I borrow the term 'critical resistance' from a grassroots collective of activists, ex-prisoners, family members and students organising against the prison-industrial complex. See Critical Resistance website at :
http://www.criticalresistance.org

58 G. Lipsitz, *The Possessive Investment in Whiteness: How White People Profit from Identity Politics*, Philadelphia, Temple University Press, 1998.

5 Segregating sexualities

The prison 'sex problem' in twentieth-century Canada and the United States[1]

Elise Chenier

In May of 1944, Ottawa magistrate Joachim Sauvé wrote to Dr J.D. Heaslip, the Superintendent of the Guelph Reformatory, Ontario's largest provincial prison.[2] 'We had lately a few charges of gross indecency,' Sauvé explained, 'the most recent involving a flight lieutenant in the air force who has homosexual inclinations.' Sauvé planned to send him to Guelph, but first wanted to know what special disposition would be made in such cases. 'This man could not of course be placed with others,' he wrote. Heaslip promptly replied, explaining that if he is caught 'practising [his] disability', the 'known homo-sexual' receives corporal punishment and is 'segregated in a special corridor of cells' known among inmates 'as "Gunzil's Alley"'.

In 1944, the practice of segregating 'known homo-sexuals' was a longstanding tradition in prisons across Canada and the United States.[3] In the late nineteenth century, social reformers' concern with the corrupting influence of degenerate inmates over less dissolute prisoners led to demands for the segregation of different types of inmates. By the early twentieth century, most prisons and courts were beginning to separate the sane from the insane, women from men, the merely poor from the criminal, and children from adults. However, while systems of classification were aspired to, rarely were they fully implemented. Though poor-houses fell out of fashion, and men and women were less likely to be housed in the same institution in the twentieth century as in the nineteenth, young prisoners continued to interact with adult inmates and, unless a prisoner was declared insane, those with even the most serious mental health problems continue to be incarcerated in jails with 'normal' inmates into the present day.

Men who displayed signs of effeminacy, known colloquially as 'fairies' and 'pansies', were also segregated from the main adult male prison population, but not in an institution of their own. Known variously as Lover's Lane, Queen's Row and, at the Guelph Reformatory, Gunzil's Alley, special wings and cell blocks were set aside specifically for these types of inmates across Canada and the United States.[4] But singling out fairies was not the invention of prison administrators. The differential treatment of 'frank' or 'true' homosexuals was a socio-cultural construct already in place in major urban centres.[5] Seen as 'queer' and like women, fairies were sexually objectified by masculine men. Thus, in prison, 'true homosexuals' were segregated as both a protective and a preventative measure. Celled apart from the main inmate population, segregation ostensibly prevented them from engaging in wanted sexual contact while at the same time protecting them from unwanted advances.

Separating fairies from the rest of the prison population did nothing to halt sexual activity in prison, however. Sex contact between inmates was not only a quotidian feature of male prison culture. It also reinforced a hierarchical social structure that organised inmates into different social groupings. Mediated by a range of factors including race, age, prison experience and social connection, prison sexual culture was predicated upon the kind of street-class masculinity that claims for itself the right to sexual gratification.[6] In the early twentieth century, normative masculine sexuality was determined less by sexual object choice and more by gesture: so long as men played the 'active' role in a sexual encounter, both their peers (and the growing number of sexologists who studied them) considered their actions a statement of the natural male need for sexual pleasure. Historians of late nineteenth- and early twentieth-century hobo, naval and urban street cultures have demonstrated that men who took the active role in sexual relations with other males were known as 'wolves'.[7] With fairies often out of reach, wolves looked to other, younger, inmates for sexual pleasure. Similar to some heterosexual exchanges, wolves' relations with younger men – known variously as 'punks', 'kids' and 'lambs' – were often based on a combination of negotiation and coercion and, particularly in prison, on the manipulative use of the threat of violence and the exploitation of shame.[8]

Prevailing cultural norms around masculinity and femininity were reproduced in male prison culture in twentieth-century Canada and the United States, and were central to the organisation of social relations. Building on Joan Wallach Scott's insights into the way gender serves as a salient reference point for the distribution of power and is therefore 'implicated in the conception and construction of power itself', this chapter illustrates how gender and power are inextricably linked in the ways that medical experts, prison administrators and inmates organised bodies, desires and pleasures.[9] I draw upon an eclectic range of sources that, taken together, reveals a great deal about the socio-sexual culture of English–Canadian and US prisons. Among these are published and unpublished books, articles, conference proceedings, government reports, archival interviews, autobiographical and social scientific accounts of 'life behind bars', as well as the administrative records. Pre World War II evidence is drawn almost entirely from New York State and Ontario provincial sources. After World War II, public discussions about managing 'the sex problem' occur more regularly, and in the 1960s inmates' own descriptions and assessment of sex in prison began to appear in a variety of media including print and film. Sources representing a much wider geographical region also began to emerge, revealing an overwhelming conformity in the structure, organisation, regulation and maintenance of sexual culture in male prisons across both space and time. With remarkable consistency, throughout the twentieth century most male inmates of Canadian and American prisons adhered to a 'wolf–punk–fairy' system of sexual organisation that had its origins in *fin de siècle* hobo and urban street culture.

In many respects, twentieth-century prisons in Canada and the United States were identical: most were run like military boot camps and, until the end of the century, were funded and operated by state, provincial and federal governments. The majority of inmates were serving sentences for crimes against property, not people. However, in Canada prisoners were almost entirely of white European extraction. This contrasts sharply with the United States, where deep spatial and cultural divisions existed between African-American and white inmates. These divisions figured significantly in the organisation of the culture of rape and coercion, and I explore them in greater detail elsewhere.[10] However, here my focus is limited to the function and deployment of gender. For this reason we must keep in mind that while masculinity and femininity is a pre-eminent axis of difference, it is but the leader of a pack.

Dealing with the sex problem

Less than a year after corresponding with Magistrate Sauvé, Dr Heaslip attended the Second Annual Superintendents' Conference in New York. 'Various methods of dealing with sex problems in institutions were described,' he reported to the Department of Reform Institutions. 'It was emphasised that discussion and talk about sex activities tended to intensify the problem and it should be dealt with quietly.'[11] Up until the 1950s, most prisons operated in accordance with the notion that sex was an ever-present but dormant force that was awakened when stimulated. In other words, thinking about sex inevitably led to it. In prison this translated into the belief that a key component to successfully repressing male sexual desire was the elimination of stimulating influences. Largely because of this, mixed-sex institutions were almost completely phased out by World War I, and partitions were placed between prisoners and visitors to prevent physical contact. In many male institutions, female employees were restricted to clerical jobs where they worked well away from the general inmate population. 'Pin-up' posters and other images of the opposite sex were prohibited.

But it was not only the opposite sex who threatened to spark the sexual longings of inmates. In 1948 psychiatrist Benjamin Karpman explained that the mere 'sight and smell of naked bodies' creates sexual stimulation, a point noted as early as 1898 in a report on overcrowding at Toronto's Central Prison. Forcing inmates to sleep two to a cell, the nineteenth-century author warned, was 'to engender vices the most odious, to neutralise all reformatory efforts, and to cause a pestilence destructive to all morals to overspread the prisoners'.[12] In the fifty years between the Toronto report and Karpman's article, prison administrators introduced a range of policy and architectural changes in an effort to eliminate physical contact between inmates. Where economically possible, dormitory-style housing was abandoned in favour of the single cell. The 'lockstep', a military march that kept men in close physical formation, was abolished because of its potential to sexually arouse.[13] Shower rooms were re-modelled to improve ventilation and create better visibility for guards who, in some institutions, were stationed on elevated platforms.[14] Prisoners were prohibited from entering another man's cell, and physical contact of any sort was discouraged unless it was on the sports field.[15]

But more than the lockstep, the dormitories and the showers put together, officials considered the greatest sex stimulant in prison to be the 'fairy'. Widely recognised in working-class public and street culture in early twentieth-century New York, the self-identified fairy assumed the styles of female prostitutes and popular movie stars and theatrical performers. 'The determinative criterion in the identification of men as fairies,' argues George Chauncey in his study of pre World War II New York gay culture, 'was not the extent of their same-sex desire or activity (their sexuality), but rather the gender persona and status they assumed.'[16] Early twentieth-century medical practitioners wrote these critical distinctions into the field of sexology. For example, prison psychiatrist Samuel Kahn relied on gender codes rather than sexual practices to determine who should be singled out for segregation on Blackwell Island (New York).[17] A homosexual was 'not just one who is in love with a member of his own sex' but who 'has an emotional makeup of the opposite sex so that he could attract his own sex'. The true homosexual, he contended, ' "falls in love" more quickly with an individual of his own sex than he would a person of the opposite sex'. Those men who were also 'capable' of loving the opposite sex were excluded.[18] For Kahn, fairies were a distinct sex 'entitled to the same rights as women'.[19] The fairy's 'feminine carriage, gestures and mannerism', observed Kahn's contemporary, Joseph F. Fishman, 'tends to keep aglow the fire of sex in even the most heterosexual of the prisoners', undermining all efforts to keep sexual arousal at bay.[20]

A fairy need only adopt one or two visual cues to indicate his preference for male sexual partners.[21] Just a 'mincing walk' and lilting voice were indications of 'the classic homosexual', easily identifiable even to a small-town prison guard in the 1950s.[22] But many went to even greater lengths to affect a feminine look. In addition to 'flamboyant' colour choices and flashy clothing, fairies moulded their bodies 'in ways that approximated the ideal gender types of their cultural group'.[23] Tweezed eyebrows, bleached hair and painted faces were all readily identifiable features of the fairy. It was a style difficult to maintain in prison, and fairies proved inventive in adapting to the limited resources available. Classroom chalk became face powder, laundry-room bleach lightened hair, hospital tweezers plucked eyebrows, grime from the cell bars became eye shadow, and tomato-can labels from the kitchen were soaked in water to make rouge.[24] Among the most difficult items to procure were creams and oils, usually only available from tightly controlled medical supply chests. In 1962 an African-American gay man imprisoned at Millbrook Reformatory in Ontario repeatedly requested shaving salve from the prison doctor, claiming that due to a chronic skin condition 'it is next to impossible to shave' without it. Though this was by all reports a model prisoner, the examining physician refused the request because '[t]his "man" is a confirmed passive homosexual who wants to be beautiful'.[25] Millbrook's Superintendent accepted the doctor's explanation, and the ointment was never provided.

Like fairy culture on the streets, men who signalled their sexual interests by adopting conventionally female gender codes did so at significant risk. Inmates who refused to abide by a code of conduct that included conformity to a military-style masculine ideal were vulnerable to a range of punitive measures including physical punishment and solitary confinement. While for the most part fairies were not regarded as a threat to the daily operations of the prison, they often became targets of disciplinary measures following internal disruptions such as riots or when political administrations aimed to project a 'tough on crime' image. Fairies proved to be remarkably resilient. In the 1920s Fishman noted that

> [d]espite the watchfulness of the prison officials and the confiscation of all their jewellery, they cannot be restrained from adorning themselves with various trinkets which they make during their confinement ... Repeated searches, and confiscation of these baubles merely put a temporary stop to this practice. A few days elapse and again rouged cheeks and lips begin to make their appearance.[26]

Punishment and permissiveness

For the most part, however, prison superintendents and guards adopted a *laissez-faire* attitude towards the segregated fairy population. Perhaps because, as George Chauncey explains, as long as the fairy abided by the conventions of this cultural script, he was tolerated in much of working-class society.

> His very effeminacy served to confirm rather than threaten the masculinity of other men, particularly since it often exaggerated the conventions of deference and gender difference between men and women. The fairies reaffirmed the conventions of gender even as they violated them: they behaved as no man should but as any man might wish a woman would.[27]

Chauncey's own look at fairy culture ends in 1940, but it is clear that well into the late twentieth century the prison fairy, variously known as pansy, flaming bitch, gal, fuck-gal, fag, queen, wife, broad, whore, freak, sissy, canned fruit, dear, and stone gear, continued to occupy the same place as they had in the pre-war era. 'So well has inmate culture created the concept of "broad" that it is accepted as if it were real,' wrote Edwin Johnson in 1971. 'It is more than a theatrical performance, it is an actual life situation.'[28]

The acceptance of fairies as 'real' women was aided by the prison staff and medical and psychiatric personnel who often treated them as women, even addressing them by their adopted female names.[29] Fairies were usually assigned to work in the prison laundry, labour generally considered more suitable to women.[30] Some were even permitted to work in the clerical unit, usually the only part of the prison (besides the hospital unit) that employed women. As a rule, male prisoners were considered sexually ravenous, but fairies posed no threat to female civilians.[31] This privilege gave them a distinct advantage over other inmates; aside from being one of the least physically demanding assignments, the clerical unit allowed easy access to information that could be bartered for valuable goods and favours in the main prison population.

But these apparent rewards were matched by equally apparent punishments. Serving time in segregated units was much more punishing than simple incarceration. In some institutions, 'segregation' did not just mean living separately from other inmates. Virtually every aspect of daily life was conducted apart from the general inmate population: fairies were forced to take their meals separately, to watch movies separately and to use the exercise yard separately. They slept one to a cell, and all efforts were made to keep them separate from each other. They also had much less freedom than did men in the general population. Prisoners in segregation were permitted less time outside their cellblock, and less time outdoors. While their femininity made them less of a physical threat to guards, their ability to provoke (or inspire) mannish prisoners meant that they were sometimes considered disruptive, and on that basis were formally excluded from opportunities to serve their time in less secure training- and education-oriented facilities that proliferated in the 1950s and 1960s.[32] Fairies were most likely to be assigned to work in the laundry or the tailor shop, the former of which was physically demanding, particularly in the summer months when the temperature and humidity rose to unbearable levels.

Ironically, because segregation kept fairies out of the main prison population, it allowed them tremendous freedom to be sexually provocative. Fairies were daily marched through the prison to get to the kitchen and to other parts of the institution. According to Joseph Fishman, as soon as other men came into sight,

> Immediately, the homosexuals take on all the mannerisms of a kittenish girl flirting with a young man. They arch their necks, smile, cast suggestive looks, and despite the vigilance of the accompanying guards, make *sotto voce* remarks, usually of an endearing or insinuating nature.

Many 'take this opportunity to throw previously prepared love notes at them'.[33] Indeed, relationships fairies carried on with other inmates were conducted mostly on paper. 'Many a time I have racked my meager brain to finagle [sic] some means of spending a few minutes of happiness with you,' despaired one fairy in a note to her lover, 'but it all seems so futile.'[34] Throwing notes was risky in itself, a fact that one recipient readily acknowledged in his reply to a message tossed at him:

> I am trying to reason out why you would expose yourself to the possibility of going to the hole [solitary confinement] by throwing me a note. You said that you liked what you saw, do you like it well enough to try and really communicate with me, through letters, so that you can determine whether you would like to spend the rest of your life, and energy, to help me create a world for you and I?

Another inmate wrote to his lover: 'I like the way you stalled in front of segregation.' Yet another inmate fantasised how wonderful it would be to finally kiss his lover for the first time. Eye contact, visual sightings and letters often formed the basis of prison relationships for fairies and their lovers and spouses. Sometimes meetings were carefully plotted: 'see you Thurs library Friday dentist.' For those inmates in segregation, actual physical contact was rare.

In this setting, 'camp' was a key cultural defence mechanism that served to deflect criticism and condemnation. In 1964 a newspaper journalist described the 'sex perverts' at Millbrook Reformatory: 'Most of them work in the tailor shop where they mince up and down the aisles between their sewing machine, smiling gaily at their co-workers and visitors.'[35] *Fortune and Men's Eyes*, John Herbert's ground-breaking 1967 play (made into an MGM feature film in 1971) based on the author's experience serving time in the Guelph Reformatory, depicts Queenie, a prison fairy, as an inmate who enjoyed institutional mobility as the library's book distributor. Like Fishman's fairies in 1930s New York, Queenie openly flirted with staff and inmates alike. However, while the evidence demonstrates that at different times and in different places prison fairies were not only tolerated but provided a much welcomed diversion with their sexually playful repartee, this image is mitigated by the ways in which fairies were made the target of brutal institutional punishment. At mid-century, Benjamin Karpman described the standard approach to controlling sex as 'violent suppression', which was usually aimed at fairies whose adopted femininity made them legitimate targets of masculine abuse.[36] In the mid 1960s a member of Ontario's provincial opposition launched an official investigation into rumours that 'sex perverts' were forced to wear baby doll pyjamas as part of their punishment.[37] The information turned out to be wrong, and the investigation closed, but there was no shortage of examples of cruel treatment meted out to Millbrook's effeminate inmates. In February 1958, a prisoner in an Ontario facility was cited for 'doing his hair in a feminine way' and was docked seven days' good conduct remission. One month later Officer Woodly submitted a conduct report on the same prisoner for '[b]iting his lips and rubbing his cheeks to make them red and also plucking his eyebrows'. This time he was sentenced to three days in solitary confinement on a rationed diet. On 1 April he received yet another misconduct report, this time for 'failing to achieve the required standard in conduct and industry for 5 weeks', and he lost another five days of good conduct. Two weeks later he was admitted to the prison hospital for a course of electro-convulsive therapy. He received a total of six treatments and was released back into the prison. It is impossible to conclude with certainty that his refusal to conform to 'normal' masculinity resulted in his receiving electro-convulsive therapy, but given the absence of any other explanation – medical or otherwise – it is possible that his persistent efforts to feminise his appearance were the 'problem' in need of 'treatment'.[38]

'Any old port in a storm'

The main inmate population could also be a source of trouble. In an anonymous article in Toronto's first gay magazine, a self-described practising homosexual and ex-con explained that homosexuals are completely excluded from the 'clubs that are part and parcel of prison life', living in almost complete social isolation.[39] Robert N. Boyd, a prisoner in Nevada, argued that the inmate attitude towards gays is the direct inverse of the staff attitude. In high-security prisons, staff tended to be indifferent to the homosexual population and therefore the 'homosexual suffers heavier problems from his fellow inmates'.[40] Fairies often submitted to sexual intercourse with other inmates, but rarely in circumstances of their own choosing. As one young inmate explained in the early 1970s, 'they can't call it rape if I let them do it'.[41] So long as fairies were considered 'true' homosexuals', the men who sought them out as sexual partners enhanced their masculinity by asserting their 'right' to sexual pleasure. No one inside the prison, including the guards, the medical staff and the prisoners themselves, considered 'wolves' abnormal.

Despite the practice of segregating fairies, tough male prisoners had little trouble finding – or rather 'making' – sexual partners. Modelled after early twentieth-century urban sexual cultures in places like Toronto and New York, inmates known as 'wolves', 'jockers' and, at the end of the century, 'booty bandits' actively sought out sex with other inmates who assumed, often by force, coercion or manipulation, a 'passive' sexual role.[42] Incoming inmates were one of three types: a returning inmate who could not avoid taking on the role in prison sex culture he had before; a first-time offender who had friends inside who were willing and able to take care of him; and finally a first-time offender who knew no one and had no friends. Of the three, the latter was the most likely to be made a 'punk', a 'lamb' or a 'kid'. 'A punk is neither a wise kid nor a small-time hood,' explained a US prison inmate in 1965.

> He is a kid that has been made, made many times in the past, and that can be made now with no difficulty whatsoever. He is what, if he were a girl, would be known as a pig. Sometimes he is actually a prostitute.[43]

Known as a jailhouse 'turn-out', the punk was not viewed as female in the way the fairies were, but occupied a demasculinised space that was either implicitly or explicitly feminine. Their lack of male sexual privilege was reinforced by referring to them as 'little girls', 'lambs' or 'boy–girls'.[44] Of course, these labels also helped to define the wolves' socio-sexual role as the dominant male who enjoyed certain entitlements, including sexual access to punks and kids.[45]

Expert studies of homosexual activity in prison continued to define homosexuality as a gender-based psychological abnormality and homosexual activity as a natural adjustment to unnatural conditions well into the 1950s. One of the first articles to make this distinction formally appeared in 1928. Working out of the State Bureau of Juvenile Research in Columbus, Ohio, Charles Ford described lesbian friendships in juvenile facilities as 'natural' since the inmates were denied any 'heterosexual outlet'.[46] The same logic was applied to male prisoners. 'All environments in which large masses of men congregate – navy, army, concentration camps and prisons – lend themselves to homosexuality,' declared Samuel Kahn.[47] Despite the scrupulous examination of military inductees and the introduction of a host of methods to get rid of homosexuals in the armed forces during World

War II, the high incidence of homosexual activity merely entrenched this view, forcing most to concede that in certain settings it was virtually impossible to eradicate. For Canadian medical and psychiatric expert Aldwyn B. Stokes, prison

> merely illustrates that the homosexual way of satisfying sex impulses is because, in most people, circumstances bring it out. That was evident in some of the prisoner-of-war camps, and other places of that kind … There is a tendency there which finds its statement when the sexes are aggregated. It was true in the women's barracks during the war, and it is a statement of sex deprivation, when one sex is aggregated.[48]

In 1952 two medical doctors penned an article on the treatment of homosexuality in prison that invited readers to reflect back on their own wartime experiences. 'Those who have served in the Navy,' they argued, 'will recall the saying, "Any old port in a storm" .'[49]

So deeply entrenched was this belief that at least three post-World War II treatment experts focused their attention on men who did not want to have sex. Psychiatrist Robert Linder maintained that prisons do not 'make' homosexuals, but rather that confinement had 'certain regressive effects'.[50] In this context, homoeroticism, a function of heterosexual starvation, should be distinguished from the 'integrated and patterned attitudes characteristic of homosexuality'. While all prisoners experience some type of mental breakdown as a result of confinement, he argued, the most common mental disturbance found in prisons is the 'acute panic episode' during which one's 'natural' defences against homosexuality begin to 'crumble'. Similarly concerned with inmates in a 'homosexual panic state', two prison psychiatrists embarked on one of the earliest medical experiments in prison related to homosexual activity. Their object was not, as one might have expected, to 'cure' the true homosexual of his 'disease', but to treat panicked inmates with insulin shock therapy.[51]

Officially, prisoners were expected to repress their sexual urges. Sexual activity of any sort, including masturbation, was strictly against prison rules despite early twentieth-century medical experts' insistence that sublimation over the long term 'is neither healthy nor possible'.[52] In 1948 Benjamin Karpman reiterated the point, describing the sex urge as 'too elemental and instinctive to be completely controlled by confinement'. Celibacy is rare, he insisted, and can only be achieved by those who 'have other diversions and stimulants'.[53] In light of these modern views, prison administrators slowly shifted away from a model of sexual repression towards a goal to channel desires into appropriate outlets. Some institutions began by removing the glass and wire partitions that had long separated inmates and their visitors, but these were mere baby steps towards the panacea widely supported by medical and social welfare experts including Wardell Pomeroy of the Kinsey Institute and the Canadian Committee of Corrections.[54] In the 1960s, implementing a programme of conjugal visitation, well established in Russia, Scandinavia, parts of South America, and Mississippi, was a popular proposal and won the support of Clinton Duffy, the retired warden of California's notoriously rough San Quentin Prison. 'All a man needs is an hour a month alone with his wife. I can't understand why this privilege isn't used to help keep order in prison and to effect rehabilitation later.'[55] Conjugal visits had little to do with issues of human dignity and compassion. Citing the 1962 case of Lawrence C. Garner, who requested two hours alone with his wife before his execution, Duffy argued 'permitting conjugal visits to condemned men would serve no good purpose'.[56] Implemented only in federal institutions in Canada and unevenly across the United States, conjugal visits were a state-funded attempt to deploy wives of inmates as a deviance-distracter, as a calming mechanism, and as a management tool. With the support of a compassionate public behind them, small home-like cabins dotted the corrections landscape in the 1970s.

As Duffy and others openly admitted, the central issue concerning prison superintendents and wardens was maintaining discipline and order. In the post-World War II era, growing concern over violent prisoners led some observers to be less concerned with the effeminate fairy and more concerned about the 'aggressive homosexual'. Such was the view of A.R. Virgin, the Department of Reform Institution's Director of Rehabilitation, who spoke during the 1952 hearings of Ontario's Select Committee on Delinquent Individuals and Custodial Questions:

Chairman:	We have seen them running around with their sideburns down to here [indicating] and swinging their hips. What can we do with them?
Virgin:	Segregate him at night, and try to keep him under supervision.
Grummett QC:	They are not nearly as dangerous as the aggressive homosexuals?
Virgin:	No.
Grummett:	But the aggressive homosexual is one who will push his aggressiveness to a point where he catches an unwary person; those are the ones we have to watch.
Virgin:	That is right.[57]

Despite his sexual interest in other males, the actions of the 'aggressive homosexual' were viewed as normal masculine desire adapted to unnatural conditions. The endless rules and regulations, the constant submission to the will of the guards, wardens and superintendents, the loss of independent decision-making power, all combined to thwart inmates' 'natural' masculinity. As Wardell Pomeroy explained it, the usual way a man asserts his masculinity is to have heterosexual sex. If an inmate 'can create a fiction with a person who appears to be feminine', he told a 1962 meeting of prison superintendents, 'it helps him assert his lost manliness'.[58]

Experts like Pomeroy, whose disciplinary orientation tended towards the study of the individual, had nothing to say of the effects of these manly assertions on those who were forced to submit to them. However, prisoners' rights activists, who were informed by the sociological and anthropological studies that viewed prisons as communities, certainly did. In a highly publicised investigation of a sexual assault complaint made against the Philadelphia Detention Center in the mid 1960s, investigators from the US Attorney-General's office described sexual assault in prison as an 'epidemic'. Interviews with prison staff and the warden in Philadelphia revealed that every man of slight build was approached within two or three days of his admission, and that those who did not seek or submit to the protection of a wolf were gang-raped and staff did virtually nothing to control it. One inmate told investigators that he screamed for over an hour while he was raped by a group of inmates, but the guards failed to come to his aid. Based on interviews with 3,304 men who had been in the Philadelphia prison system between June of 1966 and June of 1968, they estimated 2,000 assaults took place. Only 156 were documented, only sixty-four were mentioned in the prison records and only forty of those resulted in internal discipline against the aggressor.

The report dismissed the century-old claim that these were acts of sexual deprivation, describing them instead as expressions of 'anger and aggression'.[59] Two years later ex-prisoner Edwin Johnson wrote: 'There is absolutely no protection in society for the homosexual who is raped by force ... Prison officials generally feel that "faggots" are getting what they deserve.'[60] Johnson's charge was chillingly depicted in the enormously popular 1971 film *Fortune and Men's Eyes*. In a critical scene at the beginning of the film, an inmate is gang-raped. 'Why doesn't anyone do anything?' the newly arrived protagonist asks. 'Ain't nobody gonna mess with a man givin' his oats,' explains Rocky. After 1971, the image of the prison as sexually corrupted by the effeminate prisoner was replaced by the image of the wolf as a dangerous sexual predator.

Outside prison walls, gay rights activists asserted that homosexuality was defined by sexual object choice, not by gender. It was a claim made most loudly by American sex researcher Alfred Kinsey. In his 1948 report *Sexual Behavior in the Human Male* he rejected the cultural and medical inclination to equate gender non-conformity with homosexuality and instead created a system that measured 'total sexual outlet' – specifically, the frequency of sexual acts.[61] In this model, homosexual is never a person and always a sex act. Hired as a consultant to the federal prison in Terre Haute, Indiana, Kinsey's colleague Wardell Pomeroy argued that if wolves could be convinced that their activities made them homosexual, not manly, the sex problem might just solve itself. In 1962 a Terre Haute inmate known as a wolf explained to folklorist Bruce Jackson that the medical and psychiatric staff no longer distinguished between the punks and the wolves, between the masculine and the feminine. Since the interviewee did not want to be 'pegged as a homosexual', he claimed to be abstaining from sex altogether.[62] Pomeroy's recommendation appeared to be having its desired effect, but it was probably short-lived and isolated to the Terre Haute facility. Despite changes in thinking about hetero- and homosexuality as subjectivities defined by sexual object choice rather than gender performance, prison staff and inmates alike continued to recognise, reproduce and reinforce the early twentieth-century working-class male culture of fairies, wolves and punks up to the end of the century.[63]

Conclusion

What appears to be an anomalous preservation of an early twentieth-century cultural understanding of sexuality is in fact a reflection of a largely unchanged system of values grounded less in ideas about normal and abnormal sex than it is embedded in a system of power articulated primarily through gendered relationships. That young inexperienced inmates can be 'made a girl' demonstrates the malleability of sexual relations but, perhaps more importantly, it is an explicit example of how gender functions quite separate from biology, and is neither fixed, transparent nor predetermined but rather is part of a complex cultural process which bears little relation to the physical body. Despite the tremendous success of *Fortune and Men's Eyes*, the publicity garnered by the Philadelphia Detention Center complaint, and the numerous sociological studies that followed in the 1970s and 1980s, sexual domination and forced submission remains a defining feature of modern inmate culture in North America.[64] Indeed, rather than introduce new and stringent measures to ensure that inmates are protected in our prisons, abuses against them increasingly came to be seen as part of the cost of committing crime, thus relieving the state of its obligation to protect inmates from violent assault.

Normative and historically specific definitions of gender are reproduced and embedded in the culture of incarceration. And because they are premised on gender, and in particular masculinity, the socio-sexual organisation of Canadian and American prisoners is not likely to undergo significant change. The culture of imprisonment – to 'break' prisoners, to exert total control and discipline – is grounded in a masculinised, military-style conception of power, discipline and control. Regardless of changing models of sexuality and sexual identity in the outside world, a complex sexual culture, grounded in gendered expressions of social relations and understood by prisoners, administrators and medical and social scientists alike as a natural by-product of masculinity, persists.

Notes

1 Research for this paper was supported by a grant from the Canada–US Fulbright Foundation, and from the Canadian Women's University Association. In locating sources I am grateful for the generous assistance of Dr John Bancroft, Ruth Beasley and Jennifer Corbin at the Kinsey Institute for Research in Sex, Gender and Reproduction. Helpful critical comments were provided by Lynn Farrell, Mary MacDonald, Sheila McManus and Amanda Glasbeek and editors Carolyn Strange and Alison Bashford.

2 Archives of Ontario (hereafter AO) RG 20–16 Reel MS3167 'Correspondence and Administration Files on Training Schools and Other Institutions', Sauvé to Heaslip, 25 May 1944; Heaslip to Sauvé, 28 May 1944.

3 On the similarity between Canadian and US prisons' approach to managing the sex problem, see (AO) RG 20–16–2 Correspondence and Administration Files on Training Schools and Other Institutions – Microfilm Reels MS 3167: 'Minutes of the 2nd Annual Superintendents' Conference Feb 14–16, 1945'.

4 At the Ontario Reformatory, Guelph, twenty-four of the institution's 373 individual cells were set aside for homosexuals. (AO) 20–16–105.4 'Guelph – Inspections, 1955–56' Accommodation. 'Lover's Lane' is cited from R. Caron, *Go-Boy! Memoirs of a Life Behind Bars*, Toronto, McGraw-Hill Ryerson, 1978, pp. 21–2; 'Queen's Row' is cited from E. Johnson, 'The homosexual in prison', *Social Theory and Practice*, 1971 vol. 1, no. 4, pp. 83.

5 On the evolution of medical ideas about homosexuality and gender in the early twentieth century see J. Terry, *An American Obsession: Science, Medicine and Homosexuality in Modern Society*, Chicago, University of Chicago Press, 1999.

6 For practical purposes this essay is limited to an examination of male institutions.

7 G. Chauncey, *Gay New York: Gender, Urban Culture and the Making of the Gay Male World, 1890–1940*, New York, Basic Books, 1994; see also his 'Christian brotherhood or sexual perversion? Homosexual identities and the construction of sexual boundaries in the World War I era' in M. Duberman, M. Vicinus and G. Chauncey, Jr (eds) *Hidden from History: Reclaiming the Gay and Lesbian Past*, New York, Penguin, 1990, pp. 294–317.

8 Here I draw on Karen Dubinsky's analysis of heterosexual conflict in *Improper Advances: Rape and Heterosexual Conflict in Ontario, 1880–1929*, Chicago, University of Chicago Press, 1993.

9 J. Wallach Scott, 'Gender: a useful category of historical analysis' in J. Wallach Scott (ed.) *Feminism and History*, New York, Oxford University Press, 1996, p. 170.

10 Elise Chenier, ' "Stranger in our midst": male sexual "deviance" in postwar Ontario', unpublished PhD dissertation, Queen's University, 2001.

11 (AO) RG 20–16–2 Correspondence and Administration Files on Training Schools and Other Institutions – Microfilm Reels MS 3167: 'Minutes of the 2nd Annual Superintendents' Conference Feb 14–16, 1945.'

12 Report–Central Prison, 1898 (No. 11): 13; cited in D.G. Wetherell, 'To discipline and train: adult rehabilitation programmes in Ontario prisons, 1874–1900', *Histoire sociale/Social History*, 1990 vol. 23, no. 12, pp. 145–65.

13 J.F. Fishman, *Sex in Prison: Revealing Sex Conditions in American Prisons*, New York, National Library Press, 1934, p. 90.

14 Caron, *Go-Boy!* p. 120. On the role of architecture in prisoner management see E. Cummins, *The Rise and Fall of the Radical Prison Movement*, Stanford, Stanford University Press, 1994, p. 6.

15 H. Blackstock, *Bitter Humour: About Dope, Safe Cracking and Prisons*, Toronto, Burns and MacEachern, 1967, pp. 102–3.

16 Chauncey, *Gay New York*, p. 47.

17 S. Kahn, *Homosexuality and Mentality*, Boston, Meador Publishing, 1937, p. 13.

18 Kahn, *Homosexuality and Mentality*, p. 14.

19 Kahn, *Homosexuality and Mentality*, p. 160. Kahn does not indicate what these rights might be.

20 Fishman, *Sex in Prison*, p. 22.

21 In his study of the homosexual investigation at the Newport Naval Training Center in 1919 and 1920, George Chauncey found that men defined themselves not only as fairies but also according to the specific type of sexual activity they preferred. 'Christian brotherhood or sexual perversion?', pp. 298–300.

22 (AO) RG 20–42–3 Millbrook Inmate Case Files, KHD, 3000.

23 Chauncey, *Gay New York*, pp. 54–5.

24 These practices occurred in prisons across Canada and the United States. See Millbrook inmate files and W.H. Haines and J.J. McLaughlin, 'Treatment of the homosexual in prison', *Diseases of the Nervous System*, vol. 13, no. 3, pp. 2–4; Fishman, *Sex in Prison*, p. 60; interview by author with Al Maloney, August 2001.

25 27(AO) RG 20–42–3 Millbrook Inmate Case Files, KBL, 2480.

26 Fishman, *Sex in Prison*, p. 60.

27 Chancey, *Gay New York*, p. 57

28 Johnson, 'The homosexual in prison', p. 87.

29 For historical accounts of how the field of sexology was built on descriptions of the existing homosexual culture(s), see Chauncey, 'Christian brotherhood or sexual perversion?', pp. 314–15; H. Oosterhuis, *Stepchildren of Nature: Krafft-Ebing, Psychiatry and the Making of Sexual Identity*, Chicago, University of Chicago Press, 2000; and Terry, *An American Obsession*, especially chapter 7.

30 W.E. Mann, *Society Behind Bars: A Sociological Scrutiny of Guelph Reformatory*, Toronto, Copp Clark, Social Science Publishers, 1967, pp. 29, 89.

31 Johnson, 'The homosexual in prison', p. 89.

32 On policy excluding homosexuals from training centres, see (AO) RG 20–16– 2–0–173.20 'Guelph – NPC Clinic 1959–1960' Revised 1959 Psychological Standards of Students for the OTC, Burtch, and RG 20–16–2–0–75.7 'Guelph – Prisoners 1953–54', 18 December 1953 Memo to Miss G. Bownam, Bailiff's Office, from J.A. Graham.

33 Fishman, *Sex in Prison*, pp. 69–70.

34 See 'Prison diaries' [1940–1965?], unprocessed material, Kinsey Institute Archives (hereafter KIA).

35 *Peterborough Examiner*, 'No treatment given – men are just broken', 12 July 1965.

36 B. Karpman, 'Sex life in prison', *Journal of Criminal Law and Criminology*, 1948, vol. 38, no. 5, p. 482. See also R.N. Boyd, 'Sex behind bars' in W. Leyland (ed.) *Gay Roots: Twenty Years of Gay Sunshine*, San Francisco, Gay Sunshine Press, 1991, pp. 276.

37 *Toronto Telegram*, 28 September 1965.

38 (AO) RG 20–42–3 Millbrook Inmate Case Files, NTH, 223.

39 *TWO*, July/August [1966?], p. 5.

40 Boyd, 'Sex behind bars', pp. 272–8.

41 D. Tucker, 'A punk's song: view from the inside' in A.M. Scacco, Jr (ed.) *Male Rape: A Casebook of Sexual Aggressions*, New York, AMS Press, 1982, pp. 58–79.

42 Though throughout the twentieth century women were considered the passive party in a (hetero)sexual act (the male act of insertion constituting the 'active' part). Men who were similarly 'receptacles' were also considered 'passive' (and therefore feminine). Clearly the notion of passivity in this context bears little relation to the varying levels of energy output and physical engagement demonstrated by participants in a sexual act. On sexual relations between adult men and younger boys in early twentieth-century Toronto, see S. Maynard, 'Through a hole in the lavatory wall: homosexual subculture, police surveillance and the dialectics of discovery, Toronto, 1890–1930', *Journal of the History of Sexuality*, 1994, vol. 5, no. 2, pp. 207–42.

43 'Homosexuality in prison', author unknown, 1964, p. 6 (KIA).

44 See Boyd, 'Sex behind bars', p. 278; JS, Prison Letters, 1951, KIA. For an account of sex in prison as pleasurable for the 'victim', see D.L. Williams, 'Prison sex at age 16' in W. Leyland (ed.) *Gay Roots: Twenty Years of Gay Sunshine*, San Francisco, Gay Sunshine Press, 1991, pp. 279–86.

45 Wolves were acting as possessive owners but sometimes assumed a paternal role as protector and mentor.

46 C. Ford, 'Homosexual practices of institutionalized females', *Journal of Abnormal Psychology*, no. 23, pp. 442–8.

47 Samuel Kahn, *Homosexuality and Mentality*, Boston, Meador Publishing Company, 1937, p. 5.

48 Select Committee, pp. 6510, 6512.

49 Haines and McLaughlin, 'Treatment of the homosexual', p. 2.

50 R. Linder, 'Sex in prison', *Complex*, no. 6, pp. 5–20.

51 B.C. Glueck, Jr, and R.H. Dinerstein, 'Sub-coma insulin therapy in the treatment of homosexual panic states', *Journal of Social Therapy*, 1955, no. 1, pp. 182–6.

52 Fishman, *Sex in Prison*, pp. 133–9.

53 B. Karpman, 'Sex life in prison', *Journal of Criminal Law and Criminology*, 1948 vol. 38, no. 5, p. 482. See also R.N. Boyd, 'Sex behind bars' in W. Leyland (ed.) *Gay Roots: Twenty Years of Gay Sunshine*, San Francisco, Gay Sunshine Press, 1991, pp. 477–8.

54 Notes on visit to San Quentin, 1 April 1950. Unprocessed material, KIA.

55 C.T. Duffy, *Sex and Crime*, New York, Doubleday, 1965, pp. 174–6.

56 Duffy, *Sex and Crime*, p 180.

57 (AO), RG 49–131. 'Proceedings of the Select Committee', vol. XXVIII, pp. 6497–9.

58 W. Pomeroy, 'Sex in prison', 26 June 1962. Sound Recording, KIA.
59 United States District Attorney (Philadelphia Eastern District), *Report on Sexual Assaults in the Philadelphia Prison System and in Sheriffs' Vans*, 1968.
60 Johnson, 'The homosexual in prison', p. 88.
61 A. Kinsey *et al.*, *Sexual Behavior in the Human Male*, Philadelphia, W.B. Saunders, 1948.
62 Interview conducted by Bruce Jackson, sound recording, April 1962, KIA.
63 D. Sabo, T.A. Kupers and W. London (eds) *Prison Masculinities*, Philadelphia, Temple University Press, 2001.
64 C. Parenti, *Lockdown America: Police and Prisons in the Age of Crisis*, New York, Verso, 1999.

Part II

Therapeutic and preventive isolation

6 The ruly and the unruly

Isolation and inclusion in the management of the insane

Mark Finnane

Kevin Izod O'Doherty, Young Irelander, political exile, Queensland politician and medical practitioner, defined asylum management in 1877: 'The primary classification would, in effect, be between those who are easy to rule and those who are unruly – between the refractory ones and the contrary.'[1] The polarities speak as much of a political imagination in the management of the insane as of a medical discourse seeking to find, beneath the symptoms of disorder, the clues to diagnosis and future treatment. And precisely in pointing to the polarity of ruly versus unruly, O'Doherty's phrase evokes a broader set of contexts and possibilities which the asylum embodied. Its inmates were there above all because they were dangerous to themselves or others, or because they were incapable of governing themselves. The possibility of their release depended on their reaching a threshold where their unruliness had been overcome, or was simply diminished to a point where they were no longer dangerous to themselves or others. This chapter explores some of the ways in which the lunatic asylum – its location, its architecture, its regimes of personal management – functioned as an institution of isolation as well as an institution of inclusion, even of social reintegration, for those who could become once again 'easy to rule'.

The asylum being considered here was established in the earliest years of the self-governing English colony of Queensland, separated from New South Wales in 1859. The Australian settler colony was politically and culturally dominated by a European, mainly British and Irish, population but included by the late nineteenth century large populations of Chinese, Pacific Islanders and other migrants of mainly European origin. The country's indigenous Aboriginal people were violently dispossessed by the waves of colonial settlement fanning out to the west and north from the older settlements of the south-east coastal region. They too would contribute numbers to the population of the asylum. Given this colonial context, it is important to note that there has been some contention in the historiography of colonial medicine about the status of such colonial institutions. Vaughan's argument that the colonial hospital in Africa was not 'modern' has been constructed on a binary opposition that contrasts colonial/repressive with modern/individualising institutions.[2] The model has been questioned at least as far as it might apply to Indian asylums in the later nineteenth century, where Mills finds evidence of both a generalising and repressive incarceration, and of a more individualised medical practice.[3]

If the contrast between the views of Vaughan and Mills is treated as an historical continuum then the colonial asylum in Queensland was more of a type with the Indian case studied by Mills. Every colony was expected to have the range of institutions that defined what good Victorian government meant. The population to be contained by this institution would be varied in the extreme – according to the particular character of the colony itself and the range of attributes of its population. It housed people across class and racial backgrounds – including the colony's Indigenous peoples, even after the establishment of their own regimes of isolation under the 1897 Aborigines Protection Act. Even in death the colonial asylum's inmates were jumbled together – although the authorities, in a display of sensitivity to sectarian differences, at one point took advantage of reinterment occasioned by the replacement of the old cemetery to separate the Roman Catholics from the Protestants.[4]

Considering isolation in an asylum setting allows us to explore a paradox which demands attention, namely the purposeful seclusion, even invisibility, of the asylum and its inmates on the one hand, confronted on the other by the continuous efforts to maintain contact between the asylum and the outside world. In doing so we will look first at the decisions regarding the siting and construction of this institution, then at some of the material techniques for managing bodies within the asylum, before considering some of those practices, such as visiting, that brought the asylum and its inmates back into relation to the world outside. Finally we will consider some questions about isolation and inclusion of the insane as it appeared as a policy issue in the 1930s – a point in time by which new psychiatric and welfarist directions had begun to individualise the insane subject.

Siting the colonial asylum

In quite specific ways, colonial and imperial contexts mark the beginning of the asylum we are examining. The stimulus to the creation of the Woogaroo Lunatic Asylum was twofold. First, with the separation of Queensland from New South Wales in 1859, the longstanding transportation of the insane from the northern parts of the colony to Sydney institutions had to be replaced by local solutions. A second prompt came from London, with two circulars from the Secretary of State for Colonies arriving in 1863 and 1864. The circulars inquired after conditions in 'Colonial Hospitals and Asylums' throughout the Empire, following a scandal over the state of the hospital and lunatic asylum in Kingston, Jamaica. The report compiled in the Colonial Office on the asylums and hospitals stretching from Canada through the West Indies, Africa, and on to Australia, was scathing about the failures of colonial institutions. Makeshift products 'of utility narrowed by mistaken economy', the asylums were judged 'almost universally worse than the hospitals, and sometimes suggest the impression that they are, perhaps unconsciously, regarded too much as means of relief from a troublesome class, without care for curative treatment'.

The objectives of imperial policy regarding provision for the insane, so far as this despatch constituted them, were clear. The objects desired in the treatment of the diseased in curative hospitals and asylums are, that the greatest possible proportion of patients should be cured and in the shortest possible time, to which must be added in the case of asylums that the normal condition and rights of the insane should be infringed upon in as small a degree as may be consistent with efficient management. It is not justifiable to rest satisfied with a less number of cures than the disease reasonably admits of, or with a system which permits any unnecessary restraint.

Achieving such objectives depended on reform including medical supervision, continuous inspection and a system of management to ensure that the insane inmates were treated 'as nearly as may be as if they were sane, and to infringe firmly when necessary, but otherwise as little as possible, both as a matter of right and for the purpose of cure, on their habits and natural independence'.[5] This was an agenda formed by a mid-Victorian liberal imagination in social policy, still unclouded by the kinds of anxieties about health and degeneration that would characterise discussions of the asylum a generation later.

To the first of these Colonial Office circulars the Queensland government did not reply, as no asylum had been established and there were no government hospitals. A year later the government reported that the colonial Parliament had voted the funds for an institution to be opened before the end of 1864 – 'a general Lunatic Asylum which has been built on the best model procurable here, and is surrounded with nearly two hundred acres of grounds for the use and amusement of the inmates'.[6] The curative benefits of an ample supply of land around an asylum constituted a perennial theme in the design of asylums, especially since inadequate provision for the 'employment and amusement of the insane' was so common. As the Colonial Office had dryly noted of another place: 'The perpetual cry of the Canadian inspectors and physicians for more land is not answered, and the Jamaica asylum provides for the occupation and amusement of 200 lunatics a barrel organ.'[7]

Queensland's 'General Lunatic Asylum' had at least ample land, though it was to be many years before adequate consideration was given to the 'occupation and amusement' of the inmates. The asylum was built near the village of Woogaroo, from which it took its first name and its first inmates, fifty-seven males and twelve females who were transported there by the river steamer *Settler* on a Tuesday morning in January 1865.[8] The Colonial Architect had highlighted the advantages of the site and a vision of the asylum's construction:

This site being cheerfully and healthily situated on the river Brisbane would also appear very eligible for the Lunatic Asylum which is proposed to be erected by the Government, if say, 500 or 600 acres could be reserved with the quarry on the river bank. The majority of lunatics being paupers and belonging to the labouring classes, the work of farming and quarrying would be a means of giving active and healthy employment to them and they could assist in erecting their own Asylum, and in maintaining themselves. Other advantages of the site being; that it is nearly half-way between the two most populous towns in the Colony and at the same time sufficiently removed from either to ensure the quiet custody of the patients beyond the reach of tempta- tion, and the steamers passing at least twice a day, rendering a few miles on either side of little moment.[9]

The site was indeed accessible by water – regular flooding would ensure that the earliest buildings were eventually abandoned. It was also sufficiently removed from towns – far enough, in fact, to be an impediment to the kinds of visiting by relatives and friends and entertainers that some later saw as an integral part of treatment. But even worse was its distance from the northern and western reaches of the colony, making an escorted trip to the asylum a journey of some days even when available by rail. In 1925 the transportation of lunatics from the northern city of Townsville by rail to Brisbane still took about 60 hours, with no sleeping accommodation.[10] In a colony where the population was relatively dispersed, as it was in Queensland, the enforced isolation of an inmate in Woogaroo would provoke recurrent criticism against the institution and its managers.

The isolation of the lunatic asylum was also and quite early perceived as a disadvantage in terms of access and governance. Within five years of opening there had already been two public inquiries, the second judging that an asylum would be better placed within two or three miles of Brisbane on the grounds that 'one of the strongest safeguards against oppression and mismanagement would be found in the surveillance of the institution by the public'.[11] It was a view informed by the government medical officer, who had put it to the Colonial Secretary that its site was the very source of its problems: 'the asylum being out of sight, is out of mind, and like every other neglected thing, it has grown up to annoy and reproach us with its presence'.[12] The paradox of isolation, it appeared, was that it bred its own conditions of exposure. The asylum became all too visible in public discourse, but in a way that was most uncontrollable by government, through the constant generation of rumours, anxieties, fears and horror stories, all amplified by its material seclusion.

The architecture of isolation

The asylum as a Victorian institution suffered from its enduring association with the madhouse of Bedlam, with the uncontrollable behaviours of its inmates, perpetrators but more often victims of abuse and violence.[13] Yet colonial govern- ments knew they had to build such institutions, and in the Australian as in other colonies, they did so with enthusiasm during the mid-Victorian decades. Woogaroo had been built, so the Executive Council told the Colonial Office, 'on the best model procurable here'. But there was real dispute over exactly what was the best model, given local circumstances, which included not only popula- tion densities, materials and financial resources available, but also architectural fancies and preferences. Seeking to isolate the insane, asylum regimes pursued an architecture that never resolved the tension between care and constraint, let alone coercion. This might be seen in a myriad of ways, a striking one being the most material sign of the asylum's separation – walls and fences.

Walls are a definitive sign of the decisions made about the kind of isolation sought or required by the management of the asylum. A striking feature of Woogaroo from the start was its seeming absence of boundaries. In contrast to inner-city asylums frequently marked off by their heavy stone or brick walls, the asylum at Woogaroo had its boundaries marked by natural features – bushland, creek and river. Responding to the advocates of an inner-Brisbane asylum, a local architect warned the 1869 inquiry: 'Any building erected there must necessarily partake of the nature of an asylum, and look like an asylum, which I would wish to avoid … It would have to be walled in.'[14]

The seeming absence of walls at Woogaroo was an advantage born both of its isolation – there were too few neighbours to express anxiety about the danger of escaped inmates – and also economy. The absence of walls, however, did not mean an absence of fences. Indeed, the architecture of the site involved constant reconsideration of the kinds of fences that were held necessary to contain the inmates, to make them more manageable. The 116 acres of reserve around the early buildings were enclosed with a three-rail fence in 1864. This still left an enormous expanse of grounds over which the patients might wander – were it not for the other kinds of fences containing them. For from the beginning it had been intended that this was an institution whose architectural rationale had to avoid the appearance of restraint, while preventing the patients escaping. The opinion that mattered was that of the Colonial Architect, Charles Tiffen, who had consulted the authorities, like the famous advocate of non-restraint John Conolly, through their books. As Tiffen told the 1869 inquiry in response to questions about the high fence around the asylum: 'You must either have a high fence or high walls, or otherwise the patients will get out; – I never saw a lunatic asylum without high walls. We could not afford walls, and therefore we put up a fence.' The one that was constructed had the effect of blocking any view out of the buildings – a pragmatic decision shaped by the fact that the material available was in fact the old gaol fence from Brisbane, only sufficient to go around a small site, and not placed at some distance down the fall of the hill.[15]

Fences were useful for preventing escapes – and suicides. Having an asylum on the verge of a major river was a temptation to the suicidal and the wooden fences around the buildings were not adequate to stop the more determined from going through or over them.[16] The solution sought by later administrators was that preferred by many before them in other places – the sunken fence, known also as a 'ha-ha', that sought to avoid the appearance of containment while acting as an effective barrier to escape. A newly appointed medical superintendent, H. Byam Ellerton, reported in 1910 on an unusually high number of escapes – but refrained from condemning them since 'it shows at least that patients are not treated as prisoners, and it is necessary, as part of the treatment for the furtherance of recovery, to allow patients as much freedom as possible'.[17] Where the privilege of freedom could not be trusted, institutional architecture could innovate to diminish the sense of claustrophobia. In 1916 Ellerton reported on major work replacing a wooden palisade fence in front of three male wards by a sunken wire fence in a 4-feet-deep, V-shaped trench. Another new ward had its garden separated from the main drive by a combined wooden and wire fence that, by virtue of the contour of the land, allowed patients working in the garden a view of the surrounding country, while preventing the general public from seeing them.[18]

Fences isolated the insane from the outside world, from the dangers that awaited them and from the voyeurs, but equally separated the violent and the peaceful, the trusted and the unpredictable within the asylum. Pharmacological innovation might later render some of these purposes redundant, as it would other dimensions of institutional architecture. The careful cultivation of gardens, sporting grounds, recreation halls, the very park-like surrounds – all this made sense in the age of moral treatment, or of moral management, as Digby has usefully distinguished this style of institutional provision.[19] As pharmacological treatments advanced in the decades after the 1930s the rationale for such con-genial surrounds diminished, since an inmate was now individualised and the modern pharmacopoeia promised to remedy what were now seen as physiological disorders. What need was there, then, of Ellerton's bush-house 100 yards long and 20 yards wide, 'to give ample room for the gardener to rear young seedlings and to attend to sick plants coming back from the wards, as well as to keep a reserve stock in readiness for the wards and the Recreation Hall?'[20] What need even of the fences? By the 1960s the adoption of the 'modern' system of treatment meant psychiatric facilities in general hospitals, a declining asylum population and a focus on making the patients responsible through an 'open ward' system. As the Queensland Premier explained to the Australian Prime Minister in August 1960, 'the development of chemo-therapy and the successful use of "tranquillizing drugs" have removed whatever reasons there may have been for the segregation of mentally sick patients in Mental Hospitals for the purpose of their treatment'.[21] Drugs rendered redundant the walls and even the notion of the separate asylum colony, as the mentally ill person was normalised as a recipient of medical care.

Managing bodies, managing asylums

How far and in what ways should and did the asylum make subject the body of the inmate? The question was one informed by medical and administrative require-ments and fashions. The contrasting perspectives that might develop about how an asylum's techniques were related to its objectives are captured almost at the outset by ambiguity around the meanings of restraint. Woogaroo had barely opened its doors when the Visiting Justice, whose duty it was to inspect the asylum, suggested to the Colonial Secretary that 'a book should be kept ... in which all punishments or restraints to which the patients have been subjected together with the causes of the same shall be entered'. The suggestion flowed from a juristic view of the neces-sity to control and make accountable abusive behaviour in institutions. The reply rejected this proposal, which was regarded as 'not at present desirable – the restraints inflicted being not so much in the nature of punishments as part of the medical treatment of each inmate'.[22] Management of the body under medical treatment would justify interventions that would constitute assaults in other circumstances. This did not make the asylum an unregulated space but one subjected to different possibilities in the management of one group of people by another.

Management of the body was shaped by other perceptions and sensibilities. Medical authority was also gendered authority in an institution in which both genders were represented. Between 1867 and 1940 there were nearly 22,000 first admissions to Woogaroo, nearly 40 per cent of them women. This made for a large institution of nearly 1,800 residents on a daily basis by the 1930s, in the same gender proportions. There were other social distinctions in the asylum, including race, and age, and even social status, but gender was the most enduring distinction in this asylum, embodied in the segregation of wards, the fences demarcating the territory of male and female, and the regulations controlling access of male staff to female patients. The pertinence of gender is captured repeatedly in the small ways by which the asylum sought to manage the body of the inmate in ways that would re-shape their potential for entering the world once again. Equally these re-shapings reflected the status and gender differences between doctors and their charges.

Managing the bodies of inmates was a process not just of containing their unregulated and uncontrolled behaviours – of making them ruly again, or rendering them at the least more tractable. It was, for the more ambitious medical superintendents, a way of making inmates into civil beings – in short, of civilising them. Appearance, clothing, deportment, manners, useful activity – all these attributes, of course, were signs by which one could assess the state of order versus disorder, signs that conventionally marked the insane as needing confinement or care. The asylum presented an opportunity to change habits and modes of living – and the techniques adopted in pursuit of such an objective tell us much at this distance of the way in which the system of moral treatment was in so many ways a system of making the insane into civil beings. The process was captured especially in the administration of H. Byam Ellerton, the long-serving (1909–37) medical superintendent at what was now known as Goodna Hospital for the Insane. Ellerton's administration of the hospital was the target of muck-rakers who prompted a Royal Commission in 1915, but it was he more than any other superintendent in the first eighty years of the hospital who pursued the possibilities of an institutional re-making of its inmates. As one who had served his apprenticeship in some of the largest English asylums before his move to Australia in 1909,[23] his optimism about the possibilities of the asylum environment suggest some need to reassess the pessimism that is held by some to pervade the late Victorian and early Edwardian period of asylum history.[24]

Ellerton's aspiration was the cultivation of an institution that would embody high standards of care and dignity for the inmates of the asylum – and is in the lineage of the vision of the nineteenth-century asylum as a utopia.[25] His vision of moral treatment seems predicated on an institutional design that cultivates a kind of Edwardian middle-class display of discipline and manners. Patients would be given their best chance of recovery if they had opportunities of useful labour, engagement in recreations such as cricket, exposure to cultural artefacts including music, and cultivation of appropriate manners. We can capture these orientations in the careful and public documentation of asylum reconstruction that he provided over the years from 1909 to 1937. In 1911, for example, after only two years, Ellerton reported on the renovation of a dining room, a renewal in which environmental design was calculated to reform manners:

> A departure in the scheme of tables was tried in this ward – the room is furnished *à la table d'hôte*, and the tables are of sizes some to seat four, others not more than six patients, but this cannot be done unless the dining-rooms are of a generous size for the number of patients they are to accommodate. The rest of the furniture is of a light kind, and the old idea of heavy, ugly tables and forms has been discarded. Good prints and photogravures ornament the walls, and the floor is polished.

The 'marked improvement in their demeanour and behaviour' confirmed for Ellerton what he had frequently said before – 'that, with those mentally afflicted, overcrowding goes hand in hand with increased noise, confusion and rough manners'.[26]

Ellerton's constructive ideas for changing the behaviour of patients extended outside the buildings. We have already hinted at his fondness for the recuperative benefits of plants. The year of the creation of the 100-yard-long bush-house was also one for experimenting with a new scheme for the making of flower-beds in the central garden of the female wards. As he explained, 'this had been tried years ago, but it was not attended with much success, owing to the proclivities of female patients in plucking the flowers and destroying the plants'. The remedy was to involve the patients – a female patient was assigned to 'the charge of certain beds adjoining the wards in which she resides, giving her a watering can, and making her appreciate a sense of responsibility in keeping her flower-beds in good order'. The method had already been adopted with success at the male wards.[27] Its extension to the female wards was a leap of faith across perceptions of gendered capacities, or weaknesses – in his very first year Ellerton had told the Home Secretary that not only did the female patients 'simply pluck the flowers to wear them in their dresses', but 'male patients who work at gardening naturally take more pride and care in their own work'.[28]

Managing bodies, however, meant more than cultivating productive labour or encouraging mannered eating habits. The institution was also a place where gendered understandings of dignity and bodily image were played out, even provoking debate between staff over appropriate management. At hearings of the 1915 Royal Commission, the issues were highlighted by evidence of disputation between doctor and nurse over the shaving of heads. A charge nurse in a female ward gave evidence that the doctor had wanted to cut off the hair of the patients:

> I told him that the patient's friends objected to that being done, and he then said that they could not object, and that there was no difference between them and the prisoners, except that they had committed no crime.

The doctor concerned confirmed that he had wanted to cut their hair in order to control head lice. To him the Matron had said 'that she would not like to cut their hair because they were women, and it is not a very nice thing for a woman to have her hair cut short'. Earlier, his evidence recalled a distinction he had made between women in some wards and others, the more severe mental cases being an instance where 'it would not matter to them whether their hair was cut or not, from an appearance point of view'.[29] The difference in perspective between doctor and nurse on this matter of bodily image reflected both a distance between them regarding the formal status of the person/patient, and a gendered disposition on what was essential to dignity. This was a contest that, in the nurse's evidence, reflected the context of a patient as a social being, as a person with 'friends' outside the walls who valued what happened to the one inside.

Sexuality also had to be managed. On the one hand, this implied controlling the sexuality of those deemed incapable of managing themselves. When in 1937 the mother of a Goodna Park patient (a girl said to be a 'mental deficient') requested of the Home Secretary that her daughter be sterilised, the medical authorities were confronted with the political reality that such action was not legal, however much it might be regarded as commendable from the 'point of view of the betterment of the race'. The Minister's Office consulted with Dr Basil Stafford at the hospital, suggesting to him that 'the better course would be to detain this girl until such time as the Mental Deficient Bill is determined'. Stafford agreed, and the mother was informed that her daughter would be detained. The context suggests that the mother would have concurred.[30] In other countries, especially in North America, the law had been amended in the flush of eugenic fervour during the early decades of the twentieth century, though its longer-term implementation remained controversial – in places like Queensland, where the law was not amended, detention nevertheless played its own part in this management of bodies.[31]

A different management of gender relations was implicit in the norms that attended the separation of the sexes in the asylum, norms that were explicitly framed to limit sexual access of men, both patients and staff, to women. The separation began on the journey to the asylum – the transportation by rail of prospective inmates was carefully managed to ensure that nurses accompanied female patients destined for the asylum.[32] In the institution itself sexual contact was forbidden, and controlled through the segregation of wards, divided by fences. While transgression of the norm was possible, its discovery could be severely punished, especially where a staff member was involved. In 1936 the Home Secretary ordered the instant dismissal of a warder after evidence emerged that the warder had slept with a patient at his flat in Brisbane city, after she was discharged on parole to her mother.[33] Transgressing the norms against sexual contact between staff and patients was, at least in this case, met with immediate punishment of the warder concerned. Uncovering such transgressions was another matter, a continuing problem for institutional governance.

Managing bodies in the asylum was as imperfect a task as one might expect, the careful construction of asylum regulations notwithstanding. It was a process not only of training patients, it seems, but also of training staff. Regulations for the management of gender relations in the asylum were complemented by more than institutional design. As this last example suggests, they were also supported by norms about the kinds of people that an asylum might employ, and the kinds of practices that it might proscribe. In this way, of course, the asylum was part of the very process of modern government, in which individual subjects were being shaped for civil life and habits, capable (so it was expected) of distinguishing their private and public selves and interests.

Isolation and inclusion

To say that the asylum described here functioned as an institution of reintegration is to invest its history with too much unity. An inmate who did not get out within a year of admission had a high likelihood of staying many years, perhaps even the rest of their life, short or long as it might be. Yet it has been demonstrated in numerous studies that a reality of the asylum was not the long-term incarceration of the insane but the high turnover of its population. Both in public and private asylums in Victorian Britain it was the case that a high proportion of patients left the institution within one or two years, if they did not die there, being already physically ill on entry.[34] At Woogaroo/Goodna the patterns were replicated. The proportion of those discharged as 'recovered' fluctuated from year to year, but ranged between a third and two-thirds of the admissions across the seventy years considered here. The majority of those who were discharged were in the hospital for less than a year.

The isolation of the insane was sometimes purposeful, their removal being a response to their perceived danger to themselves or others. For many the isolation was truly asylum – a resort for those unable by reason of many circumstances of maintaining themselves. A large proportion of those in colonial asylums were already socially isolated people. In the homelands of the settlers, such as Ireland and Britain, the great majority (over 80 per cent at the Omagh asylum in Ireland throughout the later nineteenth century) of persons committed to the asylum appear to have had a family relative living with or near them.[35] In the colonies in the earliest decades, settlers who ended in the asylum were very frequently friend-less – with some groups markedly so, such as the Chinese in Queensland, all 132 of whom admitted to Woogaroo in the thirty years after 1868 were male and, like the great majority of their compatriots in the colony, alone.

Even for those who did have relatives or friends who were potential visitors, the geography of the colony made the asylum a distant, isolated place. Parliamentarians representing northern electorates received enquiries from their constituents asking for direct information about their incarcerated relatives – and at least in some cases appear to have taken the task in hand by occasional visits themselves.[36] The norms of family sentiment were the source of repeated appeals by politicians representing northern and western constituencies for the establish-ment of asylums in their districts. The vast distances separating some inmates of Goodna from their homes rendered visiting an impossibility – until a sympathetic government introduced a system of free travel passes to facilitate contact. The passes were available only to the 'indigent' – people such as a Rockhampton mother of five, with an unemployed husband, who was granted a rail pass to travel the 600 kilometres with one daughter to see her 20-year-old child in Goodna in 1937.[37] Such assistance to the relatives of asylum inmates suggests the value attached by democratised government to the dignity entitlement of those without means. Applications for visitors' passes make up a high proportion of the correspondence relating to the asylum in the Queensland Home Secretary's Office in the 1930s. They signify the resilience of a sentiment of contact between those inside and outside the asylum. Such governmental support is consistent with a revived interest at this time in the possibilities of recovery and reintegration of the mentally ill.

At the end of our time period stands an event that signifies the emergence of the asylum (by now known as Goodna, after the suburb of which it was now a dominant part) from a colonial past. The retirement of Byam Ellerton precipitated a series of changes in direction. The responsibility for Goodna was handed to a young Melbourne-educated doctor, Basil Stafford, whose sense of future directions was shaped by his attendance as the official Australian delegate to the Second International Congress on Mental Hygiene in Paris in July 1937.[38] Away for nine months, Stafford visited the United States, Britain, France, Belgium and Austria, preparing from his travels a report on contemporary management of mental illness and deficiency that signalled changes from Ellerton's institutional regime, embedded as it had been in a moral treatment ethos. Stafford's report helped frame new legislation replacing the colonial law of insanity, and sought to establish a new regime focused on the separation of acute diseases from chronic, but now within the nomenclature of psychiatry rather than the older psychological medicine with its preferences for moral treatment.[39] These changes came belatedly to Queensland – more than two decades after South Australia's Mental Deficiency Act, and more than a decade after that in Tasmania, and indeed a generation after the establishment of a pathology laboratory in New South Wales. They point, that is, to the belated transformation of mental health institutions that had been shaped by colonial legal and administrative requirements.

Stafford also returned from his 1937 world tour armed with a programme that would seek to distinguish more purposefully the mentally diseased from the mentally deficient. His vision of how the future life of those in the second category might be governed highlights the issue I have sought to accentuate here – how containment in specialised asylums was seen as a mechanism for managing the distinctions between those who were governable and those whose lack of governability rendered them suitable subjects for prolonged or even permanent isolation from the outside world.

For Stafford, key distinctions around the concept of mental deficiency centred on how segregation could be used to render 'the "backward" children' capable of attaining a 'socially satisfactory standard of intelligence'. Stafford contrasted with this possibility the situation of those left to compete with normal children in an 'unequal struggle, often with very marked and serious emotional disturbances, which might make a potentially humble but very productive social unit, a menace to himself and the community'. The enclosed and protected world of the asylum, a place in which those unable to govern themselves might be at least protected against danger, offered to some of its population the chance to render useful labour. There was thus no reason why the worst of the deficient, 'Idiots',

> should not be housed and cared for in an institution for chronic mental disease, where the nursing staff would have the assistance of patients. This definitely provides a therapeutic occupation for chronic psychotic patients that is often very helpful to them. Certainly the influence on chronic patients can be definitely expected to be beneficial and not harmful.

There were others among the mental defects whose future was more positive – in both London and New York he had visited institutions in which

> a few become sufficiently skilful or adaptable socially to be able to go out to employment such as domestic service in the day time and return to the institution at night, more or less using the institution as a hostel.

The problem of 'moral deficiency' (by which would be meant at this time sex offenders) was especially difficult – here the standard of treatment was 'satisfactory resocialisation', but difficult to achieve. In contrast to other modes of treating deficiency in which he stressed the advantages of the one institution, 'probably the most satisfactory institutions for this class are rural or agricultural colonies. The necessary isolation and removal from previous environment and environs are all to the good.'

Such colonies would be exceptional, both by reason of their intended population and by contrast with the governance requirements of the common mental hospital. For at the very moment of its transformation from the colonial to the modern, we can observe that Stafford highlighted once again the vital importance that should be attached to avoidance of the isolation of the institution itself from the public world. Any future institution, especially for defectives, should be in close vicinity to the metropolitan area, for reasons including availability of the required 'eminently expert professional and artisan staff'. Further, 'sufferers from mental deficiency have an especial appeal to relatives and friends, and the institution should be situated favourably for their visits'. But reducing isolation had another purpose:

> A metropolitan institution is always a public interest, and as such is ensured the attention it deserves from political and Departmental administration. Place an institution in the 'Bush' and it is 'Out of sight, out of mind', and consequently it will be hampered by inefficient equipment and very soon by inefficient personnel.[40]

Stafford's report, I am suggesting, captures nicely the functionality of isolation, its possibilities and its dangers.

It is not just the recurrence of the phrase 'out of sight, out of mind', nearly seventy years after its earlier use in an 1869 public inquiry into Woogaroo, that captures the continuities of an institution that is both isolating/isolated and inclusive. Those attributes were part of the history of the asylum from its modern origins, if we are to follow Castel. Qualifying Foucault, he suggests that therapeutic and segregative impulses were intimately connected, the latter being replaced by the former as circumstances allowed. The asylum, notes Castel, was that innovation of the revolutionary era which best continued the twin impulses of the totalitarian institution ('of both neutralizing and re-education') – a mixed form 'in which segregation would represent the first stage to be abolished, thanks to the application, in an enclosed environment, of a programme of resocialization'.[41] That stepwise replacement of segregation by a programme of resocialisation is similarly evoked in Mills' account of the asylum in British India – as in the account here of an institution in colonised Queensland. In the beginning was segregation – but always thereafter the challenge of bringing the asylum back into the fold of governable institutions, just as the inmates themselves, once isolated, would be, where possible, returned to the places whence they came, as individuals who were at least easy to rule if not totally self-governing.

Notes

1 Royal Commission appointed to inquire into the Management of the Woogaroo Lunatic Asylum and the Lunatic Reception Houses of the Colony, *Report and Minutes of Evidence*, Brisbane, 1877, q. 265.

2 M. Vaughan, *Curing their Ills: Colonial Power and African Illness*, Cambridge, Cambridge University Press, 1991, pp. 10–11, 120–5.

3 J.H. Mills, 'Re-forming the Indian: treatment regimes in the lunatic asylums of British India, 1857–1880', *The Indian Economic and Social History Review*, 1999, vol. 36, pp. 407–29.

4 Royal Commission of Inquiry into the Management of the Hospital for the Insane, *Report and Minutes of Evidence*. Brisbane, 1915 q. 20443.

5 Circular from Secretary of State for Colonies, 14 January 1864 – 'Colonial hospitals and lunatic asylums', pp. 6, 13, 17, Queensland State Archives [hereafter QSA], EXE/E10, 64/37.

6 Executive Council Minute 13 August 1864, QSA, EXE/E10, 64/37.

7 Circular from Secretary of State for Colonies, 14 January 1864 – 'Colonial hospitals and lunatic asylums', p. 12, QSA, EXE/E10, 64/37.

8 *Brisbane Courier*, 14 January 1865.

9 Colonial Architect Letterbooks ARC/6, Col. Arch. to Surv.-Gen., 61/166, 27 September 1861, QSA.

10 Comm. of Police to Under Sec., Home Dept, 16 March 1925, QSA A/44745.

11 Joint Select Committee on the Woogaroo Lunatic Asylum, *Report*, 1869, p. 6.

12 *Ibid.*, Minutes of Evidence, p. 71 (Letter of W. Hobbs, Medical Officer, to Colonial Secretary, 14 May 1869).

13 R. Porter, *Mind-forg'd Manacles: A History of Madness in England from the Restoration to the Regency*, London, Athlone Press, 1987, pp. 123–9.

14 Select Committee, 1869, Minutes of Evidence, p. 42 (Richard Suter, Architect).

15 *Ibid.*, Minutes of Evidence, p. 6 (Charles Tiffin, Colonial Architect)

16 Annual Report of the Medical Superintendent, Woogaroo Asylum [hereafter *Annual Report*], 1889, p. 1.

17   *Annual Report*, 1910, p. 5.
18   *Annual Report*, 1916, pp. 6, 37.
19   A. Digby, *Madness, Morality and Medicine*, Cambridge, Cambridge University Press, 1985; A. Scull, *The Most Solitary of Afflictions: Madness and Society in Britain, 1700–1900*, New Haven and London, Yale University Press, 1993, p. 298.
20   *Annual Report*, 1911, p. 28.
21   Premier of Queensland to Prime Minister, 9 August 1960, QSA, TR/1889/841.
22   Visiting Justice to Col. Sec., Brisbane, 16 July 1865, COL/A68 (Z/6538), QSA.
23   D. MacKinnon, ‘“A captive audience”: musical concerts in Queensland mental institutions *c*.1870–*c*.1930’, *Context: A Journal of Music Research*, 2000, no. 19, pp. 43–56.
24   See especially Scull, *The Most Solitary of Afflictions*, ch. 6.
25   *Ibid.*, pp. 296–7.
26   *Annual Report*, 1911, p. 28.
27   *Ibid.*, p. 28.
28   Ellerton to Home Sec., 18 July 1910, COL/330, QSA.
29   Royal Commission of Inquiry into the Management of the Hospital for the Insane, *Report and Minutes of Evidence*, Brisbane, 1915, ev. Maria Daly, Charge Nurse, 16544–6; ev. Dr J.C. Hemsley, 11231, 11097–8.
30   Director-General (Cilento) to Minister, 24 November 1937, QSA A/3949.
31   G. Grob, *The Mad Among Us: A History of the Care of America's Mentally Ill*, Cambridge, Mass., Harvard University Press, 1994, pp. 161–2; G. Broberg and N. Roll-Hansen (eds), *Eugenics and the Welfare State: Sterilization Policy in Denmark, Sweden, Norway and Finland*, East Lansing, Michigan State University Press, 1996; S. Garton, ‘Sound minds and healthy bodies: re-considering eugenics in Australia, 1914–40’, *Australian Historial Studies*, 1994, vol. 26, no. 103, pp. 163–81; S. Garton, *Medicine and Madness: A Social History of Insanity in New South Wales, 1880–1940*, Kensington, NSW, NSWU Press, 1988, p. 60; D. Wright and A. Digby (eds) *From Idiocy to Mental Deficiency: Historical Perspectives on People with Learning Disabilities*, London and New York, Routledge, 1996, pp. 13–14.
32   Police report, on escort of insane patients from Townsville to Brisbane, 21 May 1925, QSA A/44745.
33   Police report, 22 October 1936, QSA A/3874.
34   L.J. Ray, ‘Models of madness in Victorian asylum practice’, *Archives Européenes de Sociologie*, 1981, vol. 22, pp. 231–4. See also C. Mackenzie, ‘Social factors in the admission, discharge, and continuing stay of patients at Ticehurst Asylum, 1845–1917’, in W.F. Bynum, R. Porter and M. Shepherd (eds) *The Anatomy of Madness: Essays in the History of Psychiatry. Volume II Institutions and Society*, vol. 2, London and New York, Tavistock, 1985, pp. 147, 169; S. Garton, *Medicine and Madness*, p. 36; M. Finnane, ‘Law and the social uses of the asylum in nineteenth century Ireland’, in D. Tomlinson and J. Carrier (eds) *Asylum in the Community*, London and New York, Routledge, pp. 101–5; D. Wright, ‘Getting out of the asylum: understanding the confinement of the insane in the nineteenth century’, *Social History of Medicine*, 1997, vol. 10, no. 1, p. 143.
35   R. Adair, J. Melling and B. Forsythe, ‘Migration, family structure and pauper lunacy in Victorian England: admissions to the Devon County Pauper Lunatic Asylum, 1845–1900’, *Continuity and Change*, 1997, vol. 12, no. 3, pp. 373–401; P. Bartlett and D. Wright (eds) *Outside the Walls of the Asylum: The History of Care in the Community 1750–2000*, London, Athlone Press, 1999; M. Finnane, *Insanity and the Insane in Post-Famine Ireland*, London, Croom Helm, 1981, p. 132.
36   Cf. *Queensland Parliamentary Debates*, 14 October 1914, p. 1682.
37   Applications for visitors' passes, QSA, A/3954, 37/12189; 37/12147.
38   Correspondence with Commonwealth Government on nomination of Stafford as an Australian delegate, QSA, A/3910, 37/4077.
39   B.F.R. Stafford ‘Report on modern trends in administration and treatment of mental diseases’ (February 1938), QSA, A/31781, 45/8786.

40 Stafford, 'Report', pp. 31–4, QSA, A/31781, 45/8786.
41 R. Castel, *The Regulation of Madness: The Origins of Incarceration in France*, translated by W.D. Halls, Oxford, Polity Press, 1988, pp. 80–1.

7 From 'leper villages' to leprosaria

Public health, nationalism and the culture of exclusion in Japan

Susan L. Burns

Today in Japan there exists a system of thirteen national leprosaria where more than 5,000 patients reside, most of whom are elderly and infirm.[1] Some of them have spent five or more decades within the leprosaria, the largest of which once housed more than 1,900 people. The course of their lives was determined by the passage in 1931 of the 'lifetime confinement' law that required the forcible segregation until death of all those diagnosed with leprosy. It was not until 1996 that this law was finally repealed, after a prolonged debate that centred on the question of whether leprosy 'still' constituted a threat to public health. Since then, controversy surrounding the leprosaria has continued: hundreds of patients have filed suit in several district courts asking for compensation on the grounds that their human rights were violated by the confinement law.

This chapter seeks to examine the history of the leprosarium system in Japan from the late nineteenth century until the 1930s. The Japanese case is of significance for the project of constructing a transnational history of exclusionary practices precisely because it does not intersect neatly with conclusions that have been drawn about attitudes and policies towards leprosy sufferers in other non-Western societies. In their seminal 1970 article, Zachary Gussow and George S. Tracy questioned the view that the stigmatisation of leprosy was a historically and transculturally stable phenomenon that arose 'naturally' in response to an incurable and disfiguring disease. They argued instead that fear of leprosy was a cultural construct that emerged in the West in the late nineteenth century in conjunction with racial concerns heightened by the expansion of colonialism.[2] The characterisation of leprosy as a 'threat' posed by racial others spurred efforts to confine those infected in the colonies to prevent the spread of the disease to the 'civilised' world. The result was the production of new attitudes of stigma towards leprosy in societies where it had been 'just' a disease.

Gussow and Tracy's work is the point of departure for a series of studies on 'leper' colonies and leprosaria. Megan Vaughan, Alison Bashford and Maria Nugent, and Warwick Anderson are among those who have explored the interaction between indigenous concepts of the disease in sites such as Africa, Australia and the Philippines, and the Western policies of exclusion established in the late nineteenth- and early twentieth-century context of nationalism and racism.[3] Where these authors depart from Gussow and Tracy is in their recognition that the policies of exclusion also gave rise to new subjectivities as leprosy sufferers developed strategies to confront and negotiate the relations of power that shaped these new institutions. My discussion of the rise of the Japanese leprosarium system aims to reflect upon the issues raised by this literature – the origin of stigma, the impact of Western concepts of race and nation, and the nature of the 'leper' as subject.

Before the leprosarium – the premodern culture of exclusion

Japan's initial leprosy prevention policy was promulgated in 1907. It made doctors responsible for notifying the police in the case of a diagnosis of leprosy and gave the police the responsibility for overseeing the isolation and disinfection of sufferers who had homes and families. But the law was most concerned with those termed 'wandering lepers', afflicted people without homes or a source of income. It required that they be confined at public expense in five regional leprosaria that were to be established by 1909. To be sure, the passage of the 1907 law owed much to the international medical discourse on leprosy that emerged after Gerhard Hansen identified the bacterium that caused the disease in 1874. In 1897, the first international congress of leprosy was held in Berlin. The two Japanese delegates who had attended reported the conclusions of the meeting to the Japanese Home Ministry: leprosy was a contagious disease, no cure was known, and so prevention must focus on limiting the spread of the disease. In the aftermath of the report, the Ministry ordered the first survey of the number of leprosy sufferers in Japan, and politicians, journalists, public health officials and doctors began to call for the segregation of those infected. However, underlying the references to medical science and public health was the understanding of leprosy already in place. Even before leprosy was declared to be a 'public health problem' in the late nineteenth century, the disease was already profoundly marked, entangled in cultural assumptions and concerns.

A point of entry into popular attitudes towards leprosy before it was transformed into a public health issue are the multiple petitions submitted to local authorities by a man who used the name Nishiyama Kyozan, a resident of the temple Nishiyama Kōmyōin, located in what is now Nara prefecture. One of the earliest of these, dated 1880, states:

> I suffer from leprosy [*repura*], that is, the divine punishment disease, and am a resident of Nishiyama in this village. In this province there are two such places. One is Kitayama at Todaiji; the other is Nishiyama at Yakushiji. From long ago, those who suffered from this disease entered these two places and spent their lives there … Based upon an edict from the time of the Bunmu [*sic*] emperor, we began to receive alms of rice in two seasons … However, after the Restoration the gathering of alms was generally forbidden and since then we have no other means of receiving support, for there is no law that saves those

who are diseased, no law that offers them aid ... Even though this sickness is the result of karmic retribution, there is no method to aid those who are without support.[4]

This is but one of a series of petitions that Nishiyama Kyozan made to local officials on behalf of the residents of Kōmyōin during the 1880s. Like the one I have quoted, they were skilfully crafted, evoking historical precedent and signs of imperial favour, religious conceptions of charity and pure human need.

In his petitions, Nishiyama uses multiple terms to label both his affliction and himself. He makes reference to *repura*, a word of European origin that entered Japan in the late sixteenth century via Catholic missionaries, but also describes his condition as the 'divine punishment disease' and asserts that it resulted from 'karmic retribution'. In his early petitions, Kyozan denoted his social status by means of the term *monoyoshi*, although he later abandoned this in favour of the new class designation of 'commoner'. The term *monoyoshi*, which implied something lucky or a good omen, was used to refer to members of organised communities of leprosy sufferers in Kyoto, Nara and elsewhere in the early modern period.

The origin of these 'leper' communities, as well as the meaning attached to their members, can be traced to medieval Japanese society. According to Kuroda Hideo, by the eleventh century, sufferers of leprosy were already among those categorised as 'non-people' or outcastes, who congregated on the slope that led to the Kiyomizu Temple in Kyoto.[5] While there is some evidence that leprosy was already stigmatised in ancient times, Yokoi Kiyoshi has argued that it was the popularisation of Buddhism in the medieval period that led this disease to acquire a special status. He notes that in *sutras* such as the Hokke-kyō and Yakushi-kyō and later in the popular Buddhist fables known as *setsuwa*, leprosy is described as the consequence of karmic retribution for misdeeds in past or present incarnations.[6] It came to be regarded as the 'unclean' [*fujō, kegarena*] disease that was the corporal manifestation of the moral depravity of the sufferer.

However, if, as Yokoi suggests, Buddhism provided the logic of discrimination towards sufferers of leprosy, it also provided an impetus for compassion and charity. Among the medieval tales are many that are of the pattern of the legend of the eighth-century empress Kōmyō. According to this legend, one day Kōmyō 'as an act of charity' offered to bathe personally one thousand people. However, the thousandth person who presented himself was a 'leper' whose body was covered with open oozing sores. The empress hesitated for a moment, but then proceeded to wash him with care. When she was finished the afflicted one emanated a bright light and revealed himself to be a *boddhisatva*.[7] The proliferation of such tales reveals that the sufferer of leprosy was an ambivalent figure in medieval culture – seemingly the physical manifestation of sin, but also potentially capable of bringing salvation to one who offered compassion.

It was this conception of leprosy that in the late thirteenth century led priests such as Eizon and Ninshō to create shelters for sufferers of the disease.[8] The communities at Nishiyama and Kitayama of which Kyozan wrote in his 1880 petition were among those sites where simple shelters were constructed by these priests and their supporters. However, the aim of these shelters was not to provide care, much less treatment, for the sufferer of leprosy.[9] They were meant to facilitate his salvation – as well, of course, as that of those who as expressions of charity participated in their establishment. Those within the shelters were exhorted to engage in acts of penitence and prayer in the hope of expiating the acts that had led to their condition.

As the early modern caste system took form, the medieval outcaste communities and the 'leper' shelters were transformed, and by the seventeenth century *monoyoshi* villages, communities of leprosy sufferers autonomous from other outcaste groups, had taken form in Kyoto, Nara, and elsewhere.[10] As in medieval times, the residents of these sites were imbued with religious significance. They supported themselves by soliciting alms house-to-house several times a year: as they moved from home to home collecting offerings of rice, goods and cash, the 'lepers' announced themselves with the call '*monoyoshi*', signifying that they were bringing fortune to those who showed them compassion.

The existence of the *monoyoshi* villages thus reveals a clear continuity with the medieval construction of leprosy, but in the early modern period new associations were also inserted into the duality I have traced out above. In the seventeenth and eighteenth centuries, leprosy became the object of medical practice within Confucian-influenced medical theory, which established a link between the behaviour of the patient and his state of health. Japanese physicians explained leprosy by reference to the patient's flawed behaviour, arguing that over-indulgence in sexual activity or other 'unnatural' acts had 'poisoned' the blood. Medical theorists were in general agreement that once such 'bad blood' had formed, it was then passed from parent to child. As this suggests, leprosy came to be generally identified as a hereditary disease. This new 'medicalised' understanding of leprosy had an impact on the early modern understanding of the 'leper' communities. For example, Katakura Kakuryō, the physician-author of *A New Text on Syphilis and Leprosy* (1786), a popular and widely read medical work, pointed approvingly to the situation in the Nara area where, he stated, everyone who had leprosy lived within a 'leper village', making it easy to avoid a dangerous marriage.[11]

'The most leprous country in the world'

In the wake of the Meiji Restoration of 1868, the political revolution that brought to power a new modernising government, the *monoyoshi* communities quickly dissolved as the early modern system of status distinctions was abandoned. The one in Kyoto disintegrated after an 1872 law forbade the organised collection of alms. But as these communities disintegrated, leprosy emerged as the object of official concern in another context. In 1873, an institution known as the Yōikuin was established in Tokyo. Its mission was to house a swelling population of abandoned children, the insane, the sick and the infirm, who from the perspective of officials were 'dirtying' the streets and lowering Japan's standing in the eyes of Western visitors. Records of the institution reveal that many leprosy sufferers were among those confined.

The concern of city officials for the visibility of the sick and diseased was the product of a new political discourse on disease and its political consequences. Soon after its establishment, the Meiji government made improving the health of its citizens a state priority, and to that end it began to support new forms of medical knowledge and practice and to establish new institutions. The public health system that began to take form in the 1870s and 1880s was organised around the principles of policing and confinement, as the primary means of dealing with the 'danger' that disease posed to the creation of a large healthy population of potential workers and soldiers, necessary for the modern and powerful nation government leaders aspired to create. Espousing this view of disease, the politician Yamane Masaji, one of the advocates of a leprosy prevention law, declared: 'There is no greater problem for the nation of Japan than the poor health of its citizenry. Whatever the occupation of an unhealthy person, he will become unproductive.'[12]

The formation of public health policy was also implicated in the pursuit of national prestige. The Japanese leadership was well aware that Europeans and Americans pointed to high incidence of certain stigmatised disease in Asia and Africa as evidence that these societies were 'primitive'. As the government slogan 'Civilisation and enlightenment' suggests, in the 1870s Japan's governmental and civic élite wanted to establish their country as part of the modern world and to distance it from 'backward' Asian societies such as India and China. However, as the number of Western residents and visitors to Japan increased in the 1880s, their gaze began to fall upon Japan's newly visible leprosy sufferers. Between 1888 and 1906, Christian missionaries established five private leprosaria in Japan, and articles on leprosy in Japan appeared in publications such as the *New York Tribune*, the *Japan Weekly Mail*, and the *Medical Standard*.[13] Diet member Saitō Yoshio raised the issue of national prestige when he submitted a proposal for a leprosy prevention law in 1902. He began his remarks with the statement that 'leprosy is a frightening infectious disease that is in fact the sign of an uncivilised country'.[14]

It was in this context that leprosy began to be transformed from a personal or familial 'problem' into one with profound political and social implications. Soon after the return of Japan's delegates to the Berlin Conference in 1897, the Home Ministry ordered a survey of the number of leprosy sufferers in Japan. Completed in 1900, it contained figures that reverberated through Japanese society. According to the survey, there were 30,359 sufferers of leprosy, 19,907 households with a lineage that contained leprosy, and 990,930 people who came from such lineages. As the use of the category of 'lineage' suggests, in spite of the new scientific evidence against hereditary transmission, the Home Ministry still made use of it in the compilation of these statistics. And it was the figure of one million that came to be deployed in the post-1900 discourse on the disease. Citing this figure, an article in the *Tokyo Daily Newspaper* stated: 'In the number of leprosy sufferers, our country is second only to India, and if one considers the ratio of that number to the general population then this is indeed the most leprous country in the world.'[15] The use of the figure of one million as an index of national humiliation became an integral part of the political discourse on leprosy, and it was used in conjunction with other statistics that suggested that leprosy was rare in Western Europe and common in Asia and Africa.

But if the image of 'one million lepers' was deployed in discussions of leprosy as an issue of national prestige, it also figured in discussions of leprosy as a problem of 'public health'. A 1902 *Yomiuri Newspaper* article opened with the headline 'One million leprosy patients'. While the text of the article went on to explain that this was the number, not of sufferers of the disease, but of those who had a relative who was infected, it was the threat posed by the latter that was emphasised: 'people from such lineages work in businesses that sell food and drink and in this way the poison of this sickness is spread'.[16] Thus, the collapse of the distinction between hereditary transmission and infection was used to emphasise the 'threat' posed by leprosy. It was the 'hidden leper' who, unmarked by disfigurement, walked among the healthy, spreading 'poison'. At the same time, exaggerated claims were made about the infectiousness of the disease. In 1898, Murata Nobuyuki, head of the Institute of Infectious Disease, wrote that the danger posed by leprosy was greater than that of the eight infectious diseases (among them, cholera, typhoid and plague) designed by the Infectious Disease Prevention Law of 1879.[17]

Exclusion as 'tradition'

As the exaggerated claims about leprosy's infectiousness and the extent of its transmission were instantiated as 'fact', calls for the isolation of leprosy sufferers emanated from the medical establishment, the Diet and the press. But conversely, the figure of one million became an argument against, as well as for, isolation. As officials in the Bureau of Hygiene pointed out, the confinement of tens of thousands of people for the extent of their lives, however medically justified, was simply economically untenable.[18] It was in relation to the debate over confinement that the exclusion of 'lepers' in the premodern period came to be evoked – not as the manifestation of a flawed understanding of the disease or as a reprehensible aspect of 'feudal' society, but as a mode of social organisation worthy of emulation. In 1901, Mitsuda Kensuke (1876–1964), whose name was to become synonymous with the policy of forced confinement of leprosy sufferers, took up these communities in an article entitled 'On the need to establish isolation centres for leprosy'. He was then a young physician employed by the Tokyo Yōikuin, where in 1899 he had overseen the creation of an isolation ward for leprosy patients in order to separate them from other internees. Mitsuda's article centred on an image we have already noted, that of the 'hidden leper' who moved freely through society spreading infection:

> But before I discuss the danger posed by the wandering lepers spreading their poison through society, I must describe something more frightening, that is, the one who is not a beggar, but works on a ship, or preparing food and drink,

or something else, and there is the barber whose parents are lepers and the woman whose husband is a leper who works serving food and drink.[19]

In contrast to this situation, Mitsuda asserted that in Germany, India, Russia and South America, confinement laws were in place. But isolation, according to Mitsuda, was not a custom foreign to Japan. Rather,

> in our country too, before the Restoration, as a principle of social order those of leprosy lineages were excluded by the public, and so they naturally came together to form villages and in this way the spread of the disease was forestalled, but after the Restoration, as all the old ways were destroyed, the leper villages too came to be forgotten.[20]

The attempt to recoup the premodern 'leper' communities as a precedent for confinement was not Mitsuda's alone. In 1902, the *Kyoto Newspaper of Medicine and Public Health*, then an important journal of medicine and public health, published a series of articles on premodern 'institutions' for the sufferers of leprosy. Writing on the history of the Jūhachikenko, a 'leper' shelter established in Nara in the thirteenth century, Sawa Riichiro framed his discussion around the assertion that its 'one million lepers' made Japan 'the most leprous country in the world'.[21] He stated that his aim in examining the history of the shelter, which he described as 'something to be proud of before the rest of the world', was 'to arouse the determination of the Japanese people to create new leprosy hospitals'.[22] A few months later, the journal began to serialise a long article on leprosy shelters in Kyoto. Like Mitsuda and Sawa, its author, Takahashi Seii, lamented the fact that the premodern tradition of exclusion had been forgotten. On the Kyoto *monoyoshi* village, he wrote:

> after the Restoration, the temple was abandoned and not only its priests, but also the many lepers scattered in the four directions ... Later this area was incorporated into the pleasure district [*kagai*] and now brothels line its streets. This foul and polluted place has changed so that not only can one not tell that it stood here, but even those who know its name are few.[23]

As this suggests, like Mitsuda, Takahashi argued that the Restoration had contributed to the indiscriminate spread of the 'foul and polluted' disease throughout Japanese society.

Needless to say, the outcaste communities and leprosy shelters of the medieval period and the *monoyoshi* villages of the early modern period bore scant resemblance to the 'isolation centres' and 'hospitals' that these authors were advocating. The borders of the former had been permeable, while in the latter every aspect of daily life would come to be regulated by the officials who administered them as state employees. What the authors such as Mitsuda, Sawa and Takahashi attempted to conceal was their advocacy of a new regime of exclusion, albeit authorised by appeals to 'tradition'. Hidden beneath the rhetoric of public health and social welfare was the image of the leprosy sufferer as unclean and immoral, but now thoroughly stripped of any spiritual connotations – and this in turn rendered his exclusion from society right, proper and just. Ultimately, the 1907 Leprosy Prevention Law was premised upon the maintenance of this set of associations. It provided for the confinement of only the most vulnerable population, the so-called 'wandering lepers', but the system of notification and disinfection prescribed for those with families, jobs and social ties was designed to 'reveal' their 'shame' and to thereby facilitate exclusion on the level of daily life for those who remained outside of the leprosaria. The creation of this institutional genealogy was also a response to the Western discourse that made leprosy the sign of a 'primitive' or 'uncivilised' society. By discovering indigenous forms of exclusion and linking them to the 'modern' institution of the leprosarium, Japanese officials recouped premodern practices of exclusion as prescentially 'modern'.

Deconstructing the 'leper village'

The ideological nature of the attempt to link 'leper villages' to the leprosaria in a narrative of progress is clearly revealed by examining the fate of those communities that survived into modernity, as well as the nature of the institutions that supplanted them. As for Nishiyama Kyozan and the others of Kōmyōin, their community had been all but dissolved by the time the 1907 law was promulgated. Kyozan seems to have died sometime around 1898, by which time the residents of Kōmyōin numbered only seven or eight. The others had either died or became part of the population of 'wandering lepers' that so concerned Japanese officials.

In the modern period, the 'leper village' that attracted the most attention was located at the hot-spring town known as Kusatsu in Gumma prefecture. Unlike Kōmyōin, with its medieval roots, the Kusatsu community had taken form in the late nineteenth century. Japanese physicians had long advocated bathing in hot springs as a treatment for leprosy, as well as other skin ailments, and the springs at Kusatsu had gained a reputation for effectiveness in relieving the symptoms of this disease. It appears that in the early modern period, most leprosy sufferers in Kusatsu were transient visitors who came in search of some relief. While they bathed alongside the healthy, they seem to have resided in special inns known locally as 'leper hostels'.[24] In 1871, however, a disastrous fire struck Kusatsu, burning down much of the town. In its aftermath, town leaders began a publicity campaign designed to attract visitors in order to finance rebuilding. The pamphlet they published and circulated made much of the efficacy of the waters of Kusatsu for leprosy, with the result that leprosy sufferers, now with a new freedom to travel, began to gather there. Less than twenty years later, in 1887, town leaders had clearly begun to question the wisdom of their marketing strategy. It seems that other visitors to the town were no longer willing to bathe with the sick, some of whom had become permanent residents of Kusatsu. The decision was made to move the leprosy sufferers outside the town itself and to establish a new 'village', known as Yu no Zawa, specifically for them.[25]

In 1902, Mitsuda Kensuke, who had written eloquently on the value of the premodern 'leper villages' for forestalling the spread of disease, visited Yu no Zawa.

What he found there horrified him, as a report he later published made clear.[26] According to Mitsuda, Yu no Zawa had a population of 126 people, which included thirty-two married couples. Five children had been born there in the preceding year. The residents worked at a variety of professions: some operated rooming houses, others were peddlers or day labourers, but their numbers also included a barber, an acupuncturist, a pharmacist, a doctor and a variety of artisans.

It was not such evidence of the normalcy of this functioning community that drew Mitsuda's attention. Instead, he asserted that among the residents of Yu no Zawa,

> there are those who have lost every moral and religious concept and are addicted to food and drink, engage in gambling, and cause trouble for officials. And most of those who call themselves husband and wife started out as illicit unions, and I have heard that the evil practice of abortion is not uncommon.[27]

While Mitsuda never explicitly charged that such behaviour 'caused' their affliction, his concern for behaviour clearly evoked the well-established links between the disease and immorality. Moreover, Mitsuda was appalled at the social ties that existed between the residents of Yu no Zawa and those of Kusatsu: people moved freely between the two communities, and the children of 'lepers' attended the same school as their healthy neighbours. Mitsuda argued that if Yu no Zawa were to continue to exist, policies designed to completely separate the two communities would be necessary.

Three years after the promulgation of the Leprosy Prevention Law, Mitsuda visited Kusatsu for a second time and once again published a report on his findings. To his dismay, the establishment of the new leprosaria notwithstanding, the number of leprosy sufferers at Yu no Zawa had more than doubled. And with their increased numbers had come a new attitude of belligerency, or so Mitsuda argued. He quoted one 'leper' of Yu no Zawa as stating,

> our Yu no Zawa is flourishing more and more, and soon there will be leprosy sufferers living in the town of Kusatsu itself. Then other visitors will gradually decrease, and Kusatsu as a whole will not be disturbed by the government.

Mitsuda, a government official who had argued passionately for state intervention to control leprosy, reported that upon hearing this boast, 'he could not help but become angry'.[28] His solution was to advocate that the national government intervene to move the Yu no Zawa community away from Kusatsu to a more isolated location.

Whether Mitsuda played a role in what followed is unclear, but in that same year the town leaders of Kusatsu petitioned the prefectural government for aid in relocating the Yu no Zawa community to a new site, arguing that this was necessary to stop the 'spread of the poison of disease', safeguard the health of other visitors to the springs, and preserve the town's prosperity.[29] The response of the residents of Yu no Zawa was to submit their own letter of protest directly to the Home Minister in Tokyo.[30] In it, they charged that although the town leaders were using 'leprosy prevention' to explain their desire to remove the Yu no Zawa residents to a more distant site, the current location was adequate to prevent the spread of infection. In fact, it was a 'selfish desire for profit' that was motivating town officials, who feared that potential visitors would avoid the town because of their 'dislike' of the 'lepers'. The petition concluded by calling on the Minister to intercede on behalf of Yu no Zawa's residents to stop their forced removal. Within weeks, a response came via country authorities to the town leaders, who were told that local opposition made approval impossible. In the aftermath of this defeat, the town formulated its own solution. In 1916, a wall was constructed to physically separate the two communities and to stop the movement of people between them.

Creating leprosaria

Even in the face of such restrictions, the population of Yu no Zawa continued to grow, reaching 800 in 1930. The growth of the community suggests not only that the stigmatisation of the disease was making life increasingly difficult for sufferers, but also that they desired an alternative to confinement in the new leprosaria. Erving Goffman has argued that the rendering of prisons, asylums and sanitaria into 'total institutions' required the dismantling of the inmate's identity, something accomplished not only by the stripping of property, privacy and dignity but also by creating a system of privileges which awarded compliance to the institutions' rules. The result of this process was that the inmate was 'colonised' or 'converted' into accepting that existence within the institution was in some ways better than life 'outside'.[31] A revealing picture of how the 'dismantling' process was accomplished in Japan's new leprosaria appears in the memoirs of Mitsuda Kensuke, who became the chief physician of Zenshōen, the largest of the early public leprosaria in 1909. Written in 1950, as criticism of leprosy policy that had begun to emerge, Mitsuda's aim was clearly to refute charges of inhumane treatment. He scathingly rejected the suggestion that patients were 'victims' and portrayed them instead as a difficult and dangerous population.[32]

Until 1914, Mitsuda as chief physician was under the authority of one Ikeuchi Saijiro, a member of the provincial police force. As this suggests, it was the prison rather than the hospital that provided the model for the modern leprosarium. Patients generally arrived in police custody, because the police were given authority over the enforcement of public health laws. Upon arrival, their clothing and other personal belongings were confiscated, a policy justified by reference to the germs these articles potentially carried. Adults and children, men and women were all issued institutional garb that took the form of *kimono* of a uniform design, making those who attempted to flee the facility easily recognisable outside its walls, but also effacing the markers of gender and age that clothing typically displays. Eventually, Zenshōen and the other leprosaria instituted the policy of confiscating, as well, all cash belonging to incoming patients. In exchange, they received institutional scrip that could be used only in the leprosarium's canteen. For patients who failed to follow the institution's rules, a system of punishments was created, again closely modelled on prison practices. These included restrictions on food and drink, censorship of letters, and solitary confinement. Patient rooms were also modelled on prisons of the period: eight patients were housed in twelve-mat *tatami* rooms (each mat measuring approximately 6 by 3 feet).[33]

Within Mitsuda's account of his years at Zenshōen, no single issue concerned him more than the sexual conduct of its residents. Male and female patients were housed separately, but the policy of segregation by gender proved difficult to maintain, a problem Mitsuda attributed to the lack of 'moral self-knowledge' (*dōtoku jikaku*) on the part of the patients. As he explained, 'for such hopeless people, it was perhaps naturally that they thought of nothing but the ephemeral pleasures of each single day of life. Within the leprosarium the pleasures they sought were gambling and fornication'.[34] According to Mitsuda, he put into place a number of measures designed to maintain the policy of segregation and prevent sexual contact, but all proved unsuccessful. Ten-foot-high walls were constructed, only to be quickly vandalised. Night-time patrols by the staff members were carried out, but each one revealed fleeing visitors of the opposite sex. Of particular concern to Mitsuda was the fate of young unmarried girls in this environment in which, he charged, seduction was common and rape not unknown. He converted a building near the staff quarters into housing for these residents and gave them the task of raising ducks, with the intention that the birds would quack and awaken the staff in the case of amorous male intruders. But this plan backfired when, explained Mitsuda, 'the mating of the duck stimulated the girls and had the effect of making them become more [sexually] active'.[35]

Mitsuda's depiction of the 'leper' as subject to pronounced and unnatural sexual desires referenced the longstanding associations of the disease with immorality, but his concern was a specifically modern one: the sexual activities of the residents were threatening the order of the institution itself, and their resistance to the institution's regulations called into question its authority. Moreover, he regarded with palpable alarm the fact that sexual acts between patients were leading to the birth of children within the leprosarium walls, thus increasing the diseased population that the institution was established to control. Mitsuda's solution was to begin a campaign to encourage sterilisation in 1915. Male patients who agreed to receive a vasectomy got not only the right to 'marry', but also a week of rest that included meals of eggs, chicken and even red wine. Mitsuda noted with clear satisfaction that it 'became the normal practice for young men to receive this operation'.[36]

Towards a 'leper' identity

In their work on leprosy communities in the Philippines and Indonesia, Warwick Anderson and Rita Smith Kipp have emphasised the way in which administrators tried to create 'new social worlds' for those confined to these sites of exclusion. According to Kipp, at Lau Si Momo in Sumatra, aspects of village life were incorporated into leprosaria so that they could be presented to residents as 'like a real village – only cleaner'.[37] In contrast, in Culion, under the direction of the American staff, it was small-town America that provided the model, with the result that the island came to have an elected town council, Boy Scout troops and a volunteer brass band.[38] For those in Japan's leprosaria, the introduction of aspects of 'normal' social life came slowly and in a piecemeal fashion. Even the 'marriage' that was the reward for accepting sterilisation had little in common with how that relationship was defined outside the leprosarium. It meant nothing more than permission to have conjugal visits in the overcrowded dormitory room where one's 'spouse' resided, free of the harassment of the staff. Gradually, however, the administrators of Japan's leprosaria began to organise celebrations for traditional holidays, to establish shrines and temples, and to sponsor the formation of poetry clubs and amateur theatre groups.

But the process of 'colonising' the patients included not only measures such as these but also the final destruction of 'leper villages' such as Yu no Zawa, which had continued to provide a vision of an alternative form of exclusion. As even Mitsuda noted, at Zenshōen, patients evoked the dream of Yu no Zawa routinely as they went about their assigned tasks, chanting, 'Kusatsu is a good place, I want to go there sometime'.[39] In response, in the 1930s the government began the process of dismantling Yu no Zawa and other such communities. In 1931, with the passage of the lifetime exclusion law, all the existing public leprosaria came directly under the control of the national government, and plans were made to construct several more, with the new goal of confining all of Japan's 'lepers'. One site chosen for the construction of a new leprosarium was Yu no Zawa itself. This institution, called Kiriu Rakusen'en, was completed in 1931, thereby effectively bringing Yu no Zawa under state control and rendering the dream of 'going to Kusatsu' meaningless.[40]

After 1931, as all of Japan's leprosy sufferers were gradually forced into leprosaria, these institutions gave rise to a new 'leper identity' that affirmed, even valorised, the culture of exclusion. The most explicit expression of this identity were the poems, short stories and essays that came to be categorised as 'leprosy literature' [*rai bungaku*], a term that reflects not only their authorship but also their content. 'Leprosy literature' explored the meaning of 'being a leper' in a society in which that disease was labelled a national shame and a political problem and viewed as evidence of immorality, even perversion. The inaugural and best-known work of this genre was 'The first night of life', which was originally published in the prestigious literary magazine *Bungakkai* (World of Literature) in 1936. Its author, Hōjō Tamio (1914–37), was then a patient of the Zenshōen, which he had entered at the age of 20. Soon after entering the leprosarium, Hōjō began a correspondence with the novelist Kawabata Yasunari, an influential author and one of the founders of *Bungakkai*. At the urging of Kawabata, *Bungakkai* published a series of Hōjō's short stories, all of which dealt with life as a 'leper'.

Narrated in the first person, 'The first night of life' describes the arrival at a leprosarium of a young man named Oda Tamao. It relates his anxiety as he journeys towards the institution, his fear that everyone he meets knows his 'secret', his struggle with thoughts of suicide, and his humiliation when, after his arrival late at night, he is stripped of his belongings and forced to bathe before several young nurses, who are elaborately masked and gowned. Eventually, Oda is turned over to another young man, Saeki, a long-term resident of the leprosarium and the patient 'on duty' that night. While the two converse quietly amid their sleeping fellow-patients, Oda gazes with horror at the disfigurement and disability around him. As he is overcome with despair, Saeki tells him,

> At the moment when someone catches leprosy, then his 'humanness' is destroyed. He dies. It is not just that he has ceased to be a 'human being' in the social sense. It is clearly not just that kind of superficial death ... But when you succeed in completely living as a leper, then you can be reborn again as a human being. That can be the beginning of your new life as a human being. Mr Oda, now you are dead. And because you are dead, you are not a human being. Where does your pain and hopelessness come from? Think about it, please. Isn't it because even though you are dead you are still aspiring for your former life?[41]

By the end of the story, Oda has embraced the ethos of resignation that Saeki advocates. He has decided to give himself over 'to being a leper' within the walls of the institution.

The theme of 'The first night of life' became the theme of 'leprosy literature' as a whole. Acceptance of the disease and the stigma it brought assumed a new kind of moral authority in the 1930s, 1940s and beyond. What 'leprosy literature' left unquestioned and therefore unchallenged was the ethicality of the policy of exclusion itself. Rather than contesting exclusion, 'leprosy literature' put forth the notion that life within the leprosarium had its own value and meaning. Hōjō's protagonist Oda bears little in common with Nishiyama Kyozan, who in the 1880s had so persistently petitioned local authorities as the representative of Kōmyōin, or with the residents of Yu no Zawa, who in 1910 had called upon the Home Ministry to intervene on their behalf. Ultimately, Japan's modern leprosaria succeeded in producing subjects who embraced their own exclusion.

Conclusion

In this paper, I have explored the complex set of relations, geographical, historical, ideological and imaginary, that have linked the spaces of the 'leper village' and the 'leprosarium' in order to explore the rise of Japan's leprosarium system, so remarkable in its longevity. As we have seen, leprosy had been the object of stigma since medieval times, but the forms of exclusion that emerged in the premodern period did not require isolation or confinement. In the late nineteenth century, however, a new culture of exclusion took form, which transformed leprosy from an individual or familial problem into a disease with profound social and political implications. Civic leaders and political élites alike came to view leprosy as a national shame that marked Japan as an uncivilised country and threatened the goals of economic strength and military power. As they worked to implement a policy of leprosy prevention, the 'leper villages' of the past were held up as 'proof' of Japan's prescient modernity, an indigenous tradition that paralleled the practices of the modern West. However, once the leprosy policy had been promulgated, the 'leper villages' assumed a different meaning for the proponents of exclusion: they were insufficient forms of isolation, the existence of which threatened the healthy population. In contrast, for leprosy sufferers themselves, sites such as Yu no Zawa, offered up the hope of a 'normal' life within the culture of exclusion, a life in which work, family and community might be possible. In the 1930s, the tension between these two spaces was finally resolved, with the dismantling one by one of Japan's 'leper villages' and the transformation of the leprosaria into total institutions, which made those within define themselves as 'lepers', in terms unthinkable until modernity.

Notes

1   F. Ōtani, *Raiyobōhō no rekishi* , Kyoto, Keisō Shobō, 1998, pp. 18–19.
2   Z. Gussow and G.S. Tracy, 'Stigma and the leprosy phenomenon: the social history of the disease in the nineteenth and twentieth centuries', *Bulletin of the History of Medicine*, 1970, vol. 44, no. 5, pp. 425–49.
3   M. Vaughan, *Curing Their Ills: Colonial Power and African Illness*, Cambridge, Polity Press, 1991, pp. 77–99. A. Bashford and M. Nugent, 'Leprosy and the management of race, sexuality, and nation in tropical Australia', in A. Bashford and C. Hooker (eds) *Contagion: Historical and Cultural Studies*, London, Routledge, 2001, pp. 106–28. Warwick Anderson, 'Leprosy and citizenship', *Positions*, 1998, vol. 6, no. 3, pp 707–30.
4   R. Miyagawa, 'Kyūrai shiseki Nishiyama Kōmyōin ni tsuite', in *Hida ni umarete*, Tokyo, Shinkyō Shuppan, 1977, pp. 179–80.
5   H. Kuroda, *Kyōkai no chūsei, shōchō no chūsei*, Tokyo, Tōkyō Daigaku Shuppankai, 1986, pp. 241–4.
6   K. Yokoi, *Chūsei minshū no seikatsu bunka*, Tokyo, Tokyo Daigaku Shuppankai, 1975, pp. 307.
7   S. Kobayashi, 'Kodai chūsei no "raisha" to shūkyō', in Y. Fujino (ed.) *Rekishi no naka no raisha*, Tokyo, Yumiru Shuppan, 1996, pp. 32–6.
8   T. Shinmura, *Nihon iryō shakaishi no kenkyū*, Tokyo, Hōsei Daigaku Shuppan, 1985, pp. 206–11.
9   Y. Fujiwara, 'Chūsei zenki no byōsha to kyūsai', *Rettō no bunkashi*, 1986, no. 3, pp. 79–114.
10 N. Yokota, 'Monoyoshi kō–Kinsei Kyōto no raisha ni tsuite', *Nihon shi kenkyū*, 1991, no. 352, pp. 1–29.
11 Held by the Fujikawa Yū Bunkō, Kyoto University Library.
12 *Dai Nihon shiritsu eiseikai zasshi*, no. 141 (12 June 1903), pp. 37–49.
13 S. Yamamoto, *Nihon rai shi*, Tokyo, Tōkyō Daigaku Shuppankai, pp. 25–34, 50–1.
14 *Dai Nihon shiritsu eiseikai zasshi*, no. 126 (25 March 1903), pp. 34–42.
15 Quoted in Y. Fujino, *Nihon fashizumu to iryō* , Tokyo, Iwanami Shoten, 1993, p. 12.
16 Y. Nakayama (ed.), *Shinbun shūsei: Meiji hennenshi*, vol. 11, Tokyo, Honpō Shoseki, p. 414.
17 Yamamoto, *Nihon rai shi*, p. 46.
18 Yamamoto, *Nihon rai shi*, pp. 39–83.
19 K. Mitsuda, 'Raibyō kakurijo setsuritsu no hitsuyō ni tsuite', in *Mitsuda Kensuke to Nihon no rai yobō jigyō*, Tokyo, Tōfū Kyōkai, p. 6.
20 Mitsuda, 'Raibyō kakurijo setsuritsu no hitsuyō ni tsuite', p. 7.
21 R. Sawa, 'Nihon saisho no raibyōin ni tsuite', *Kyōto iji eisei shimbun*, 1902, no. 101, p. 3.
22 Sawa, 'Nihon saisho no raibyōin ni tsuite', *Kyōto iji eisei shimbun*, p. 18.
23 S. Takahashi, ' Kyōto no raibyōin ni tsuite', *Kyōto iji eisei shi*, 1902, no. 101, p. 6.

24 N. Suzuki, 'Kinsei raibyōkan no keisei to tenkai', in Y. Fujino (ed.) *Rekishi no naka no raisha*, Tokyo, Yumiru Shuppan, 1996, p. 133.

25 On these events, see Kuriu Rakusen'en Kanjya Jijikai (ed.) *Fūsetsu no mon: Kuriu Rakusen'en kanjya gojūnenshi*, Gumma, Kuriu Rakusen'en Kanjya Jijikai, 1982, pp. 14–15; and K. Furumi, 'Yu no Zawa buraku rokūjunen shikō' in S. Sakai (ed.) *Kindai shomin seikatsushi*, vol. 20, Tokyo, San'ichi Shobō, 1995, pp. 426–7.

26 K. Mitsuda, 'Jōshū Kusatu oyobi Kaishū Minobi no okeru raikanjya no genkyō' (1903), in *Mitsuda Kensuke to Nihon no rai yobō jigyō*, pp. 10–11.

27 Mitsuda, 'Jōshū Kusatu oyobi Kaishū Minobi no okeru raikanjya no genkyō', pp. 12–3.

28 Mitsuda, 'Meiji yonjūninen igo ni ha Kusatsu ni okeru raikanjya wa ikan ni shochi serarubeki ya' (1910), in *Mitsuda Kensuke to Nihon no rai yobō jigyō*, p. 33.

29 Kuriu Rakusen'en Kanjya Jijikai (ed.) *Fūsetsu no mon*, pp. 30–6.

30 Kuriu Rakusen'en Kanjya Jijikai (ed.) *Fūsetsu no mon*, p. 33.

31 E. Goffman, *Asylums*, New York, Doubleday, 1961, pp. 62–3.

32 K. Mitsuda, *Kaishun byōshitsu: Kyūrai gojūnen no kiroku*, Tokyo, Asahi Shimbunsha, 1950, p. 41.

33 Mitsuda, *Kaishun byōshitsu: Kyūrai gojūnen no kiroku*, p. 41.

34 Mitsuda, *Kaishun byōshitsu: Kyūrai gojūnen no kiroku*, p. 46.

35 Mitsuda, *Kaishun byōshitsu: Kyūrai gojūnen no kiroku*, p. 48.

36 Mitsuda, *Kaishun byōshitsu: Kyūrai gojūnen no kiroku*, p. 55.

37 Rita Smith Kipp, 'The evangelical uses of leprosy', *Social Science Medicine*, 1995, vol. 39, no. 2, p. 168.

38 Anderson, pp. 70–1.

39 Mitsuda, *Kaishun byōshitsu*, p. 178.

40 Kuriu Rakusen'en Kanjya Jijikai (ed.) *Fūsetsu no mon*, pp. 87–108.

41 Itō Sei, Kamei Kotsuichirō, Nakamura Michio, Hirano Ken and Yamamoto Kenkichi (eds) *Makino Shin'ichi, Kamura Isota, Hōjō Tamio Shū*, Tokyo, Kōdansha, 1967, p. 329.

8 'Houses of deposit' and the exclusion of women in turn-of-the-century Argentina

Kristin Ruggiero

Among the widening range of places of isolation in the late nineteenth and early twentieth centuries was a generic category of 'houses of deposit', used throughout Latin America and southern Europe. These institutions, which isolated delinquent and non-delinquent women alike from society, had a long tradition going back at least to the seventeenth century.[1] In their colonial guises in Latin America, historians have likened them to jails and to shelters for battered women. By the national period in the nineteenth century, houses of deposit had become primarily institutions of female incarceration, in which particularly contradictory rationales unique to the history of state formation and modernism operated.

Argentina presents a rich case study of state, church and individual complicity in the development of institutions of isolation. After protracted political and military struggle over the centralisation of federal government in Argentina, Buenos Aires finally became the capital in 1880. Political control was in the hands of liberal democratic elites who promoted European models of constitutional rights and guarantees, centralism, urbanism and modernism. An important addition to this array was the promotion of massive immigration, especially from southern Europe, to the point where Buenos Aires' population was often half foreign-born. The swell of population from foreign immigration as well as from rural migration necessitated a thorough overhauling of the city's transportation, sanitation, social services, and legal and policing apparatus. A colonial institution that lingered in this now bustling world capital was the house of deposit. While these houses served as schools and asylums for girls, places of worship for the neighbourhood, and refuges for widows and other women in need of 'family', they also isolated and excluded women and girls from society at the request of husbands and fathers, police and judges, employers, the state agency for minors, and charitable groups.

This chapter focuses principally on wives and daughters who were placed in isolation as a result of their defiance of patriarchal norms, and examines the conditions women faced and resisted in the Women's Hospital and the Good Shepherd House of Correction.[2] These institutions shared the ethic of several institutions: a religious and/or work regimen managed by nuns; a relationship with a civil charitable organisation, the Beneficent Society, and the police and courts; and an extra-legal approach to and control of their inmates. The institutions differed in their mission, however, in that the purpose of the Good Shepherd was to moralise and regenerate, while the purpose of the Women's Hospital was medical care without an overt moralising goal. The institutions also differed in the age of their inmates in that the Good Shepherd was the institution most commonly used by the Defence of Minors for placement of minors.

The uniqueness of houses of deposit arose first from the fact that in an age of increasing secularism, they depended on an anachronistic combination of civil, judicial and penal authorities, federal subsidies and Catholic religious orders. Second, while political and professional élites were trying to centralise judicial and penal authority in the state, they were also giving to men, as fathers and husbands, a substantial degree of punitive and judicial control through the system of depositing women against their will. Third, while the models of government being developed in Argentina held individual rights and personal liberties to be sacred and modern, houses of deposit denied their inmates these same rights and liberties. Instead, the law and tradition gave the state and individual men wide latitude to manipulate access to these rights. Finally, while feminists such as the French woman Luisa Michel were invited to speak publicly in Buenos Aires, and challenges to the inequities of the adultery law were openly being made by legal professionals, women were regularly consigned to houses of deposit for disobedience to fathers, for 'scorning' and 'dishonouring' of husbands, for 'irascibility', and for initiating legal cases of adultery and divorce. Nonetheless, the system of depositing was accepted by many Argentines as appropriate for, and legal within, a liberal democracy.

This legality and sense of appropriateness rested on deeply gendered understandings of the patriarchal family, and of women as walking vessels of potential immorality: thus women were rendered more legitimately confineable than men. There was no parallel institution for men, nor any parallel power of deposit. Nevertheless, court testimony shows that women strongly resisted depositing, and that they had the support of the occasional official or professional who broke the chain of male/state/church coercive power. As more cases of adultery and divorce began to be heard over the turn of the century, women's resistance appears more frequently in the court records, making cases of adultery and divorce more contentious as husbands fought to keep their marital authority intact and as wives fought to decrease it.

Gender and the system of deposit

Depositing figured in Argentine law as an essential part of fathers' and husbands' rights to exercise the authority and responsibility of *patria potestad* and *marital potestad*. Fathers could legally avail themselves of houses of deposit, according to the civil code of 1869, to protect the honour of their daughters when fathers were out of town, or to repair their honour when a daughter had 'stained' it by becoming pregnant, by selecting an inappropriate suitor or by disrupting family harmony. Although the maximum amount of time of reclusion was fixed at one month by the code, the majority of women in the court cases read by this researcher spent at least several months incarcerated.

Spousal cases, however, afford the best opportunity to study the full picture of the contentious character of depositing and the complexities of the system in which men worked closely with civil and church authorities. According to civil law, once the action of divorce had been introduced, or even before this in urgent cases, the civil judge could decree the separation of the spouses and the deposit of the wife in an 'honest house'. It was important to do this because spouses living separately during the judgment of divorce were charged with being mutually faithful, or else could be accused of the criminal offence of adultery. In the case of the action of divorce, civil and ecclesiastical judges often worked together to construct the case. The ecclesiastical judge was usually involved in the beginning stages of separation cases, if the spouses were Catholic, and was charged with researching the case. The secular judge's role included the assigning of the place of deposit, fixing the amount of the wife's support, and making provisions for the care and education of the children while the wife was in isolation.

Several grey areas existed where conflict could occur. For example, by law only a secular judge could solicit police force to put a woman in deposit. However, it was not uncommon in practice for ecclesiastical judges to solicit police force on their own, and for the police to comply with the Curia's wishes. Also, the intervention of the ecclesiastical judge was supposedly justified only in cases of divorce, and his authority was technically limited to the gathering of information about the requested divorce. Ecclesiastical judges intervened in all kinds of cases that did not involve divorce and went beyond their prescribed roles. Normally, secular judges upheld the decisions of the ecclesiastical judges, but in some cases there were disputes over jurisdiction. There were a few radical thinkers, including the judge who handed down a sentence in 1885 that *neither* the husband nor the ecclesiastical authority had the right to deprive a woman of her freedom and that deposit had to be at the wife's request, in accordance with her own will, and in a respectable house rather than a house of correction.[3] This judge's opinion was, however, unusual.

Although legally a husband could not choose his wife's place of deposit, nor deposit her against her will, the criminal cases indicate that in practice this occurred.[4] For men, though they might regret the estrangement from their wives, invoking the law meant the opportunity to assert their marital authority and perhaps improve their wives' behaviour. This dynamic was even more marked when the depository was a public institution. A 'deposited' wife was a husband's investment in his honour, much as money invested in a bank earned interest.[5] Knowledge of the location of houses of deposit, their monthly cost and so on, circulated widely among men. Witnesses' testimony frequently included references to men giving advice to each other to end a wife's unruliness by 'putting her in one of those houses that take away her liberty'.[6] Domestic scandals could be circumscribed this way and men's honour restored, which was also beneficial to the political élites' felt need for harmonious family life.

Men also explained to judges that their desire to deposit their wives was motivated by not wanting to harm them in a fit of passionate rage. This dovetailed with the state's desire to curb private vengeance but yet retain an outlet for private justice. While acts of private justice by husbands against wives, such as hair cutting, did not endanger lives, they could serve as a prelude to more serious acts such as uxoricide.[7] As such, depositing was presented by some as an advance for women because it gave them the option of leaving the conjugal home if their husbands were abusive, or if they had been accused of adultery and did not want to live with their accuser, and of being able to pursue their own legal cases. Under Spanish colonial law, the courts had only been able to excuse a wife from the obligation of living with her husband if her life was in danger. A far better way to protect women and ensure that they were free to pursue their legal cases, however, was to place them in private homes with relatives or friends. If a husband chose not to do this, it was usually because he preferred a public institution where, as some of the men in the court cases maintained, they could be sure of the level of morality. In tune with this era's abhorrence of violence to women by the public authority, the house of deposit was portrayed as preferable to jail, since the inmates tended to willingly obey the staff out of respect for the nuns, without the need for the unseemly use of force.[8] Often there was no resolution in these cases, but husbands achieved their principal objective of restoring their honour and asserting their authority by using the system of deposit.

In some ways, depositing in houses for women was similar to preventive detention in jails for men, while allegations were being investigated and cases heard. The depositing of women, however, went far beyond preventive detention for men. When a woman initiated a divorce case based on adultery, her husband was not infrequently placed in preventive detention. When she initiated a case and was counter-sued by her husband, however, she was the one who was put in detention. Husbands who were sued for adultery and divorce were usually quickly forgiven by their wives, released after paying bail, or absolved by the courts. Thus, husbands did not spend as long in preventive detention as wives did in internment. The most striking difference, however, was the moral chastisement associated with deposit for women and the fact that women could be incarcerated for long periods at the request of their husbands for seemingly personality and character issues. In fact, the most important Spanish legal dictionary from the 1870s, which was one of the principal sources cited in Argentine trial records, defined 'house of correction' as a 'public establishment where a woman of bad conduct is put for a time, and her children who have been perverted are put here too to correct them'.[9] There was an added layer of shame in forced consignment to a house of correction before being convicted. Even if she were acquitted and released, a woman who had been sent to a house of deposit would often become morally and socially isolated from family and friends. In addition, once she was enclosed in a house, a woman's stay commonly stretched out for several months or even a year, based on the theory that the more time in isolation the better the chance for reform. Moreover, when a court declared a woman's freedom, it could be some time before her lawyer could obtain her release.

Ironically, the system of depositing wives against their will was upheld in a period when Argentine statesmen produced numerous political treatises lauding the ideals of democracy, and under a constitution that affirmed personal and civil rights. It was norms of gender and authority within the patriarchal family and state that reconciled this paradox for many. But for others the contradiction was the object of protest. According to the Constitution, all civil legislation that contradicted the rights proclaimed by the independence revolution should be abrogated. Yet regressive social and gender relations were captured in the Republic's first civil code of 1869. The incongruity between the regressive legislation contained in the 1869 civil code and democratic ideals did not go unnoticed. Statesman Juan Bautista Alberdi, for example, argued that the mere declaration of rights and guarantees was not enough: they had to be converted into rules of practical living. A progressive constitution and an outdated system of civil legislation could not co-exist. Argentina could not expect to have state or personal democracy as long as it had outmoded civil laws that allowed the presence of 'autocracy in the family' and 'absolutism in the male'. Argentine socialist Mario Bravo, also critical of the civil code, charged that it contained profound inequalities between men and women and was as restrictive as a 'Chinese shoe' for married women, who with marriage were reduced to the status of incapable persons, such as minors, the mentally ill and the deaf and mute.[10]

There was an extreme disjuncture between these views of what was required for democracy and the conviction that domestic democracy was impossible because of the basic and scientific inequality of men and women. Luis María Drago, for example, maintained in his thesis of 1882 that women's subordination to men was an actual fact and not a legal fiction, as feminists of the period were trying to assert. Science had shown that special organs had created special functions in nature, and the same organ was not equal in men and women. Each had biologically based roles that were natural and should not be transgressed. Since men and women were unequal, Drago argued, they could not possibly have the same rights, because 'their organic formation had destined them for different goals'.[11] Thus it was part of natural law that husbands could deposit their wives in places of incarceration.

In some cases, the 'natural law' of patriarchal authority came up against not only democratic critique, but also feminist-influenced critique. For example, Graciana brought a complaint to the ecclesiastical judge in 1882 accusing her husband, Juan, of entering a prostitute's house. He had reportedly been seen by witnesses, one of whom was his own son, and had stolen money from Graciana in order to set up credit for his concubine at a local store. Wounded and angered by these accusations, Juan increased the severity of the case and went before the criminal court, charging calumny and serious injuries. His wife's statements were false and malicious, he said; she had damaged his dignity and honour; and she had physically attacked him. Because Juan's son was introduced as a witness against his father, Juan claimed that his wife had 'incited [his] own blood against [him] and wrenched from [him] the affection of [his] children and the respect that [he] deserve[d] from them'. Juan's tone of indignation throughout this testimony was motivated by two things: first, his wife's physical ferocity, and second, her strident and offensive feminism which, he argued, was to blame for the physical nature of her attacks. At lunch one day, with everyone, Juan emphasised, at the table, Graciana enthusiastically praised a speech given by the French feminist Luisa

Michel, which Graciana had just read about in the newspaper. 'These are the ideas that I like,' she announced to the whole family. 'These are the doctrines that I want to see triumph before I die. Man is a pygmy; woman is a giant.' The children were 'stunned' by this clear challenge to marital authority. From then on, in Graciana's words, it was a 'war to the death' with her husband.[12]

Husbands were able to convince judges to uphold their right of deposit to 'repair [their] lacerated honour', to 'stop public gossip', to 'teach [their wife] the respect due to a husband', to 'punish [her] for acting against [a husband's] honour and interests by filing unjust judicial cases', to 'punish [her] holy impudence with prison', to teach her to 'accommodate [a husband's] wishes, to acquiesce to [his] authority, and to respect [his] position as head of the family'. Argentines' notion of male honour and men's increasing sense of their need to defend it were at issue here. Duelling was a thriving practice in late nineteenth-century Argentina, as was litigation for calumny and personal injuries. Although a wife could charge her husband with adultery and sue for divorce, her own adultery and other offences to her husband were considered much more serious than her husband's. Public punishment for women's adultery was deemed more effective than private, because it was considered to be a manifestation of a deeper social evil: namely, prostitution. Further, anthropological criminologists held that an adulterous woman could be expected to go on to commit more heinous acts, even murder.[13]

According to the penal code of 1886, wives were punished when they engaged in, or in practice appeared to have engaged in, any sexual act with a man who was not their husband. Husbands were punished only for their habitual intercourse with the same woman: that is, when they had a 'concubine inside or outside the conjugal house'.[14] Criminal court evidence indicates that husbands who cohabited with their mistresses for several days running, even 'publicly and scandalously', argued successfully that this could not be considered *mancebo* but was simply fornication, which was not punishable for a husband. In contrast, wives who disappeared for as little time as an hour behind closed doors with another man could be successfully prosecuted for adultery, even though there was no more proof than the closed door. The questions that were drawn up by husbands, and that judges then posed to the men's wives concerning their relations with other men – such as, 'Did you eat at the same table with him?' 'Did you walk arm in arm with him?' 'Did you use the *tu* form of address with him?' – indicate how little freedom women had in their relationships with men other than their husbands. With husbands, evidence of their having shared a meal with another woman, been seen in public with her and so on, was not enough to make the judge allege that adultery had occurred.[15] Thus, while the least flaw or mistake of a wife could dishonour her husband, his own sexual mistakes did not dishonour him.

Depositing had everything to do with the seat of honour. Spanish author Severo Catalina del Amo wrote that Spanish law was original on this point. 'Keep in mind that the part of honour that the husband loses is not his. It belongs to the honour of his wife, which he has on deposit.' Of course, there were other ways that he could lose honour, hence the popularity of duelling in this period as a way of restoring honour. Peace within families depended on the mother's reputation, and gender norms, helped by the law, gave men the right to judge women's honour and to declare a woman unworthy of her husband's name and companionship if she offended him, and the right to request deposit of her in a house of internment where her honour would be on deposit and accrue 'interest' for him.[16] Normally, the length of time that a wife was to be kept isolated from society was unspecified at the time of deposit. According to one husband, the correct amount of time his wife should be separated from her family should be enough 'to absorb the advice and good teaching of the nuns, to reform her character and teach her to respect the principle of authority'.[17]

The houses of deposit

Conflicting rationales of isolation and its role in both punishment of women and their cure are seen in the General Hospital for Women and the Good Shepherd, staffed by personnel from religious orders and supported by subventions from the civil government and charitable contributions. The Beneficent Society, the police and courts, and the Defence of Minors office worked together, although not always harmoniously, in placing women in these institutions as the need arose and as space permitted. The depositor was responsible for the upkeep of the depositee. If a husband could not afford the cost of his wife's maintenance in a house of deposit, he could hire her out to a private family or to the Women's Hospital to work off her own support during depositing. Fathers and husbands of the élite classes seemed to think little of putting their daughters and wives in these places, to live poorly alongside the lower classes and criminals. Well-to-do women from business and ranching families, middle-class professionals, merchants and artisans, and lower-class laundresses, servants and seamstresses shared internment.[18] These houses functioned to punish women by isolating them from family, work and society, by imposing carceral practices within the houses, by exposing them to 'immorality' to increase their sense of shame, and by separating them from their identities as wife, mother and, often, professional that they had worked hard to establish. There was informal segregation within the house of deposit as well, as women accused of minor affronts tried to maintain their identities and self-respect. Interestingly, a report from 1980 on the Good Shepherd in the city of Córdoba, Argentina, reveals that inmates socialised little and primarily with women of the same class and/or educational level. The report criticised religious personnel for not distinguishing between mere 'sinners' and 'delinquents', and for turning the institution into an 'enclosed penitentiary'.[19]

The Women's Hospital, first built in the central section of Buenos Aires in 1774, was turned over to the women of the Beneficent Society for management in 1852. With the federalisation of Buenos Aires in 1880 and the growth of the city, many institutions were moved north of the city centre, to what became the élite area of Palermo and Belgrano. The Women's Hospital, which moved to Palermo at Las Heras and Bustamante Streets in 1887 and today is known as Hospital Rivadavia, was one of these.[20] The Women's Hospital was obliged to accept depositees of the state, and found that by the 1880s these women were undermining the medical goals of the hospital. They numbered around forty depositees in a hospital of three hundred beds. Though the depositees appeared to be the main source of manual labour for the institution, their presence was not appreciated by the Beneficent Society, and a hospital inspector accused the Defence of Minors office and the police in 1878 of attempting to convert the hospital into a correctional institution.

During the day, wrote the hospital inspector, these 'unfortunate' women were 'busy doing the work of the hospital and at night there were no beds for them and they had to sleep under the beds of the patients'. Crowded together on mattresses under the beds, badly covered in winter on the damp floors and suffocating from heat in the summer, the detainees 'used up' the air needed by patients, he explained, and at the same time were themselves contaminated by the 'noxious air' of infectious disease. It was inhumane, he wrote, to expose healthy people to illnesses.[21] The state was also sending a second population of women to the hospital in that the majority of the women who used the maternity ward of the hospital, some two to three hundred, had been sent there by the Defence of Minors office as under suspicion of having committed infanticide or abortion. These women were not allowed to leave the hospital without an order from the judge, which exacerbated the overcrowded conditions. Further, women with allegedly questionable morals discouraged other women, who were free from the stigma of being under suspicion of crime, from using the maternity ward.

The Good Shepherd, located in the older San Telmo section of Buenos Aires at the corner of Umberto Primo and Defensa Streets, was not beset by the problem of combining the confinement and medical treatment of women. Instead it served both as an asylum (*asilo*) and a jail (see Figure 8.1). The institution evolved from a Jesuit institution founded in the 1760s to become a public institution, also under the direction of the women of the Beneficent Society. It remained a women's correctional under nuns until 1974. The Good Shepherd was a place of deposit for women of all ages deemed in need of correction, as well as for those whose need for correction was only alleged. An estimate of the average number of inmates gleaned from the scattered records is about two hundred a year.[22] It too became overpopulated with women being detained for correctional reasons in the later nineteenth century.

Descriptions of life at the Good Shepherd are scarce and scattered, but almost all are negative. Much of the description and criticism survives in the records of a government agency, the Defence of Minors office. The Good Shepherd's large population of minors, as well as adult women, positioned it to be the target of the rancour between the liberal democratic institutions of the new Republic and holdovers from the colonial period. The first area of criticism was that the Good Shepherd systematically violated article 278 of the civil code of 1869 that fixed the maximum period of time for depositing at one month for women under the age of 21. Due to the lack of time and personnel for sufficient oversight by government, the staff of the Good Shepherd were able to prolong incarceration two to four years, which the nuns considered necessary to rid inmates of immorality and instil in them religious sensibilities and a work ethic.[23] The second area of contention was

Figure 8.1 A barred view of the interior courtyard at the Good Shepherd House of
Correction, Buenos Aires

Source: Author's photo

the Beneficent Society's assertion of *patria potestad* over minors at the Good
Shepherd even when a minor opposed it. This attempt to control was counter to
'good sense' and 'civilisation', argued the Defence of Minors office. The Society
had been created in colonial times by an absolute monarchy, after all, and its claim
to judicial authority was an 'anachronism' in a democracy. In contrast, in the new
democracy everyone was equal before the law, and the law stated that a minor girl
could choose a guardian.[24]

Two articles from the popular press suggest that the negative feeling towards the
Good Shepherd was fairly widespread. One, from the newspaper *La Pampa*, had a
field day with a moral scandal that broke out at the Good Shepherd in 1882, in
which the sacristan was reported as having had sexual relations with the inmates.
The article mocked the immorality of a place that advertised itself as a sanctuary
for falling and fallen women and ridiculed the pastor for his care of his flock.[25]

Several years later, in 1891, an article from *El Diario* attributed fighting that had recently taken place at the Good Shepherd to its indiscriminate mixing of different social classes, and criminals with orphaned girls, in an intensely confined area where there was reportedly less than half a foot between inmates' beds.[26] A police report from 1899, on the other hand, praised the Good Shepherd for its 'severe discipline' in the house, without having to use force; for its training of inmates in basic domestic skills; and for nuns' 'self-sacrifice'. Unlike the Defence of Minors office, the police were receptive to the nuns' view that the month allowed for incarceration by law was insufficient to moralise women's habits.[27]

Two longer examinations of the Good Shepherd, published in the mid twentieth century, portray a continuation of a world of isolation from the outside world, forced acceptance of the house's routine and regulations, mixing of women from different social and economic backgrounds and different levels of 'criminality', and an atmosphere of religiosity and indolence. According to a study from the 1930s, the civil police daily deposited women of 'drunken habits, habitual disorders, and indecent scandals' at the Good Shepherd, 'renewing the human material' of the house. From the moment the women entered the house, they were conscious of its monastic character, mandatory chapel, incense and prayers, a dress code of striped pinafores, and a certain degree of silence. The grated windows, whitewashed walls and dirty old floors, odour of grime and cheap lotions, and humidity created a sense of 'desperation'. The correctional contained about a hundred women locked in a large room at night with no sanitary facilities except a pail. Beds were so scarce that many women slept on the floor. Besides the prayers and work, especially sewing, there was a daily recreation period in the patio, where in the 1930s the women reportedly were accustomed to insulting the nuns, although observers mostly stressed women's awe of the nuns. While physical punishment was supposedly unnecessary in these houses because of their religious character, 'crude punishments' were reported at the Good Shepherd in the 1930s.[28]

Another study of the Good Shepherd, a thesis written in 1952 by a member of the order of the Buen Pastor on the re-education of women, could have easily been written a hundred years previously. Its message – that Argentina needed women who would dignify the nation with their virtues and not degrade it with their vices – resonates with the prescriptive literature of the mid to late nineteenth century. Starting with the admission that women naturally feared and felt antipathy towards the Good Shepherd because it meant a loss of their freedom and punishment, and that they often suffered from altered states in their nervous systems, the author stressed the need for a preliminary observation period before integrating a new inmate into the house. Obviously, the defect of mixing had not been resolved even in the 1950s. A 'poor vagabond girl' who had succumbed to her passions, argued the author, should not be mixed in with women from an 'honourable' home, whose parents or tutors had deposited them for 'preventative' reasons that resulted from them 'keeping bad company, or being disobedient or capricious'.[29]

These girls and women from honourable homes in the 1950s could have related quite well to the unhappiness of 16-year-old María when she was placed in the Good Shepherd in 1890. She had been living in the élite neighbourhood of El

Norte, off Plaza Vicente López, when her father suddenly put her in the Good Shepherd, in the working-class neighbourhood of San Telmo. The case involved María's pregnancy, ostensibly from her relationship with 26-year-old Lucio, a provoked abortion, and his breaking off of their engagement. He came from Argentine stock and old money; she came from Italian immigrant parents and new money. María's father tried to blackmail Lucio, but when these efforts failed, María's father brought a case against Lucio and the attending midwife in 1891 for abortion. The father's attempt to establish an equivalent honour for his family, through money and through depositing his daughter, to compete with Lucio's family, is interesting. The strategy of depositing put the community on notice that the father knew the right thing to do to 'recover what, in an hour of sad memories, was snatched away from [him] unjustly' and to secure María's confession. Depositing María also showed him as a good father:

> I had an honest family and the future of my children ahead of me. All of this was my capital, and I laboured to increase it, doing all those demonstrative acts of paternal sentiment. María is the oldest of my daughters and the one in whom my wife and I had put our best hopes. I sacrificed so that she would have a careful education, which she continued until she was 16, when these events became clear and left my home cold, and my illusions stained which as a father once formed me. María wants to remain in reclusion until a condemnation of the guilty parties opens the doors of society to her. I'm acting for her honour as her legitimate representative.[30]

Contrary to her father's statement that she preferred to remain in the Good Shepherd until the resolution of the case, María had no such intention: she pencilled the following message on a scrap of cardboard and arranged to have it smuggled out to a friend.

> Yesterday afternoon, papa put me in the correctional of women. I beg you to tell Lucio to get me out of this martyrdom; the reason is my stepmother. That's why he put me here. I hope that you can do what's possible to tell Lucio to get me out. Say that you're my cousins. I beg you to tell Lucio to get me out, because I'm dying and I'm being martyred by that crazy woman [her stepmother].[31]

María's father was criticised for putting his daughter in the correctional of the Good Shepherd, a breeding ground for nervous diseases and even madness, which science had shown was contagious. Seven months in such a poisonous atmosphere, observers said, 'asphyxiated noble sentiments and taught lessons of perversion'. In a reversal of the effect intended by María's father, her deposit was also used as proof that María was in fact immoral, because only this could explain why a father would put his daughter in a 'place of that sort' for seven months, 'exposing her to all sorts of women, a true school of prostitution and vice. Is this how you deal with a girl with pure sentiments? Is it this society that is suited to a young honest girl?'[32]

Conclusion

Integral to the system of depositing was the contradiction that Argentina's liberal democratic political élites promoted the legal and scientific isolation of women while attempting to convince women that exclusionary systems like depositing actually increased their chances of being good and modern citizens. Traditional beliefs in male authority, now bolstered by the sciences of biology and criminology, continued to be propounded. Just because women had the right to challenge their husbands in court, argued a judge, it was far better for her to attempt change through the use of tears, kind words and submission. Liberal institutions took a back seat to traditional patriarchal and church power.

Was it just an overlap of historical periods of colonial and national, of church/patriarchal authority and new democratic state power that accounted for the state's acceptance of houses of deposit in a modern world, or was it a modern strategy of governing? I argue that it was the latter. First, the state's support of the depositing system was an important part of its plan to curtail instances of private vengeance, yet retain an outlet for private justice. By strengthening its own control of women, the state could avoid the anarchy of passionate husbands' criminal acts. Husbands referred in court to having placed their wives in houses of deposit in order to avoid violence against them. Only seemingly contradictory was the fact that honour and the passion that went with it, far from being tied to a traditional world, became more valuable with the process of modernisation. The increase in the depositing of women and in duelling were ways in which the state maintained a controlled outlet for the sphere of private justice. Second, positivism was the working framework for jurists and political élites who were well aware that exclusion and isolation were important concepts in the development of a society informed by positive science and striving to be civilised and progressive. Now that science had turned traditional arguments of women's inequality into verifiable facts, the use of systems such as depositing made sense in new ways. This may have been especially welcomed in light of the increase in wives' litigation against their husbands, the increase in feminism, and the growing representation of women in the workforce and educational institutions. Third, the medical and criminological concern with the origin of the 'disease states' of contagion and degeneration, both of which had moral as well as physical dimensions, were credited in part to 'deviant' women. While contagion within houses of deposit was clearly a problem, what was considered a larger concern was the need to contain the spread of social and moral contagion by isolating questionable and questioning women from the rest of society.

Notes

1 For an early explanation of depositing, see Bartolo da Sassoferrato, *Commentaria in corpus iuris civilis (codice e istituzioni)*, Venice, 1567, cited in *Enciclopedia del diritto* in the entry 'Adulterio', vol. 1, Verese, Giuffrè, 1958.

2 Information about houses of deposit and the system of depositing in Argentina is difficult to find and fragmentary. Yet evidence does appear in civil and criminal cases in testimonies, arguments of the prosecutor, the defence lawyer and the judge, and

texts cited by these men. I have treated a third institution, the House of Spiritual Exercises, which also acted as a place of deposit for women, in Ruggiero, 'Wives on "deposit": internment and the preservation of husbands' honor in late nineteenth-century Buenos Aires', *Journal of Family History*, 1992, vol. 17, no. 3, pp. 253–70.

3 J.L. Aguirre, *Autos y sentencias del Juez del Crímen*, Buenos Aires, Mayo, 1885, pp. 637–8.

4 Aguirre, *Autos y sentencias del Juez del Crímen*, pp. 637–8.

5 A. Carette (ed.) *Diccionario de la jurisprudencia argentina, ó síntesis completa de las sentencias dictadas por los tribunals argentinos*, 2 vols, Buenos Aires, Lajouane, 1917–21, *voce* 'Divorcio' (clause 112).

6 Archivo General Nacional (AGN), Tribunal Criminal (TC), 2, B, 22, 1883, against Clara Barghelli for poisoning of Aquilino Semino and attempted poisoning of Santiago Semino, and against the accomplice, Andrés Pagano.

7 J.L. Duffy, 'Curiosidades fiscals. Otro dictámen del Dr. Quesada', *Revista de Policia (RP)*, 1899, vol. 3, no. 57, pp. 139–42 passim; Duffy, 'Curiosidades fiscals. Sentencia del doctor Barrenecha', *RP*, 1899, vol. 3, no. 58, pp. 151–2 passim.

8 'Asilo de Mujeres, 1899', *RP*, 1900, vol. 3, no. 64, pp. 260–1.

9 J. Escriche y Martín, *Diccionario razonado de legislación y jurisprudencia*, vol. 2, Madrid, Cuesta, 1874, *voce* 'Casa de corrección'.

10 E.S. Zeballos, 'Discurso', *Revista del Derecho, Historia y Letras (RDHL)*, 1902, vol. 5, no. 13, pp. 461–2 quoting J.B. Alberdi; M. Bravo, *Derechos civiles de la mujer. El codigo, los proyectos, la ley*, Buenos Aires, El Ateneo, 1927, pp. 69, 119.

11 L.M. Drago, 'El poder marital', thesis, Facultad de Derecho y Ciencias Sociales, Buenos Aires, El Diario, 1882, pp. 12–18.

12 AGN, TC, 1, U, 2, 1882, against Graciana Urrutigarray by her husband, Juan Bautista Bonnement, for calumny and serious injuries (including divorce).

13 Argentine Penal Code (1886), Titulo Tercero, Capitulo Primero, Artículo 123.

14 AGN, TC, 2, C, 118, 1899, Brunette Wal de Catton against her husband, Julio Gasten Catton, and his lover, Agustina Villain, for adultery.

15 Escriche, *Diccionario*, vol. 1, 1874, *voce* 'Adulterio'.

16 S. Catalina del Amo, *La mujer, Apuntes para un libro*, 2nd edn, Madrid, San Martin, 1861, p. 117.

17 AGN, Tribunal Civil (Trib. Civil), Index no. 116, A, 347, 1892, Dionisio Anglada against his wife, Ana Arrix, and request to put her in a convent.

18 R.D. Salvatore and C. Aguirre (eds) *The Birth of the Penitentiary in Latin America: Essays on Criminology, Prison Reform, and Social Control, 1830–1940*, Austin, University of Texas Press, 1996.

19 Inter-American Commission of Women, *Situación de la mujer en centros de reclusion: estudio de la unidad penitenciaria 'El Buen Pastor'*, Córdoba, Argentina, Washington, DC, Organization of American States, 1980, pp. 11–17, 27–8, 38, 53–4.

20 Rodio Raíces, *Breve historia del Hospital Rivadavia*, summary online at http://www.medicos-municipales.org.ar/rivadavia.htm.

21 AGN, SB, 51, Asilo del Buen Pastor, 1855–91.

22 AGN, SB, 51, Asilo del Buen Pastor, 1855–91.

23 'Seccion: Derecho civil', *Revista de Lejislación y Jurisprudencia (RLJ)*, 1870, vol. 5, pp. 14–20, 26, 35, 37.

24 AGN, SB, 179, Defensoría de Menores, 1824–95.

25 AGN, SB, 51, Asilo del Buen Pastor, 1855–91, pp. 116–17, citing article from *La Pampa*, 20 October 1882.

26 'Buen Pastor', *El Diario*, 12 October 1891.

27 'Asilo de Mujeres', *RP*, pp. 260–1.

28 A. Mendoza, *Carcel de Mujeres; Impesiones recogidas en el Asilo del Buen Pastor*, Buenos Aires, Coleccion Claridad 'Problemas Sociales', 1930/9.

29 M. Gomez, 'La obra de la reeducación de la mujer', thesis, Buenos Aires, 1952, p.17.

30 AGN, TC, 2, C, 64, 1891 and AGN, TC, 2, C, 68, 1891, against Lucio Cascallares Paz and Susana Breuil de Concerc for abortion.
31 AGN, TC, 2, C, 64, 1891 and AGN, TC, 2, C, 68, 1891, against Lucio Cascallares Paz and Susana Breuil de Concerc for abortion.
32 *El Diario*, 24 August 1891.

9 Cultures of confinement

Tuberculosis, isolation and the sanatorium

Alison Bashford

The early twentieth-century sanatorium for consumptives was a hybrid place with a peculiar genealogy. Recognisable as a classic disciplinary institution, the sanatorium emerged from ambiguous and multiple traditions of corrective, therapeutic and educational sites and practices of isolation: part hospital, part prison, part school, and in its variously classed public and private versions, part asylum or part health resort. Sanatoria were disciplinary institutions yet often voluntary; they were places for the isolation of the dangerous yet also for their instruction; they were highly policed but aiming to produce self-policing subjects; and they were places of both therapy and prevention. In this chapter I focus on sanatoria as interesting transitional sites between methods of preventive public health based on coerced spatial isolation of the dangerous, and methods based on self-governance and the instalment of civic responsibilities.[1]

Public health sociologists and historians have schematised various strategies of spatial management over time in the West. An historical trajectory leading from quarantine, implemented very early in the development of administrative government, to the post 1970s 'new public health' has been suggested and taken up with some enthusiasm in critical medical sociology.[2] If quarantine was an example of 'sovereign' power in which the unclean were isolated coercively, or the dangerous were cast away in a move of 'exile-enclosure' in Foucault's famous example of the leper, the 'new public health' is sustained rather more by self-governance and by a desire for healthiness as a core part of the modern self.[3] In other articles I have tried both to utilise this schema and to qualify it at the same time, for a close reading of the evidence shows overlapping, emerging and receding logics and practices, as well as different public health measures being applied to different populations and 'dangers' simultaneously, thereby suggesting a chronology far more complicated and difficult to pin down than that implied in the sociological literature.[4] The schema 'from quarantine to the new public health' is both generally correct and nonetheless very general. What interests me about the case of tuberculosis is that both new quarantining strategies and, within quarantined space itself, new modes of training-into-healthiness came together: tuberculosis management at the turn of the century represents a complicated simultaneity of public health measures and rationales involving isolation, rather than a progressive teleology of measures.

Public health literature has dovetailed recently with a related strand of scholarship (which was never entirely separate) on dangerousness, risk and methods of prevention in liberal and neo-liberal societies, which directly addresses the use of isolation as a strategy for prevention. In his seminal 1991 article, Robert Castel argued that there has been a qualitative shift in modern strategies of prevention 'from dangerousness to risk'.[5] Castel writes that the question was posed in the nineteenth century: 'How will it be possible to prevent without being forced to confine?' He suggests that governments and experts were finding confinement measures of prevention crude and limited, in that 'one cannot confine masses of people', and unresponsive, in that the strategy 'can only be carried out on individual patients one by one'. Like many recent sociologists he identifies (and criticises) 'risk' as the major late twentieth-century solution to the problems of prevention-through-isolation.[6]

Both Castel in this article and Foucault in 'About the concept of the "dangerous individual"' focus their analyses on criminal psychiatry. They argue that the dangerous individual was not necessarily 'diagnosed' as such because of their criminal action, but because of a quality inhering in the individual, which suggested that such asocial action *might* happen. What one *is*, not what one *does*, became key to the psychiatric and legal response: 'Are there individuals who are intrinsically dangerous? By what signs can they be recognised, and how can one react to their presence?'[7] Unpredictability was the problem to work with, for 'even those who appear calm [or, I might add, healthy] carry a threat'.[8] Thus, in order to *prevent* the threatened pathological act, the dangerous individual needed to be diagnosed as such by increasingly specialised medical/psychiatric experts, and confined in a prison, or an asylum. Isolation was a preventive measure rather more than, or as well as being, a punishment measure: 'to confine signified to neutralize, if possible in advance, an individual deemed dangerous'.[9] In a similar way, the dangerous individual might be the infected but symptomless person, a 'carrier' – a category invented in public health discourse of the very late nineteenth century. The threatened pathological act in that case was not violence, but was rather the spread of contagion. In the way that the criminal individual *appeared* calm, the carrier appeared healthy, but both were nonetheless dangerous. Although there is very little analysis of the infected as dangerous within this theoretical framework, it is clear that the infected-as-social-threat were managed in ways which crossed over with and borrowed from penal systems of confinement and denial of liberty, and vice versa. Moreover, as I show in this chapter through the case study of tuberculosis, 'danger' was not infrequently the precise language used by experts and governments as the safety and health of the population became increasingly an object of intervention.

In the field of public health, institutions for isolation of the dangerous expanded prolifically around the turn of the nineteenth to the twentieth century.[10] The phenomenon of 'isolation hospitals' was not new. There were early modern syphilitic hospitals, separate maternity wards in the nineteenth century, and Lock Hospitals for prostitutes with venereal diseases, which in many ways stands as the modern template for the exclusion of the undesirable. Yet in the early twentieth century both the measures to enforce isolation on health grounds and the number and specialised kinds of places of isolation were newly expanding, as bacteriology offered both better diagnostic tools and new rationales for the location and confinement of the (medically) dangerous, and as progressivist and liberal-welfare states created new imperatives for the pursuit of bureaucratic information on individuals and populations. Spatial isolation was far from the *only* public health response, but what is significant is the expansion and refinement of spaces of isolation, which very clearly characterised this period.

The common legislative and management innovation of the late nineteenth century was the technique of notification, which had a twin – isolation. Measures for compulsory notification were not in themselves new, but they expanded exponentially in this period, and were accompanied by all kinds of novel measures and powers for the compulsory examination and detention of the infected. In Britain, notification increased incrementally from the middle of the nineteenth century, with some 'setback' after the public reaction to the series of Contagious Diseases Acts in the 1860s, but then mushroomed after the 1889 Infectious Diseases (Notification) Act and the Act's significant intensification in 1899.[11] Although the reasons for the introduction of notification in specific years in specific locales are multiple (particular governments, particular epidemics, particular diagnostic possibilities), notification and isolation proliferated without precedent in the turn-of-the-century period. Sometimes these places and institutions were for the sick, but they were also for the 'carrier', the infected but symptomless person.[12] Isolation hospitals began to appear in this period, some specialising in particular diseases, for example smallpox hospitals, others for particular populations, especially children's infectious disease hospitals. This is the period also of the expansion of the leper colony, the epileptic colony and, as I discuss here, the sanatorium for consumptives.

At the same time, though, the period is also characterised by the evolution of hygienic self-governance. The case of tuberculosis management in sanatoria stands as a perfect example of the simultaneity of these measures, both of isolation-of-the-dangerous and of modes of hygienic self-governance characteristic of 'the new public health'. Sanatoria are also significant because consumptives often entered the institutions voluntarily, albeit for a range of reasons and some with little choice due to their severely impoverished state. Once 'inside', the aim of open-air treatment in sanatoria was to reform consumptives into responsible self-governing, non-infective ('safe') and hygienic citizens. The sanatorium was one institution where the 'soul of the citizen' came to be intensively governed.[13]

Here, then, I locate this literature on isolation, public health spaces and management of the dangerous with respect to tuberculosis – or consumption – in early twentieth-century Australia. In the first section I show how the language of 'dangerousness' drove new strategies of institutional and isolated therapy and prevention. In the second section, I discuss the instruction and training which went on within these isolated spaces, as not only bodies but souls became the project of the experts and, significantly, of the consumptives themselves. And finally I discuss healthy citizenship and civic responsibility to be 'safely' released back into the community, as part of this new cultivation of the hygienic self.

Throughout, I explore isolation in the turn-of-the-century sanatorium as situated *between* coerced confinement and 'voluntary' confinement, which itself signalled new modes of governance-through-freedom.[14]

Isolation and the dangerous consumptive

'Open-air' treatment in sanatoria became common in Europe, Britain, North America and Australia very suddenly at the turn of the century. It was no radical departure from the dominant nineteenth-century climatic understanding of consumption, but rather was derivative of it; a systematised, institutionalised and ordered (that is, 'modern') rendition of long-established therapeutic and preventive techniques involving pure air, the regulation of diet and exercise, and exposure to (and often struggle with) 'nature' in one version or another. Modelled on German private institutions for open-air treatment, the first British sanatorium was established in Edinburgh in 1889 and, as Linda Bryder has demonstrated, there was a phenomenal proliferation of institutions for the prevention and treatment of tuberculosis over the turn of the century. She notes nineteen specialist hospitals in England and Wales in 1886 and 176 institutions in 1920.[15] In the US the sanatorium treatment was popularised from about 1884, and Michael Teller notes a similar mushrooming of institutions for various kinds of open-air treatment.[16] In Australia, sanatoria and institutionalised open-air treatment were also established from around 1900 and, as in the German and British example particularly, this institutional management of tuberculosis was closely linked to the emergence of important new forms of social welfare, including sickness benefits and health insurance schemes.

There was a discernible shift in focus around the turn of the century from the individual and often aestheticised consumptive towards an imagining of the disease as a product of urbanisation and industrialisation. Katherine Ott notes, with respect to the US, that conceptualisations of tuberculosis changed from an 'allure of delicate consumptions' towards association with 'poverty and the dangerous classes'.[17] At one level this continued to justify and explain removal to the 'open air' on the part of middle-class as well as working-class consumptives, as 'nature' counteracted the effects of urban living. Thus, as one proponent of sanatorium treatment put it, tuberculosis 'is one method by which nature protests against an unnatural system of living'.[18] Open-air treatment made some sense as the offsetting of 'unnatural' urbanised life with 'nature', whether that be rural settlements in England, bracing mountain air in Germany or ocean breezes in Australia. In this instance, 'isolation' held a double meaning: both segregation from other people and therapeutic, restorative removal from urban life and its effects. But at another level, and this is largely what interests me here, tuberculosis was drawn into, and was in part productive of, a bureaucratised and institutionalised *public* health – that is, a classed disease to be managed at population level: as such it came to be problematised explicitly as 'dangerousness'.

'Danger' and 'dangerousness' were the lexicon through which tuberculosis was understood by Australian public health and hygiene experts when they turned to consider tuberculosis as a public health issue around the turn of the century. 'Every consumptive [is] a source of danger,' announced a 1911 government *Report on Consumption*.[19] In 1909 one doctor asked: what is to be done with the consumptive who 'cannot manage himself, and is a perpetual or intermittent source of danger to his neighbours'?[20] And the editor of Sydney's *Daily Telegraph* warned that consumptives were 'at present a source of danger to themselves and to all around them'.[21] This language of dangerousness both recommended and justified new legal powers and institutional isolation, both compulsory and voluntary, among the preventive responses. When the state health ministers met in 1911 over the issue of consumption, they recommended five measures to be implemented uniformly across the states, based on the creation of new legal powers: compulsory notification; legal powers to regulate the home management of consumptives; legal powers to 'remove dangerous or infective consumptives into segregation'; powers to detain them in segregation; legal power to medically examine contacts of consumptives.[22]

In practice, diagnosis with tuberculosis rarely resulted in immediate segregation, in the way that those diagnosed with smallpox, plague or leprosy were placed in emergency quarantine. Rather, the new powers of compulsory isolation in the case of tuberculosis were implemented over people who were proving ungovernable in some other respect as well, usually working-class people without identifiable homes which could be inspected and sanitised by a visiting nurse or a sanitary inspector. Their indigence meant untraceability in a public health system which relied on spatial tracking; their lack of place was understood as dangerous 'roaming', spreading the disease in unknown ways as they moved uncontrolled through the city. This was a longstanding classed understanding of the urban-ungovernable, linking twentieth-century isolation and institutionalisation with early modern confinement of beggars, 'wild children' or the unemployed and, indeed, with late-modern projects of 'cleaning up' of urban spaces detailed in other chapters in this book.[23] For example, the Melbourne psychiatrist and eugenicist J.W. Springthorpe wrote in 1912:

> The danger, the greatest danger of all, is from careless, generally advanced patients, walking about at large, using ordinary handkerchiefs, and spitting here, there, and everywhere. Such actions should be regarded as a grave crime against the community. Such patients should be taught the danger, that it affects themselves, also, and how to cease being a danger … in many cases, especially among the poor and ignorant, the sufferers must be aggregated into suitable homes or institutions which need not be dangers to others.[24]

The consumptive who could not manage himself was understood as wholly infective and dangerous, and requiring total management in isolation.

Institutions for the isolation of the consumptive did appear in both charitable and state-run versions for working-class people and private versions for those who could afford them. To take examples from the Sydney region, a philanthropic organisation, the Queen Victoria Homes of Consumptives Fund, opened two sanatoria, one south of the city (1899) which became a women's sanatorium when a second opened for men in the Blue Mountains west of the city (1903).[25] The large government institution at Waterfall, again on the southern fringes of the city, was opened in 1909. This investment on the part of government indicates the sudden sense in which tuberculosis shifted from being understood as a disease of individuals (over which government had no responsibility) to a disease of population and infectious disease control (which liberal and welfare governments increasingly took up as their responsibility). It was a direct result of a challenge posed at a string of public meetings, that tuberculosis control was a 'duty of the State' because it was an infectious disease threatening the community, and thus uninfected citizens should expect protection.[26]

Across the world the movement towards sanatorium treatment aimed to institutionalise people in the earliest stages of tuberculosis, and even those who were diagnosed but symptomless. The model of the sanatorium-proper was not intended as an institution for those about to die. However, the case records show that the NSW government sanatorium was rather more like an asylum for incurables than this kind of sanatorium-proper, at least in its earliest years. Of the first hundred admissions, thirty-four died at the sanatorium, many having been referred from existing government asylums.[27] The medical superintendent argued for a better system of classifying and separating patients, so that some, at least, could benefit from proper open-air treatment.[28] And over time the Waterfall institution, like the non-government institutions, functioned as a sanatorium-proper, with 'chalets', rest and exercise routines and strictly monitored diets, all of which I discuss below.

In the re-casting of tuberculosis as a dangerous infectious disease of the public, progressivist and liberal governments struck many new problems, the sorting out of which can be seen as instrumental in the twentieth-century shifts towards 'risk management', primarily through insurance rather than through confinement-of-the-dangerous. Tuberculosis management is at the heart of the earliest experiments in health insurance. Unlike acute diseases like smallpox (primarily significant in Australia) or cholera (primarily significant in Britain), tuberculosis was a long-term chronic disease of the individual, and endemic, not epidemic, in populations. As Castel has argued of the consideration of other social problems, universal confinement for the infected, which now included the possibility of diagnosing the *carrier*, was in fact more or less impossible for governments to implement as a method of prevention. This was compounded by the understanding, which I discuss below, that tuberculosis was never completely eradicated in an individual, once infected. Rather, the individual would always carry the disease, and thus intervention was concerned with minimising its effect and rendering that person responsible and safe in the community.

In the recasting of tuberculosis as a chronic infectious disease of the populace, there was considerable discussion of the precise nature of its dangerousness. That is, did the dangerousness inhere in the person him or herself, as an integral aspect or element of the person, a 'quality of the subject', something like the criminal personality?[29] Or was the dangerousness arbitrarily attached, a substance, if you like, that could be detached? Bacteriology and germ theories, themselves being refined over the turn of the century, offered limited ways in which the consumptive subject was de-pathologised, de-psychologised and in many ways de-mythologised. Their 'dangerousness' was sometimes comprehensible not as an inherent quality, but simply as microbes in the body. The report of a meeting of combined state ministers on consumption in 1911 argued thus:

> In what does this dangerousness consist? Only in the expectoration they give off. Their dangerousness is proportioned to the amount and virulence of their expectoration ... the actual danger ... depends entirely on the care they take of their expectoration. If they collect and destroy it, others are in no danger ... but if they spit about carelessly, and soil their clothes, floors and handkerchiefs ... the danger to others is great.

Minimising danger, then, was sometimes about isolating the unmanageable in institutions, but it was also about teaching habits, certain safe and responsible modes of conduct. Consumption, the ministers reported, 'can be easily managed with safety'.[30]

> [S]egregation of the sick from the healthy should be our aim. But it would be unnecessary, useless, impracticable and improper, to advise segregation as a routine measure to be inexorably carried out in every case. All consumptives are not dangerous; few consumptives are dangerous throughout their illness; and even those consumptives who are most dangerous can surely live among the healthy with safety to them, by punctual observance of simple and easy precautions.[31]

Training the consumptive, body and soul

Sanatoria were more than simply places of isolation, they were also places for instruction: 'A sanatorium is not merely a hospital in the ordinary sense ... it is also a training school where patients are taught how they must live.'[32] Unlike the 'dangerous' leper, whose conduct and psychology were of no particular interest to experts and authorities once they were confined or removed,[33] the conduct and psychology of the consumptive was precisely the *project* of sanatorium treatment-in-isolation. The ideal sanatorium's disciplinary regime aimed radically to reform the tuberculous person, who not infrequently voluntarily submitted themselves, their selves, for re-making. The voluntary nature of their submission to institutional discipline and isolation, their complicity in the project of learning a new way of being, especially in the private middle-class sanatorium, was itself evidence of new modes of governance at work. The extent of this voluntary participation and the nature of the re-training of the self in open-air treatment were highly class-dependent. In the charitable and government sanatoria, re-training largely took the form of work (which kept the cost of the institutions down), and in this way sanatoria form part of the lineage of the workhouse. In private sanatoria, re-training was

focused on a programme of exercise and mental engagement, a re-training of attitude, which placed these sanatoria more in the tradition of the ascetic community
on the one hand, and the health resort on the other. In both, however, and I
discuss this in the next section, consumptives were instructed in the social responsibilities brought by their own (perpetual) infectiveness.

Sanatoria were 'total institutions' in that every aspect of the patient's life was
regulated and monitored.[34] Both temporally and spatially the consumptive was
entirely directed, and was to follow a precise series of verbal and written rules about
bodily conduct and interaction, as well as the imperative to live out of doors as
much as possible. For working-class consumptives, rule-following in institutions was
part of an established class dynamic, reworked in the sanatorium as therapeutic. For
example, the state-run Greenvale Sanatorium in Victoria presented its rules in a
manner similar to any public institution of the period: 'Any patient found communicating with another patient in his ward or tent by speech, signs, or writing, or found
moving about or otherwise disturbing the quiet of the tent during the silent rest
period is liable to immediate dismissal.'[35] Yet for a consumptive, unlike other kinds
of patients or prisoners, silence and compliance with the regime was not *just* about
maintaining institutional order: it was a specific aspect of the treatment, part of the
regime of therapeutic isolation. For middle-class consumptives, who might have the
option to undertake a version of open-air treatment at home, it was the imposed
discipline of the institution that recommended it, which aided one in self-discipline.
Thus a 1908 medical congress was told:

> In a sanatorium, the close relation of patient and physician is especially
> conducive to recovery, and where a good result so often depends on strictly
> following out orders in apparently trivial details. It is the regularity and
> precision that count for so much, and are only to be gained as a rule in a
> sanatorium.[36]

Precisely what constituted 'open-air' treatment? Simply, patients were to spend
as much time outdoors as possible. That rural 'outdoor' place was carefully located
by experts, according to ever-changing opinion on the benefits of mountain air, sea
air, temperature and prevailing winds. Activities usually undertaken inside – rest,
sleep, schooling, eating and so forth – were to be transferred outside wherever
possible; hence the vogue for 'open-air schools'. Possibly most emphasis was placed
on breathing 'outside' pure air through the night. Thus consumptives were urged
(and in the case of sanatorium patients *required*) to sleep in tents, or on verandahs,
or in the peculiar innovation of the period, the consumptives' chalet. The chalets
were designed to accommodate a single patient; in them, air constantly circulated
around the tuberculous person, day and night, summer and winter, in virtually any
weather, including rain.[37] The verandah remained a staple of hospital architecture
through the first half of the twentieth century largely because of the perceived
value of outside, pure air. Conversely, the peculiarities of Australian domestic
architecture, in which verandahs were common, were consistently praised as especially health-promoting.

Open-air treatment usually meant a disciplined programme of rest and exercise. As in many kinds of institutions, from the military to the religious to the therapeutic, eating and rest signified the temporal divisions of the day. Beginning with total bedrest, the consumptive, under close and very strict medical and nursing direction, would gradually increase their daily regime of exercise and exertion. Initially involving short walks at a very slow pace, this might increase over several months to walks of several miles with substantial inclines.

> Before meals we lie on lounges silent for one hour … After meals we lie again on lounges, like gorged boa-constrictors, for half an hour, and then, if ordered, walk out at a snail's pace. When I first saw the patients creeping about, I pitied the poor feeble creatures, but found that it was regulation pace, and I was frequently pulled up for my jaunty tread.[38]

Public, charitable and working-class sanatoria reformulated this exercise programme as 'graduated labour' and required patients to undertake work as therapy – for example, gardening or scrubbing floors. In that tuberculosis management was so tied to national economic problems of labour, there was an explicit intention to return the consumptive from dependent invalidity to being viable, or productive even, in a limited way, as a worker. Betraying its genealogy as a corrective institution, therapy became part of work in the sanatorium, and work became part of therapy, in ways not dissimilar to other institutions-of-isolation considered in this book.[39] In England such an establishment came to be called an 'industrial sanatorium', an institution in which 'graduated labour' and training into employment ('industrial training') was a central objective.[40] In Australia, the (state-run) Greenvale Sanatorium established a detailed progressive plan for returning consumptives from invalidity to usefulness. Although treatment began with total bedrest, it then entailed 'a gradually increasing amount of actual manual labour under supervision. Under such conditions, patients benefit, and they also learn to help themselves, as well as others, and so become better fitted to return to the stress of ordinary life'.[41] The so-called 'graduated labour' was clearly therapy for working-class consumptives, but, as Robin Walker has noted, was not unimportant for the economy of such institutions.[42] The idea of 'farm colonies' as an institutional step *after* sanatorium treatment also arose.[43] 'Picton Lakes Village' was opened in New South Wales in 1929, modelled largely on the earlier British Papworth Village.[44] Both were enclosed communities of consumptives and (failed) attempts at creating permanent settlements-in-isolation. Extensions of the sanatorium, these curious villages carried many rationales of isolation simultaneously. They were at once permanent solutions (or so their designers hoped) to the need for preventive segregation; they were certainly sanctuary-asylums, 'homes' for those who had nowhere else; and they sustained the idea of isolation as a therapeutic measure.

In all sanatoria, diet was carefully regulated, with many institutions forcing large meals on consumptives, seeking significant weight-gains as evidence of recovery. All the consumptive's activities were monitored; all rewards were granted or withdrawn according to their weight, as well as their normal or abnormal temperature. One consumptive wrote in 1907:

> There is a regular rule about temperature. If one is 98.8 early, must stop in bed; and if 100.2 at 5 p.m., must retire ... I wanted to stay in bed for break-fast, and couldn't (without a regulation temperature) ... Four times a day we take our temperatures, and we do the same thing every day.[45]

Consumptives were to learn all kinds of new practices, new ways of being, in a re-education programme usually recommended for six months.

There was certainly a notion that eating in the right way, resting and being surrounded by pure air had concrete effects upon the body. But there was an important sense in which the discipline itself, succumbing to rigidly controlled institutional life, and subjecting oneself to certain hardships of 'nature', produced 'character' and 'strength' rather than, or as part of, 'cure'. Discipline and struggle produced stronger bodies with a greater capacity to resist and contain the effects of the disease. Like a range of quasi-military, character-building, 'outdoor' cultural institutions such as the Boy Scouts, both the body and soul were tested and invigo-rated. For most experts and patients, enhancing 'resisting power' meant working on character and attitude as much as bodies. One successfully treated advocate of the system wrote: 'A stiff-upper-lip is needed, a certain amount of brains are needed, character is needed; a little money is needed; also a mind and imagination kept pure from contaminating thoughts and desires.'[46] Open-air treatment was a 'hardening' treatment.[47] And still another consumptive wrote: 'No pampering. Everything to harden one and make one independent.'[48] The treatment regime, then, was not only about forming certain bodily habits, it was about forming a resisting character, cultivating a strong self out of struggle. The more that psycho-logical discourse became available, the more it integrated into the purpose of a sanatorium: 'A sanatorium is not an institution, it is an atmosphere.'[49] By 1924 one Australian expert argued strongly for far greater emphasis on 'the psychological side of the tuberculous patient's character'. At the very least, he suggested, doctors and public health administrators should note the palpable difference in the 'atmosphere' between the graduated labour programmes and 'the old system of monotonous rest'. He wrote that 'there is a psychological advantage in that the improvement is made visible by tangible steps'.[50] A sanatorium regime was conceptualised as much as a 'mental' treatment as a physiological treatment. As such, isolation was a tool to separate consumptives from families and friends, and to facilitate the total discipline required for re-training into healthiness and safety.

Cultivating healthy citizens

Nikolas Rose has written that: 'The citizens of a liberal democracy are to regulate themselves ... to be educated and solicited into a kind of alliance between personal objectives and ambitions and institutionally or socially prized goals or activities.'[51] Such an alliance is clearly articulated in a fascinating set of letters written by a middle-class consumptive in a private sanatorium, published anonymously in Melbourne in 1907. The letters suggest how this particular consumptive learned to regulate herself and to desire a new way of being through mechanisms of severe institutional discipline and isolation, which were nonetheless voluntarily entered into.[52]

The author of *Letters from a Sanatorium* wrote: 'I am in a Reformatory ... hedged with bye-laws, where the days are cut into lengths for rest and exercise, with intervals for temperature taking and meals. The Doctor's word is law.'[53] At another moment she described it more as a convent: 'here in these conventual precincts I am restrained, guarded, protected, preserved'.[54] The shift between imagining herself in some kind of corrective institution on the one hand and in a religious community on the other, is not accidental. The sanatorium functioned well within a culture of total order, obedience and punishment, which took the form of withdrawal of reward, characteristic of both the prison and the ascetic religious community. For her, the sanatorium also had the ambiguity of the asylum, both as place of protection-because-vulnerable and as place of isolation-because-dangerous. She wrote with a certain irony and humour about life in the sanatorium, and with a fascinating insight into her own 'institutionalisation', as we would now call it. 'My world seems bounded by Sanatorium hills,' she wrote. 'I tremble at the thought of going forth into the wide reckless world without the Doctor to direct my steps from the time I open my eyes at dawn until I shut them again at night.'[55] She was very much aware of the deliberate process of re-making herself, of allowing herself to be re-made, which was precisely the aim of the treatment and of the isolation. She described another patient who had become so totally dependent that he could not leave the institution, even when pronounced well: 'I am not as frightened as Mr Bunny is. He has been here five months, and is perfectly well, but cannot make up his mind to leave ... Mr Bunny hugs his chains.'[56]

Mr Bunny was a failure of the sanatorium system because, even though he had been technically and physically treated successfully, he had not become a self-policing 'independent' consumptive: his psychological treatment, as it were, had failed. The anonymous letter-writer, on the other hand, was a success because she left the institution as a fully self-monitoring convert to 'open-air' life, having internalised the sanatorium's instruction in a new mode of conduct, having developed a new sense of self, even as she had all kinds of insights into this very process. She understood that not only was she the 'project' of the doctor and nurses who ran the sanatorium, she was her own project. She had to cultivate a new consumptive self, and with that she could be released from isolation and returned to her family as a safe and responsible mother, and to the community as a safe and responsible citizen.

Within the sanatorium system, the consumptive was imagined as a *tabula rasa* project for reform, and many of the peculiar practices should be understood as modes of imagining the patient as a blank slate on which to then build up the new strong and responsible embodied self. The discipline and excessive order of the sanatoria not only represented conventional institutional culture, but were also ways of re-making the consumptive from first principles, as it were. In this system, total bedrest and silence constituted a symbolically blank and neutral starting point. The will of the patient was to be neutralised and replaced by the will of the doctor and the institution. Ultimately, and almost necessarily through struggle, the patient would will herself into new modes of conduct and a new hygienic subjectivity. The consumptive's freedom was removed (or voluntarily forfeited) – 'we do the same thing every day and have no will of our own'[57] – and it was to be regained or earned back in an incremental process of instruction and acceptance of a new way of life, by developing 'the will to persevere and beat the microbes'.[58]

At the most mundane but certainly not the least important level, this meant being trained in precise new bodily habits. The minutiae of bodily conduct – coughing, chewing, kissing, washing, sleeping – were all considered reformable in the interests of the patient, and governable in the interests of the public. The reform of consumptive conduct was centred on the mouth and on spitting. But if 'Don't spit' was the simple order on public health posters of the period, instruction for consumptives was far more detailed:

> When coughing or sneezing hold a rag lightly in front of the mouth or nose in order to catch the cough spray … Do not swallow any spit which comes up from your lungs or which comes from the back of your throat.[59]

And while spitting was the primary focus for the reform of habits, not only for consumptives but for the general public, it was certainly not the only bodily habit under scrutiny. For example, in 1912 the medical officer at the Greenvale Sanatorium in Victoria instructed thus: 'Do not kiss or allow yourself to be kissed on the mouth.' And as for eating and resting:

> Always wash your lips and hands, and rinse out the mouth, before eating … food must be eaten slowly … Half-an-hour at the very least must be spent over each meal … Rest, especially before meals, should be as complete as possible, and is best obtained by lying at full length on the bed or couch, and refraining from talking.[60]

The sanatorium training of the consumptive body and soul extended into the cultivation of citizenship. Civic responsibility was one of the major attributes which sanatorium instruction aimed to instil as a core part of the consumptive self. When the States met in 1911 on the question of tuberculosis, they concluded that preventive measures should be grounded in 'the education of the consumptive, and the awakening of a sense of responsibility in himself'.[61] This need for responsibility was based on the idea that tuberculosis was never eradicated, only 'arrested', in the common medical parlance. Something like the 'alcoholic' produced by AA discourse, sanatorium treatment produced a permanent consumptive. And in some ways like the contemporary subject who learns to 'live with HIV/AIDS', the consumptive learned to live with the disease in the least harmful way, rather than to expect cure. Consumptives were to think of themselves as always potentially infective. If their symptoms disappeared, it was because the infection had been contained within them, rather than eradicated, and inattention to their open-air regime could threaten a recurrence of symptoms at any time. Thus part of the re-education of the consumptive concerned the instalment of a constant vigilance about their conduct, as well as a recognition that they were always a potential danger to those around them if they did not remain vigilant. They were to be responsible for their habits of living both in their own interests and in the interests of the community. This was part of the bargain of their release from institutional isolation. The aim was to make certain modes of conduct and interaction entirely habitual, yet at the same time to instil a mentality of constant self-monitoring on the part of each consumptive.

Training in responsibility to others worked from complicated premises, some emotional and moral and some drawn from social contract imperatives. Competing obligations and rights were one of the languages for the education of consumptives in civic responsibility. For example:

> The patient's conscience may be appealed to, but his self-interest will form the most effective lever in dealing with him. He must be taught that even public carriers are subject to regulations ... and that while consumptives have legal and moral rights, the general public, too, have theirs.[62]

Being responsible as a consumptive was about citizenship, both in terms of conscientious monitoring of one's own infectiveness and in terms of reciprocal obligations to the community.

If successfully trained in the sanatorium, consumptives were not only considered 'safe' in the community, but were also a means by which hygienic conduct was to be disseminated to the public. Consumptives successfully instructed in the open-air regime 'provide the whole community with conspicuous object lessons in hygiene'.[63] For example, the anonymous 1907 consumptive wrote: 'The Sanatorium is an education centre, and from it light is expected to shine into dark places, every patient acting as a torch.'[64] In the community, the consumptive was not only 'hygienically harmless' or 'safe' but was a positive object lesson for those around her, a kind of missionary who actively taught by example. Rather than spreading the disease, she was to spread a new way of living. And the anonymous letter-writer, for one, seems to have done this successfully. In the coda of the book she writes that she and her family are healthy, that she is a 'convert' to open-air living and that her family now all sleep outdoors.[65] Sanatoria aimed to produce, and evidently did produce, reformed rather than 'cured' consumptives, whose hygienic conduct not only prevented further infection but who were advocates of open-air living in the community, exemplars of hygienic citizenship.

Conclusion

In the introductory chapter to this book, we discussed the multiple rationales of isolation which often co-existed in any given place or practice of exclusion: rationales of prevention, of therapy, of correction, of cure and of restoration. And we discussed the common constitution of the isolated as simultaneously dangerous and vulnerable, qualities of individuals and populations which often invited and incited the intervention of paternal and welfarist states. The early twentieth-century sanatorium aptly illustrates these ideas. Newly imagined as an infectious disease associated with urbanisation and industrialisation, tuberculosis was re-conceptualised within longstanding spatial strategies of segregation. Those with symptoms and, importantly, those who were symptomless carriers, found them-selves caught within a discourse of dangerousness, one manifestation of which was a modern form of quarantine: the sanatorium. But I have also discussed and suggested the nature of this institution *as modern*, as one which worked as much through 'voluntary' submission to an institution of isolation, and disciplinary practices therein, as through coerced and legislated means of exclusion. Sanatoria represented preventive isolation, thus protection of the general community, but also therapeutic isolation, which took the form of a programme of re-training and disciplining into healthy and safe living. Part of this programme was removal from family and home influences to restorative sanctuary-isolation in 'nature'.

Studying the sanatorium as an institution of isolation also poses questions about modes of governance. In the management of tuberculosis one can see not only the retention of sovereign powers of removal, quarantine and detention which had long been used in epidemics of various kinds, but also their extension to other cat-egories of 'dangerousness'. Powers of notification and removal expanded around the turn of the century, and specialist institutions of isolation like the sanatorium for consumptives became expensive responsibilities of welfare governments, as well as of charitable and private organisations. These extensive and, importantly, new powers, mechanisms and imperatives for the confinement of the diseased and dangerous need much further explanation within medical sociology and within scholarship on dangerousness and risk: as innovations of the late nineteenth and early twentieth century, they sit uncomfortably with the implied chronology of the scholarship. But it is also the case that this theoretical framework offers an impor-tant and fresh way to assess the sanatorium. If the emerging 'new public health' of the twentieth century was based on widespread self-policing and self-governance, then one can see the sanatorium as a site for this kind of disciplining of the self, but importantly still within a bounded carceral space. That some people were placed in this carceral–therapeutic space by law, and others by 'choice', not only represents the working of a highly classed culture, it also suggests the sanatorium as a transitional site between modes of governance of (the health of) populations.

Notes

1　This argument is developed with respect to tuberculosis, smallpox and leprosy in A. Bashford, *Imperial Hygiene: A Critical History of Colonialism, Nationalism and Public Health*, London, Palgrave, forthcoming.

2　D. Armstrong, 'Public health spaces and the fabrication of identity', *Sociology*, 1993, vol. 27, pp. 393–410.

3　M. Foucault, *Discipline and Punish*, Harmondsworth, Penguin, 1991, p. 198; A. Petersen and D. Lupton, *The New Public Health: Health and Self in the Age of Risk*, London, Sage, 1996. See also T. Osborne, 'Of health and statecraft', in A. Petersen and R. Bunton (eds)

Foucault, Health and Medicine, London and New York, Routledge, 1997, pp. 173–88; A. Petersen, 'Risk, governance and the new public health', in Alan Petersen and Robin Bunton (eds) *Foucault, Health and Medicine*, pp. 189–206.

4   A. Bashford, *Purity and Pollution: Gender, Embodiment and Victorian Medicine*, London, Macmillan, 1998, pp. 78–83; A. Bashford and M. Nugent, 'Leprosy and the management of race, sexuality and nation in tropical Australia', in A. Bashford and C. Hooker (eds) *Contagion: Historical and Cultural Studies*, London, Routledge, 2001, pp. 106–28.

5   R. Castel, 'From dangerousness to risk', in G. Burchell, C. Gordon and P. Miller (eds) *The Foucault Effect: Studies in Governmentality*, Chicago, University of Chicago Press, 1991, pp. 281–98. Castel's article draws from M. Foucault, 'About the concept of the "dangerous individual" in 19th century legal psychiatry', in D.N. Weisstub (ed.) *Law and Psychiatry*, Toronto, Pergamon Press, 1978, pp. 1–18.

6   Castel, 'From dangerousness to risk', pp. 283, 286.

7   Foucault, 'About the concept of the "dangerous individual"', p. 17.

8   Castel, 'From dangerousness to risk', p. 283.

9   Castel, 'From dangerousness to risk', p. 283.

10 Linda Bryder argues for the proliferation of sanatoria as part of a culture of institutions and institutionalisation. But it is worth pursuing her insight by asking further questions about what institutionalisation meant, as a practice of isolation of the undesirable and as a practice of reform and correction. See L. Bryder, *Below the Magic Mountain*, Oxford, Clarendon Press, 1988, p. 29.

11 See G. Mooney, 'Public health versus private practice: the contested development of compulsory infectious disease notification in late-nineteenth-century Britain', *Bulletin of the History of Medicine*, 1999, vol. 73, pp. 238–67; D. Porter and R. Porter, 'The enforcement of health: the British debate', in E. Fee and D. M. Fox (eds) *AIDS: The Burdens of History*, Berkeley, University of California Press, 1988, pp. 97–120; J.M. Eyler, 'Scarlet fever and confinement: the Edwardian debate over isolation hospitals', *Bulletin of the History of Medicine*, 1987, vol. 61, pp. 1–24.

12 See especially J. Walzer Leavitt, *Typhoid Mary: Captive to the Public's Health*, Beacon Press, Boston, 1996.

13 See N. Rose, *Governing the Soul: The Shaping of the Private Self*, New York, Routledge, 1990, p. 2.

14 N. Rose, *Powers of Freedom*, Cambridge, Cambridge University Press, 1999. But on the recent trend towards detention see R. Coker, *From Chaos to Coercion: Detention and the Control of Tuberculosis*, New York, St Martin's Press, 2000.

15 L. Bryder, 'The Papworth village settlement – a unique experiment in the treatment and care of the tuberculous?' *Medical History*, 1984, vol. 28, p. 373.

16 Twelve institutions in 1899 and 223 by 1916. See M.E. Teller, *The Tuberculosis Movement: A Public Health Campaign in the Progressive Era*, New York, Greenwood Press, 1988, p. 82.

17 K. Ott, *Fevered Lives*, Cambridge, Mass., Harvard University Press, 1996, p. 70.

18 H. Hyslop Thomson, *Tuberculosis and Public Health*, London, Longmans, Green, 1920, p. 1.

19 States of Australia, *Report on Consumption*, Melbourne, Government Printer, 1911, p. 6.

20 W. Ramsay Smith, *On Consumption*, Melbourne, Mason, Firth and McCutcheon, 1909, p. 9.

21 'The greatest enemy of the human race: the duty of the state', *Sydney Daily Telegraph*, 1 October 1901, in Newspaper Cuttings on Tuberculosis, 1901–17, Mitchell Library Folio 616.2/N.

22 *Report on Consumption*, p. 8.

23 See chapters by P. Gay y Blasco and E. Blue respectively.

24 J.W. Springthorpe, 'The Great White Plague', in *Social Sins*, The Church of England Social Questions Committee, Melbourne, 1912, p. 46.

25 See Queen Victoria Homes for Consumptives Fund, *Annual Reports*, 1899–1921.
26 'The greatest enemy of the human race', *Sydney Daily Telegraph*, 1 October 1901, in Newspaper Cuttings on Tuberculosis, 1901–17, Mitchell Library Folio 616.2/N.
27 Waterfall Home for Consumptives, Case Histories, 1909–10, X648, State Records Authority of NSW.
28 Report of the Director-General of Public Health, NSW LA, *Papers*, 1914–45, p. 153.
29 D. Lupton, *Risk*, Routledge, London, 1999, p. 92.
30 *Report on Consumption*, p. 7.
31 Sir P.S. Jones, 'Discussion upon the dissemination of tuberculosis', *Australasian Association for the Advancement of Science*, 1911, vol. 13, p. 701.
32 Department of Public Health, Victoria, *Greenvale Sanatorium for Consumptives: Notes on Pulmonary Tuberculosis (Consumption) and on the Sanatorium Treatment of the Disease*, 5th edn, Melbourne, J. Kemp, Government Printer, 1912, p. 5.
33 See Bashford and Nugent, 'Leprosy and the management of race, sexuality and nation in tropical Australia', pp. 106–28. But for the counter-argument in a different context, see W. Anderson, 'Leprosy and citizenship', *positions*, 1998, vol. 6, pp. 707–30.
34 E. Goffman, *Asylum*, Harmondsworth, Penguin, 1961.
35 *Greenvale Sanatorium for Consumptives*, pp. 8–9.
36 F.J. Drake, 'Sanatorium treatment of pulmonary tuberculosis', *Australasian Medical Congress, Transactions*, Session 8, 1908, p. 153.
37 See Anon, *Letters from a Sanatorium*, Melbourne, George Robertson, 1907, p. 15.
38 Anon, *Letters from a Sanatorium*, pp. 10–11.
39 For example, the penitentiary, the Argentinian 'houses of deposit' and psychiatric institutions. See chapters by K. Ruggiero and M. Finnane respectively.
40 H. Hyslop Thomson, *Tuberculosis and Public Health*, London, Longmans, Green, 1920, p. 75.
41 *Greenvale Sanatorium for Consumptives*, p. 13.
42 R. Walker, 'The struggle against pulmonary tuberculosis in Australia, 1877–1950', *Historical Studies*, 1983 vol. 20, p. 439–59.
43 J.G. Hislop, 'The control of pulmonary tuberculosis: sanatorium treatment', *MJA*, May 1924, vol. 31, p. 528.
44 Walker, 'The struggle against pulmonary tuberculosis', p. 456.
45 *Letters from a Sanatorium*, pp. 10–11.
46 A. Evelyn, 'A cure for tuberculosis', *The Lone Hand*, 1 August 1911, p. 312.
47 A.H. Gault, 'A plea for the sanatorium treatment of consumption', *Intercolonial Medical Congress of Australasia*, 1902, p. 515.
48 Anon, *Letters from a Sanatorium*.
49 Sir J. Kingston, cited in J.G. Hislop, 'The control of pulmonary tuberculosis', p. 531.
50 Hislop, 'The control of pulmonary tuberculosis', p. 529.
51 Rose, *Governing the Soul*, p. 10.
52 This is a very different kind of isolation from the arbitrary detention which Coker argues is becoming more common in the current global management of tuberculosis. R.J. Coker, 'Civil liberties and public good: detention of tuberculosis patients and the *Public Health Act* 1984', *Medical History*, 2001, vol. 45, pp. 339–56.
53 *Letters from a Sanatorium*, p. 9.
54 *Letters from a Sanatorium*, p. 59.
55 *Letters from a Sanatorium*, p. 59.
56 *Letters from a Sanatorium*, pp. 59–60.
57 *Letters from a Sanatorium*, pp. 10–11.
58 *Letters from a Sanatorium*, p. 21.
59 *Greenvale Sanatorium for Consumptives*, pp. 11–19.
60 *Greenvale Sanatorium for Consumptives*, p. 19.
61 *Report on Consumption*, p. 7.

62 W. Ramsay Smith, *On Consumption*, Melbourne, Mason, Firth and McCutcheon, 1909, p. 9.
63 C. Bage, 'The treatment of consumptives in private practice', *Australasian Medical Congress Transactions*, 1911, vol. 1, p. 221.
64 *Letters from a Sanatorium*, p. 13.
65 *Letters from a Sanatorium*, pp. 61–2, 70.

Part III

Banishment, exile and exclusion

10 Patterns of exclusion on Robben Island, 1654–1992

Harriet Deacon

Robben Island, probably best known as Nelson Mandela's prison between 1964 and 1982, has played a key role in South African history. Since the sixteenth century, it has been used as a place of exclusion: variously for political dissidents, criminals, people and animals under quarantine, sex-workers, 'lunatics', 'lepers', and black and female military trainees. While the historical construction of the space has been deeply exclusionary, after the democratic transition of 1994 the Island has been reinterpreted in the official imagination as a site of nation-building and a symbol of national reconciliation. Always a geographically marginal and isolated site, Robben Island has operated as a symbolic container within which the contradictions[1] inherent in the development of a mainland identity have been played out.

Apartheid South Africa (1948–94) was modelled on a fantasy of exclusion. Following their colonial predecessors, but becoming more rigorous and violent in its methods, successive Nationalist governments after 1948 radically restructured society in less than a generation, implementing the 'most ambitious contemporary exercise in applied geography'.[2] The apartheid system defined people as 'Africans', 'Indians', 'coloureds' and 'whites' during the 1950s and then forcibly segregated them territorially (into 'homelands'), residentially (in towns and cities) and through petty apartheid practices (in public amenities and commercial enterprises).[3] This had benefits for the white population, white government and white industry by ensuring disproportional benefits, ownership of capital and political rights. Those participating in the growing opposition to these practices were imprisoned, put under house arrest, detained without trial, tortured, murdered, or removed from society in other ways. After the 1960s, because of anti-apartheid lobbying locally and abroad, the country was itself excluded by some nations from international cultural exchange, sport and trade opportunities. Both in its internal and its international relations, therefore, South Africa was marked by exclusion.

As an apartheid prison, Robben Island was both agent and symbol of the exclusionary state. From 1960 to 1992 it housed over 2,000 political prisoners,[4] all of whom were black men serving prison sentences. By sending them to the Island, the state attempted to isolate them from news of mainland struggles and to prevent their mainland supporters from seeing them or helping them. News blackouts about the Island and its prisoners were broken only briefly for pro-government propaganda. In fact, prisoners often knew what was happening on the mainland.

Prisoners communicated with supporters and each other, while campaigns for their release intensified at home and abroad. With increased mainland instability and economic decline, negotiations between the Nationalists and the African National Congress (ANC) began in the 1980s, and all political prisoners were released by 1992. By this time, used as a rallying point by anti-apartheid campaigns, Robben Island began to symbolise resistance to oppression, the reintegration of South Africa into the democratic world, and the development of a democratic human rights culture. Ironically, former prisoners like Mandela have sometimes referred to their time in prison in positive terms as well as negative – as a time of personal growth and education in preparation for democratic rule, unfettered by police harassment and day-to-day concerns on the mainland.

How does one understand a site of exclusion such as Robben Island both as a geographical entity and as a symbolic container for broader political discourses? Using maps to 'inject geographical sensitivity'[5] into Robben Island's history, this chapter will examine the ways in which the physical space of Robben Island has become inscribed with exclusionary discourses. Maps both represent and construct these meanings and relationships – in this context, representing a nexus of imperial power, knowledge and capital.[6] In addition, the chapter will explore some of the interrelationships between different exclusionary discourses on the Island. During the course of this discussion, I wish to make two major points: first, that the construction of a discourse of exclusion about Robben Island was firmly connected to its role as a 'mother-node' of colonialism in Southern Africa; and second, that different exclusionary discourses have produced complex gradations of isolation on the Island itself.

Exclusion: mother-node and margin

Robben Island was the first site to be effectively controlled by Europeans in Southern Africa. It was a launching pad for the colonial effort in Africa and the East Indies, playing an important, even essential, role in provisioning European sailors after 1498 and ensuring the survival of the Dutch East India Company (DEIC) 'refreshment station' established at Cape Town in 1652.[7] Robben Island also protected Cape Town from outside incursions during times of instability, as it was perfectly positioned to guard both sea channels into Table Bay. Robben Island was thus a mother-node of colonialism, a safe haven from which colonists established and protected their interests on the African sub-continent.

Because it was so firmly under colonial control, Robben Island could be used to silence and exclude those who presented a threat to the advance of colonial power on the mainland. One can map the expansion of the colonial frontier in South Africa by tracing the origins of political prisoners who were sent to Robben Island. The first prisoners came from the Cape Town area in the 1650s. During the eighteenth century, prisoners trickled in from indigenous groups in the hinterland and from Dutch incursions into East Asia. By the nineteenth century, as the British colonial frontier advanced in a new series of bloody encounters, political prisoners were sent to the Island from each new area of conquest – mainly in the north and east.[8] At the same time, Robben Island was used to police internal boundaries on which rested the power and safety of the colonial state: employer–employee and master–slave relations, political activity, criminality, white poverty, infectivity and unreason. These internal boundaries could be seen as new frontiers of control. The increased use of political imprisonment under apartheid rule from 1960 onwards was part of a state project to crush opposition to new oppressive and discriminatory legislation, and particularly the emergence of strong and increasingly militant political organisations after 1960. Key black leaders were picked out of these organisations and sent to the Island, in the same way that leaders from East Asia and South African colonial frontiers had been banished in the past.

Robben Island is a geographically and symbolically marginal site which, paradoxically, came to represent the core of apartheid and colonialism, and later, the essence of the new South Africa. Geographical position (midway along the European spice route) and natural resources (penguins, seals, water and a harbour) played an important role in the development of Robben Island as a mother-node of colonialism, but these resources only became useful within the specific historical context of an extractive colonialism focused on the spice trade and the lack of a local seafaring population at the Cape. For much of its history, Robben Island has been a place of banishment, associated with political opposition, insanity, criminality, dirt, disease and the poorer classes.[9] The usefulness of the Island as both pantry and prison depended on *controlling* access and egress, not preventing it. Most of the land on Robben Island has always been state-owned; private use has been limited, and access to the Island and information about it has been strictly monitored and controlled. Its reputation as a secure citadel of colonial power has also been bolstered by the long tradition of imprisonment and banishment of people there. These factors have all heightened the symbolic power of the place.

Oliver Tambo commented in 1980 that '[t]he tragedy of Africa, in racial and political terms [has been] concentrated in the southern tip of the continent – in South Africa, Namibia, and, in a special sense, Robben Island'.[10] Although the Cape is not actually the southernmost tip of the African continent, it is often symbolically referred to as such.[11] For much of the last five centuries, the Island has represented a no-man's land on the frontier between Africa and Europe – a political purgatory. As J.H. Jacobs has argued: 'Topologically and symbolically Robben Island … represented the ultimate margin to which the Pretoria Government banished its opposition.'[12] Just as a boundary line defines the size and shape of a country, Robben Island's very marginality makes it critical to the visualisation of the centre. This symbolic function is strengthened by the fact that Robben Island is positioned at colonialism's origin, its mother-node, as well as its extremity in Southern Africa.

Mapping exclusionary discourses on to the Island

Maps and paintings can be read in conjunction with documentary and oral sources to help understand how broad discourses of resource exploitation, protection and exclusion were mapped on to the Island site, creating their own interrelationships and patterns there. Before the mid seventeenth century, maps of Africa were usually drawn on a relatively large scale and thus show little detail on Robben Island, if they show it at all.[13] This changed with Dutch settlement of the Cape as the DEIC took mapmaking very seriously. Early Dutch maps were mainly portolan charts of bays and coastlines, but this information was gradually incorporated into larger maps of Southern Africa.[14] There has been some debate as to whether the Dutch cartographers were abreast of eighteenth-century developments in mapping technologies,[15] mainly caused by the fact that the DEIC guarded its maps very closely from the prying eyes of the British.[16]

After the British took the Cape in 1795 and again in 1806, new cartographic surveys were done, but many of the Robben Island maps published in the early nineteenth century were simply copies of early eighteenth-century maps. Maps of Robben Island did not reach the level of accuracy of modern maps until the mid 1890s.[17] Better mapping methods were introduced during the South African War (1899–1902), because of the need for military intelligence. After this war, two survey commissions recommended a general survey programme for the Union, and in 1933 aerial photography first began to be used for this purpose in South Africa, partly as a result of the advances in military aircraft use during World War I.[18] Under military security during the war and prison regulations after 1960, however, maps were not publicly available. Even today, it has been more difficult to get access to twentieth-century maps of the Island than to find eighteenth-century maps.

For the purposes of this paper, we are less interested in technological change in cartography or in assessing accuracy than in the cultural process of mapping.[19] In examining the maps, it is clear that there are continuities in the spatial expression of exclusionary discourses, and that these are racialised and gendered. There are also differences in the degree to which various groups on the Island, such as prisoners, patients and staff, were separated from each other at different times and segregated within different institutions. Much has been written about discriminatory treatment in this context,[20] but little attention has so far been paid to spatial distributions.

The north-eastern end of the Island has been repeatedly associated with the political imprisonment of black men. The critical importance of control over the sandy anchorage and beach at the north-east of the Island was a key factor in the situating of the first dwellings here in 1654. The Dutch prison was established just behind the beach in 1657, housing staff and slaves close to both black and white prisoners, mainly male. Although institutional staff and most prisoners were shifted to the village area in the south-east of the Island under British rule from 1808 to 1846, black male political prisoners were housed in huts just north of the landing-place until 1869, if not later. The naval-run criminal prison (c.1952–61) and the first apartheid prison (1960–4) – for black men only – were also situated near the landing-place. The maximum-security prison built by prisoners in 1963–4 was sited just inland of the original DEIC prison structure and the harbour. An interesting exception to this trend was the building of a female leprosy settlement north of the landing-place in 1887. Its extreme distance from the village and the male leprosy settlement (moved to just outside the village in 1891), and the fact that female patients were moved off the Island entirely for twenty years before 1887, indicates the concern about leprosy being spread through sex, and about the patients' supposedly heightened sexuality.

The highest point of the Island, in the south, was used as part of the security apparatus of the DEIC from the 1650s. Here, the current lighthouse was erected in 1863–4. In 1808 a British prison was constructed at the foot of the hill, on an area that had been used for gardens in the late eighteenth century. With the addition of a church, parsonage and class-differentiated housing, it grew into a prison village by the 1840s. In 1846 when the prison was relocated to the mainland and a 'leper', 'lunatic' and 'chronic sick' asylum was established, the buildings were simply reused, accommodating all institutions within the bounds of the village. Over the next century or so, the village was shaped symbolically and physically as a 'whites-only' domestic space. By the turn of the twentieth century, asylum staff began to be formally assessed for 'whiteness' – one applicant deemed too 'black' for employment was sent home.[21] All prison and hospital institutions with black inmates had been moved outside the village or off the Island by the 1920s. When fear of contagion from leprosy reached its peak in the 1890s, leprosy patients were relocated outside the village, separated from it by a 'Boundary Road', which they were not permitted to cross. The chronic sick hospital in the village was closed in 1891 and the asylum in the 1920s. In World War II, 'coloured' gunnery trainees were accommodated not in village barracks but in tents to the north of the village. 'Coloured' warders, removed from the Island after 1963, also seem to have been housed on the northern edge of the village.

The village was thus gradually domesticated and whitewashed, with male leprosy patients and criminals forming a first line of exclusion, before the most threatening of all – political prisoners. Since at least the eighteenth century, Robben Island had been an unusually 'perfect' colonial community: all black residents were institutionalised, and staff were overwhelmingly white. These groups were gradually polarised geographically, with the south-east village area becoming whiter and the north-east blacker. This required some effort because Robben Island's white residents were tainted by the negative image of the Island as a site of exclusion and 'blackness'. In the eighteenth, the nineteenth, and to a certain extent also the twentieth century, Island staff were made up of people who had struggled to gain social status on the mainland and thus achieve whiteness.[22] This resulted in a particularly marked social anxiety around the representation of the village as white and middle-class. The dialectic between black and white, male and female, prison and village, was expressed in spatial terms on Robben Island. One could thus describe the Island as a place that held within it all the contradictions and tensions of colonial rule.[23]

These broad trends will now be explored in greater detail with reference to specific maps.

The lure of empty land, 1654–1700

In the first years of colonial settlement in South Africa, Robben Island was a Dutch East India Company *buitenpost*, a rough farm more pantry than prison.[24]

Many of the early Robben Island maps can be found on larger maps designed to aid navigation of the Cape coastline. As Paul Carter argues,[25] where a land's interior had not been adequately surveyed using triangulation methods, inaccurate hand-drawn patterns of mountain and bay profiles along the coastline were the only way of surveying extended lines of coast. He suggests that coastline mapping should be read as a 'desire for signification', for power over the interior.[26] In the Robben Island case, where the Island could be mapped before the mainland, sailors and early settlers derived powerful benefits from their knowledge and control of the Island: water, food, protected grazing and shelter from storms – all without having to barter with indigenes. These early maps also help us to understand the key role played by the access point for boats on the sandy beach in relation to later patterns of settlement on the Island.

Its small band of Khoi having left after only eight years for more abundant pastures in 1638, there was no one living on Robben Island when the DEIC settlers arrived in 1652. The first map we have of the Island after 1652 depicts an easy anchorage off an empty, fertile island (see Figure 10.1).[27] This emphasised the need to control resources, which was necessary because Company employees at the Cape were already in conflict with indigenes on the mainland. Robben Island was at the edge of the contact zone, giving both symbolic and material support to settler representations of an empty land of opportunity on the continent, where indigenes had already been erased from the contact zones on European-made maps.[28]

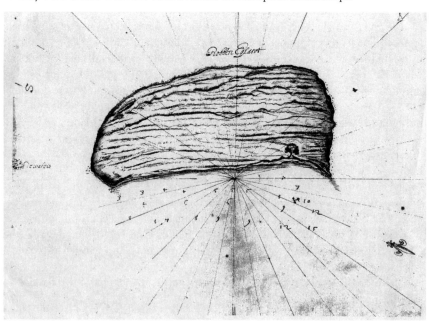

Figure 10.1 Map of Robben Island in 1654 by Blaeu, showing empty landscape and tree
Source: Cape Archives M1/10

Most maps of the period before 1700 were designed for sailing to or past the Island.[29] This, and the role of the Island, affected both what was felt worthy of representation on maps of this period (rocks, the landing-place) and what was sometimes not included (hills, buildings, quarries). A particular tree was shown prominently on several early maps.[30] It offered sailors a natural landmark close to the only natural landing-place and a source of fresh water. The tree may also have been used to mark the site of the postal stone. On a map of 1722 by Van Keulen, a note next to the tree says (in Dutch), 'This tree used to be the mark, but is no longer'. Next to the building, which has a flag, he notes, 'Company's house on which the mark is now placed'.[31] This could explain why depictions of the tree are more common on maps drawn before 1700 than are depictions of dwellings on the Island. A shed was erected for two DEIC employees and their sheep as early as March 1654, acting as a prison from 1657 onwards. Robben Island was a base for lime-digging and stone-cutting activities too, critical for building the new settlement on the mainland, and a signal fire served as both lighthouse and warning of enemy ships. Some of the early maps omit these dwellings entirely, but it seems that by the 1660s there were at least two dwellings near the landing-place.[32]

Knowledge of the landing-place on the sandy beach and the location of dangerous rocks was essential for the access of European boats at this period. It was not only the key piece of information sailors needed to know from their maps, but also the only point of access and egress from the Island. The landing-place, marked on every map, was almost certainly the most important factor in the siting of the first dwellings. Controlling the access point essentially meant having control over the resources (including imprisonment) that the Island offered the DEIC.

'The boss's house', 1700–80

Although many of the maps in this period still show little detail of the Island, they are testimony to the increasing interest of and control by the DEIC of the immediate hinterland, and the exploration of the coastal areas to the north-west and south-east of the Cape.[33] Sometimes Robben Island's resources are thus ignored in favour of documenting potentially fertile areas on the mainland.[34] Nevertheless, maps now more regularly show detail on the Island: the two small bays;[35] two dwellings and the tree near the landing-place;[36] the signal post on the hill and the *posthouder*'s house. An undated but probably early eighteenth-century map shows three buildings (one with a flag) at the southern end and two (one with a flag) at the northern end of the Island.[37] Potentially dangerous rocky outcrops start being named,[38] and the placement of guns at the southern end and on the landing-place is noted on some maps.[39] Both the lighthouse and the guns were part of an early security warning and defence system.

Before the nineteenth century, imprisonment was not a major form of punishment in any European country or colony, hanging, mutilation and transportation being far more common.[40] Robben Island thus functioned more as a hard labour camp and transportation site than as a formal prison. Before the 1780s the Island prison was represented in many maps as a house or *loosje*,[41] marked also as '*d baas zyn woning'* (the boss's dwelling).[42] The prison was thus presented as an extension of the settler household, where slaves lived and worked under the often harsh rule of their masters, rather than as an institution whose function was to remove criminals from society. Prison labour outside the institution was key to its functioning. Van Keulen's map of 1700 is titled *Robben Eylant – Daer de Slaven Inde Ketting Loopen* (Robben Island – there the slaves *walk* in chains). From the very beginning, prisoner mobility within the bounds of the Island was critical in exploiting Robben Island's natural resources.

The importance of the Island's natural resources begins to be expressed in the maps during this period, which indicates their changing focus from sailing past the Cape to settling it. One of the most interesting views of Robben Island during this period is a rare panorama drawn by R.J. Gordon in 1777, a detailed view of the eastern coast of the Island.[43] The farm-like quality of the Island prison is evident in the wide distribution of activities outside the prison buildings (stone-cutting, lime- and stone-quarrying, gardening, travelling to Dassen Island for seal culling), and the description of the prison itself as 'prisoners' living quarters'.

The Dutch prison, 1780–95 and 1803–6

After 1780, Dutch and French concern to protect their interests in the Cape from the British[44] intensified the process of map-making on both sides. The defence system at the Cape was rapidly developed, using French consultants. There are many more maps of Robben Island during this period therefore (see Figure 10.2), showing greater detail than before: rocks, soundings, landing-places and hills, buildings, quarries, gardens, wells, paths.

Once the British had taken the Cape for the first time in 1795, they sent one of their naval lieutenants to survey the Island (see Figure 10.3).[45] Although the prison rolls seem to indicate that prisoners were still held on the Island during the first British occupation (1795–1803) and Batavian rule (1803–6),[46] this 1798 map describes the buildings (similar in position and size to those represented in the Gordon Panorama of 1777) as 'ruined',[47] as did a survey in 1805.[48]

By the end of the eighteenth century, Robben Island was firmly associated in the colonial imagination with the exclusion of negatively defined elements and thereby with blackness. Even at the beginning of colonial settlement at the Cape, when racial relations were relatively fluid, Company employees with black wives were chosen to be Robben Island's first *posthouders*. Since all slaves were black, the sub-title of the Van Keulen map of 1700, *Daer de Slaven Inde Ketting Loopen*, is also testimony to the developing iconic status of the Island as black, although white Company servants were also banished to the Island. (In fact, the earliest surviving prison rolls show that in 1728 there were twenty-six white and only sixteen black prisoners.)[49] The association of the Island with blackness was both informed and cemented by the later predominance of black inmates in the colonial prisons, the hospitals and the apartheid prison after 1960 in which almost all of the prisoners were black men.

As racism became entrenched on the mainland, segregation of white staff and white inmates from black inmates at Robben Island became more important both

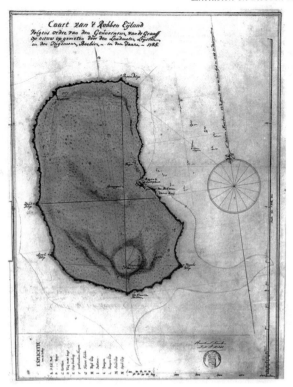

Figure 10.2 Map of Robben Island in 1785 by Leijsten and Barbier, showing gardens, quarries, signal places and houses

Source: Cape Archives M1/902

to white residents of the Island and to the authorities. By 1803 at least, prisoners on the Island were racially segregated.[50] Prisoners, who were divided into *Indiaanen* (black) and *Europeaanen* (white) on the prison rolls from 1728 onwards, may have been racially segregated during the eighteenth century too, with black prisoners housed in a section called *die kraal*, probably a former sheep shed, and white prisoners in the *bandiet huisje* (prisoners' house) as early as 1735.[51] In line with segregatory trends in mainland institutions, however, black and white inmates in the Dutch colonial prison were still housed in the same building, and spatial distinctions between staff and inmates were probably only slightly exaggerated compared to those between master and slave on Dutch colonial farms. This was to change in the years to follow.

The village, 1808–1931

From the eighteenth century onwards, the focus of larger-scale maps of the Cape moved inland, affirming and recording the growth of the colony, and further marginalising Robben Island. With the increased use of Simonstown as a winter

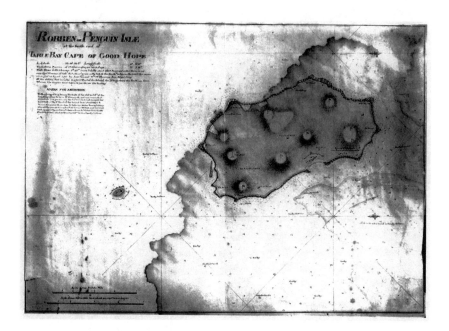

Figure 10.3 Map of Robben Island in 1798 by Rice, showing ruins of Dutch prison
Source: Cape Archives M288

anchorage, the establishment of a more self-sufficient settlement and the exclusion of Khoisan from the peninsula, the use of the Island as a safe anchorage in stormy weather, or as a pantry, had become less critical by the mid-eighteenth century. Late eighteenth-century maps of the Island were relatively numerous and drawn in some detail mainly because of the security advantages the Island offered during wartime. Although a detailed map of the Island was drawn by a British lieutenant, Rice, in 1798 (see Figure 10.3), one of the maps of the Cape Peninsula coast just after the first British occupation began in 1795 did not show Robben Island at all – an omission that would have been unthinkable in the seventeenth century.[52] By the late nineteenth century, maps of the Island show buildings in great detail, which demonstrates growing colonial interest in the erection of new buildings for the Island institutions. By this time, maps of the Cape of Good Hope are maps of a mainland settlement rather than of a port as viewed from the sea. Robben Island had become an institutional site outside the town rather than an intrinsic part of the settlement.

Before 1808, all colonial dwellings on Robben Island were located either on the signal hill or around the landing-place. When the British took the Cape for the second time in 1806, they granted a tract of Robben Island land to the British-born whaler John Murray at his request. At this time, it is relatively certain that the Robben Island prisoners were being held in the Amsterdam Battery near the Cape Town harbour,[53] and the British authorities may have decided to stop using the Island as a prison. Two years after Murray had set up his whaling station on the

Island, when the authorities decided to re-establish the prison, they had to build a new settlement in what is now known as the village area, in the south-east of the Island. The British authorities soon appreciated the value of controlling the landing-site when a group of prisoners escaped in Murray's boat in 1820. They ordered Murray to leave immediately, paying him out for his improvements.

Many boats still used the beach for landing, according to paintings and photographs of the time. This may not have been far from the village: according to contemporary maps,[54] the main beach was now situated more or less in the middle of the eastern coast of the Island. What is now a small stony cove in the village area was also used for landing – it may have been more sandy 150 years ago. Although beaches may have shifted since the eighteenth century and disappeared by now, the differences between nineteenth-century maps in their depiction of beaches and landing-places is also quite marked. The authorities became so confident of control over boats at the old landing-site, or so tied into a negative stereotyping of the north-eastern end of the Island, that it became the most marked exclusionary zone. They located political prisoners there from 1858 to 1869, and female leprosy patients there from 1887.

During the course of the nineteenth century, maps of the Island show the development of the village as the main dwelling area.[55] A French map of 1824 suggests that there may have been use of the northern end of the Island but British maps of the early to mid nineteenth century suggest that the village area was the only significant settlement, interestingly labelled as the 'fishery' rather than the prison or the hospital.[56] Detailed maps before 1890 are rare, although there are two good maps of the village area.[57] By 1933, when the leprosy wards had all been destroyed, the only buildings remaining on the Island were south of Boundary Road.[58] The village was increasingly constructed as a domestic zone as well as an institutional one. The Anglican church, built in 1841 and prominently marked and labelled on most subsequent maps, formed the central core of the village. Aside from the church, parsonage and main house, for much of the nineteenth century the village was dominated by its institutions, with staff housing adjunct to them. Ordinary staff housing only began to develop a separate identity in the 1870s, with the development of 'Irishtown' to the south-west and the Beach Road cottages to the north-east of the main road (see Figure 10.4). In the 1890s, a recreational club and sports facilities for staff helped give a middle-class gloss to the village.[59]

The general association of the Island with exclusion and blackness made it particularly important by the late nineteenth century for staff to create and preserve a white middle-class veneer. There was an added tension in the nineteenth century between the dominant image of the Island as a prison and its use as a hospital after 1846. Although nineteenth-century hospitals tended to be custodial institutions for the poor, and the Robben Island ones were particularly associated with exclusion and danger, there was an attempt to develop a curative rather than punitive approach to white institutionalisation in the asylum in the 1850s and the leprosy hospital in the 1890s.[60] In the 1850s and 1860s, the anomalous position of wealthier white inmates within the asylum was resolved within a 'moral-management' model based on cure, minimal restraint and recreational activity, such as

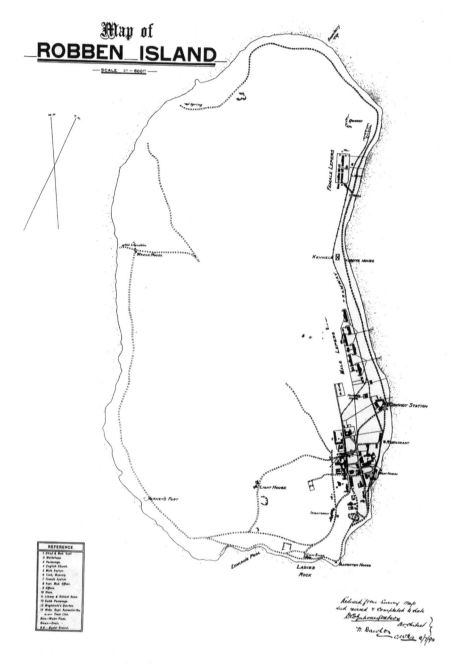

Figure 10.4 Map of Robben Island in 1894 by Watson and Dawson, showing the relocation of the leprosy institutions outside the village

Source: Cape Archives CCP 1/2/1/92 G4a–95

gardening. Gender and racial segregation were thus a feature of the asylum. Towards the end of the century, a curative model for white lunatics was well established, against a custodial model for black lunatics. The Robben Island asylum was associated with the latter, and housed only black inmates and 'incurable', dangerous whites.[61]

By the early twentieth century the brief tension between custody and cure at Robben Island was resolved in favour of custody, primarily for black inmates, and strongly associated with forced labour. Relations between staff and inmates were deeply influenced by master–servant models. Although this was true to some extent of all contemporary institutions, it was exaggerated by the particular polarisation of the Island community within a racialised colonial environment. The use of black prison labour has always characterised the South African prison system,[62] and for centuries provided the main vehicle for resource exploitation, construction and maintenance on the Island. The prison probably became gender-specific (male) and racially segregated by the early nineteenth century. Certainly by the 1950s, but probably as early as 1866, it housed only black male inmates. For black inmates of the hospitals and prisons on the Island, the experience of institutionalisation would have been very similar. Black female inmates of the nineteenth-century asylum did laundry and domestic work for the institutions and for senior staff, just like criminal prisoners in the 1980s. Labour needs often influenced institutional development. The application of moral-management systems, mainly to white patients, created a need for more labour in the 1860s, for example, so a criminal prison was re-established on the Island in 1866. In the early twentieth century, black lunatics who worked well at Robben Island were transferred to separate wards near a new white asylum at Valkenberg on the mainland, where there was a shortage of workers and no associated black prison to provide cheap labour.[63]

The importance of race, class and gender prejudice in the development of segregation within the Island's medical institutions was influenced by broader segregatory trends and the shift of power from Britain to the more openly racist Cape government after 1872. However, different stereotypes of disease and different race, class and gender patient ratios within each institution played a key role in determining when segregation was applied. Formal racial segregation emerged at different times in the three medical institutions: in the 1860s in the class- and racially mixed asylum, in the 1870s in the largely white but poor chronic sick hospital, and in the 1890s in the largely black leprosy hospital.[64] With the development of separate institutions for different racially defined groups on the mainland in the 1890s, the Robben Island institutions became blacker, housing only those white inmates considered most dangerous to the institutional system (dangerous lunatics, and leprosy patients who could not be segregated at home). Gender segregation was considered much more important in the asylum than the chronic sick hospital, which functioned more like a retirement home for poor white immigrants than a workhouse. In the leprosy hospital, gender segregation was not considered important at all until a resurgence of the notion that the disease was transmitted hereditarily in the 1860s led to the female leprosy patients being removed from the Island altogether until they were segregated in the harbour area in 1887.

With the shifting of the criminal prison outside the village area after 1866 and the gradual closure of village-based institutions after 1890, the village was on the way to being constructed as a white domestic space for staff families. Photographs of picnics, sports events, tram rides and spring flowers characterise the record of domestic life left by residents during this period. Patients and prisoners, although they would have worked in staff houses and interacted with staff families, were not depicted as part of village life. Photographs of prisoners during this period are entirely absent, as far as I can tell, but leprosy patients were photographed in organised recreational activities, monitored by staff, to show how well they were being treated, in spite of being forcibly incarcerated.[65]

Wartime barracks and military village, 1939–59

Except for the lighthouse keeper, the Island was abandoned between 1931 and 1939. After this date, it was redeveloped as a military defence and training station. At this time, more accurate mapping techniques were possible because of the introduction of aerial photography in the 1930s. The first contour map of the Island was drawn in 1933, presumably after an aerial photograph was taken (although we have not yet located it), and later maps were also based on aerial photographs. Accurate maps were necessary in wartime, but they had to be carefully protected for security reasons.

During the war, the Island housed a gunnery training school, but most of the other wartime facilities (gun batteries, observation points, degaussing ranges, naval sub-depot) were located outside the village. More houses for officers and female staff were built in the village and the old female asylum was converted into male barracks. In veteran reminiscences of wartime the village is characterised more as a barracks (complete with ghost stories) than a domestic space,[66] and this institutionalised identity only really changed once the war was over and naval officers relocated their families to the Island. In the 1950s, the idyllic image of semi-rural domestic village life evoked by the early twentieth-century residents was taken up again.[67]

A racialised and gendered construction of military service in South Africa meant that neither women nor black men were supposed to carry arms. In the 1940s, lack of sufficient white male volunteers (given that many Afrikaners supported the Nazis) forced the military to draft white women and black men into service as non-combatants and support personnel (although unofficially many black soldiers eventually carried arms). Because of the sensitivity of this issue within a sexist and racist milieu, much of the training of these new recruits took place on the Island.[68] One of the interesting features of this period is that although many black and white male soldiers came back from fighting on various fronts outside the country with a new, largely positive, appreciation of each other, few white veterans of Robben Island during the war, male and female, even remember any of the black soldiers as individuals.[69] Since the black soldiers were housed in tents outside the village during the war, they left no trace on the map of 1948 either. Even their memorial is unofficial, private and isolated – two circles of concrete inscribed with some of their names hidden in the bushes near the 9.2-inch gun battery. The relative invisibility of black gunners on Robben Island in the white, official account of the war may have had something to do with the fear in white society of sexual relations between black men and white women. This concern resurfaced with the use of criminal prisoners as domestic workers and cooks in the village after 1960.

The apartheid prison, 1960–91

Very few maps of this period were publicly available at the time, for security reasons. Some maps and plans have been retrieved from the Department of Public Works, the Office of Mapping and Surveys and the documentation handed over by the Department of Correctional Services when Robben Island ceased to be a prison in 1996. However, for this period there are still, ironically, many gaps in the documentary record.[70]

From 1960 the apartheid regime used an existing criminal prison system on Robben Island that had been developed by the navy in the early 1950s. The new prison used the same buildings and initially some of the same warders.[71] Now, however, the prison housed political as well as criminal prisoners.[72] The 1950s prison (for criminal black prisoners) had been a violent one. This institutional violence, too, was adopted and perhaps even embellished in the 1960s. Until they successfully challenged the system of forced labour quotas in the 1970s, prisoners were marched to the north-western quarry to fulfil their quotas of stone along the same routes documented by the maps of the 1780s and probably walked for the same purpose by eighteenth-century prisoners.[73] The quarried stone was used to build a new maximum-security prison, completed in 1964. Given the relative decline of prison walling in twentieth-century democracies,[74] it is interesting to note that boundary fencing for the Robben Island prisons was first introduced in the mid twentieth century under the repressive apartheid regime.[75] Ex-prisoner Robert Wilcox and others have suggested that within the maximum-security prison, internal walling to separate prison sections from each other actually increased during the 1980s.[76] Walling, fencing and dog runs were used to intimidate and divide prisoners; in preventing escapes, the ocean was a far more effective barrier.

At first, criminal and political prisoners were held together. After about 1970, however, they were separated.[77] Criminal prisoners were taken out of the maximum-security prison and moved nearer the village to what is called the 'Medium B' prison. According to some former political prisoners, this was necessary because they had converted criminal prisoners to their cause. Similarly, some former political prisoners suggest that 'coloured' warders were removed from the Island in 1963 because they were too sympathetic to the anti-apartheid cause.[78]

Apart from the conversion of the cricket pitch into a rugby field, the building of a putt-putt course and a swimming pool and the addition of a fake Cape Dutch gable to a flat-roofed house built in 1841, little structural change was effected in the village until a number of new houses were built in the 1980s.[79] As before, village life was often represented as a rural idyll, separate from the violence of the prison, although in practical terms this would have been impossible. Warder reminiscences dwell on the safe, farm-like atmosphere, in which they did not have to fear urban 'unrest' and common crime, although some also tell of drinking, domestic violence and the problems caused by criminals working as domestics for warders' wives.[80]

Conclusion

The construction of a discourse of exclusion centred on Robben Island was firmly connected to its role as a mother-node of colonialism in Southern Africa. It was one of the first sites controlled by European sailors and settlers, a starting point for colonisation of the African hinterland and therefore constructed as the 'tip' of Africa. Known and controlled by the colonial state, located behind the lines of advance, it was also an effective place of banishment for opponents on the colonial frontier. This was true of the expanding geographical frontier as well as the shifting frontiers of social control in the colony – control over infectious disease, white poverty and mental illness, for example. Robben Island was both agent and symbol of the exclusionary colonial and apartheid state, which sought to suppress mainland resistance by imprisoning leaders there, and to eliminate certain other undesirables through institutionalisation. It played a key role in defining the colonial ideal by excluding those who threatened that ideal.

An analysis of the cultural geography of the Island can show how exclusion from the mainland was only the first step in a series of further exclusions on the Island itself. Robben Island held within it all the contradictions of colonial society, policing both internally and externally the boundaries between white and black, good and bad, sane and insane, safe and dangerous, male and female. Along the eastern coast, different uses for the north- and south-eastern ends of the Island emerged over time. Although initially the only settlement, the north-eastern end has been primarily associated with imprisonment, mainly of black male political opponents, while the south-east has become a domesticated, feminised, white village space. In the liminal space between these two poles, criminals, leprosy patients, graveyards and a few special political prisoners occupied positions determined by gradations of social and physical exclusion. Within institutions, too, social distance was carefully regulated, based on social class, gender and racial classification. Continuities in the use of particular spaces, such as the use of the northern end of the Island for black male political prisoners, emerged over time.

The Island as a whole, and specific sites within it, have thus been used over and over again to exclude, to isolate and to differentiate. The Island is therefore both a liminal space and a defining space for the nation as a whole. It is a heavily overdetermined place, layered with repetition and meaning. With the transition to democracy in the 1990s, the Island has been as important in redefining the mainland ideal as it was during the various phases of colonial and apartheid rule. Since 1994 it has provided a location for the Mandela story, championing the ideal of human rights and, specifically, the role of reconciliation as forgiveness in effecting a democratic and peaceful transition. The Afrikaner nationalists' Great Trek towards freedom from British rule has been replaced as the official icon of national pride by Mandela's symbolic 'Long Walk to Freedom' from Robben Island. Always a place where boundaries were policed through exclusion, the Island has now become a museum representing the country's new inclusionary ethos. Because the Island is simultaneously central and marginal to the new nation, and is a bounded and separated site, it could also, more dangerously, represent the notion of reconciliation as forgetting or distancing of the past, locating the legacy of apartheid outside contemporary society, rather than within it.

Robben Island's value relies on holding the contradiction between past and present, the tension between old structures and new interpretations. This is particularly important in the absence of a major public building programme to represent the new South Africa. A cynic might argue that the success of the whole project of reconciliation between black and white in post-apartheid South Africa relies on a 'working ambiguity' of meaning attached to public places, an ambiguity that admits new interpretations without completely disrupting old ones. Less cynically, Robben Island works as a museum of the new South Africa precisely because it evokes both the horror of apartheid and, by its mere existence as a museum, apartheid's demise. As Bissell argues in the case of Zanzibar: 'How is it possible to create a post-colonial future out of the colonial past?'[81] It is difficult, and perhaps unnecessary, to see symbolic reinterpretation as a denial of the past. It may be essential for key nation-building sites to be inscribed with the scars of South Africa's past. New building projects would thus be inappropriate, not because the existing meanings of places are malleable or irrelevant, but because of the need to deal with the past in order to move forward.

Notes

1 P. MacKenzie, personal communication, 2001.
2 D.M. Smith cited in A. Lemon, 'Imposed separation', in M. Chisholm and D.M. Smith (eds) *Shared Space Divided Space*, London, Unwin Hyman, 1990, p. 195.
3 *Ibid.*, pp. 195–6.
4 In this paper, 'political prisoner' is used in the limited sense of a person who commits an illegal act for an organisation opposed to colonial or apartheid rule. Prior to the twentieth century, it is difficult to ascribe motive in this way, or to find political organisations of the type described above, so the term is used more loosely to include indigenous leaders or prisoners of war.
5 C. Philo, 'History, geography and the "still greater mystery"', in D. Gregory, R. Martin and G. Smith (eds) *Human Geography*, Minneapolis, University of Minnesota Press, 1994, pp. 252–81, p. 252.
6 A. McClintock, *Imperial Leather*, New York, Routledge, 1994, pp. 1, 3.
7 N. Penn, 'The Island under Dutch rule', in H.J. Deacon (ed.) *The Island: A History of Robben Island, 1488–1992*, Cape Town, David Philip and Mayibuye Books, 1996, p. 14.
8 Khwezi ka Mpumlwana and Deirdre Prins of the Robben Island Museum's Education Department have pointed out, quite rightly, that speaking of the northern or eastern frontier assumes that one is speaking from the perspective of the coloniser rather than the colonised.
9 This affected its place in the broader cultural geography of the Cape. See H.J. Deacon, 'The politics of medical topography in the Cape during the nineteenth century', in R. Wrigley and G. Revill (eds) *Pathologies of Travel*, Amsterdam, Rodopi,

2000, pp. 279–98 and H.J. Deacon, 'Landscapes of exile and healing', *South African Archaeological Bulletin*, 2001, vol. LV, no. 172, pp. 147–54.

10 Accepting the Jawaharlal Nehru Award for International Understanding in New Delhi, 1980, on behalf of Nelson Mandela who was then imprisoned on Robben Island. O. Tambo, *Preparing for Power: Oliver Tambo Speaks*, London, Heinemann, 1987, p. 199.

11 Z. Bialas, *Mapping Wild Gardens*, Essen, De Blaue Eule, 1997, p. 49.

12 J.H. Jacobs, 'Narrating the island', *Current Writing*, 1992, vol. 4, p. 74.

13 See, for example, the map of 'Aethopia' by J. Martinez, MS Douce 391 in the Bodleian Library, Oxford, UK.

14 This caused the exaggerated representations of bay areas in the early general maps. C. Koeman, 'Introduction', in C. Koeman (ed.) *Tabulae Geographicae Quibus Colonial Bonae Spei Antiqua Depingitur*, Cape Town, NV Hollandsch-Afrikaansche Uitgevers, 1952, p. 21.

15 Koeman, 'Introduction', in Koeman, *Tabulae Geographicae*, p. 17, says the Dutch maps were relatively accurate; J.C. Visagie, 'Karte, kartograwe en landmeters I', *Archiefnuus*, June 1966, p. 6, suggests that there was a decline in their accuracy during the second half of the eighteenth century, compared to the maps made by cartographers from other European countries, and that they only used triangulation techniques after 1850. This may be a result of the fact that many of the Dutch maps were secret: early triangulation of an area of the western Cape done by the French cartographer Abbé de la Caille (Cape Archives, Cape Town (CA) M1/166–7, 1752) was, however, used in a later map by the Dutch cartographer Tirion (CA M1/318, 1763).

16 Koeman, 'Introduction', in Koeman, *Tabulae Geographicae*, p. 14.

17 P. Riley, personal communication, 1993.

18 D.J. Buckley, 'Official maps of South Africa', in *Maps of Africa*, proceedings of the Symposium on Maps held at the South African Library, Cape Town on 24–26 November 1988, Cape Town, South African Library, 1989, pp. 73–4, 76.

19 D. Cosgrove, 'Introduction', in D. Cosgrove (ed.) *Mappings*, London, Reaktion Books, 1999, pp. 8–9.

20 H.J. Deacon, 'Racial segregation and medical discourse in nineteenth-century Cape Town', *Journal of Southern African Studies*, 1996, vol. 22, no. 2, pp. 287–308; H.J. Deacon, 'Racism and medical science in the Cape Colony', *Osiris*, 2000, vol. 15, pp. 190–206.

21 H.J. Deacon, 'Outside the profession', in A.M. Rafferty (ed.) *Nursing, Women's History and the Politics of Welfare*, London, Routledge, 1996, p. 94.

22 *Ibid.* p. 90.

23 Penny McKenzie, personal communication, 2001.

24 Penn, 'Robben Island 1488–1805', in Deacon (ed.) *The Island*, pp. 14–5.

25 P. Carter, 'Dark with excess of bright', in Cosgrove (ed.) *Mappings*, p. 125.

26 *Ibid.*, pp. 130–1.

27 CA M1/10.

28 Bialas, *Mapping Wild Gardens*, pp. 34–7, speaks of the depopulation of the contact zone in maps of the Cape after Dias.

29 An excellent example is the map CA M2/2, 1687, showing Robben and Dassen islands, the mainland coastline and minimal interior detail.

30 CA M2/5, 1661, is essentially a map for the sailor, showing only the Robben Island tree and anchorage, as well as the profile of Table Mountain and the Cape Town landing-site. CA M2/6, 1663, is similar in purpose, showing profiles of the whole coast, rocks, landing-places and, on Robben Island, a tree, anchorage, dwelling and grasses. Possibly an indigenous milkwood, the tree may have been the same one described in the 1777 Panorama as a 'bush, six foot high, the only one on the Island' (Gordon Panorama, CA M1/1106–7, 1777).

31 Table Bay MLC 0002003, maps by Van Keulen the elder, Amsterdam 1722, c.12.f.3, British Library, London.

32 See CA M1/11, 1656 (one dwelling at landing-place) and CA M2/6, 1663 (two dwellings at landing-place). In the British Library an undated seventeenth-century map shows one dwelling at the landing-place (Sloane Mss Add 5027, no. 15 – possibly a copy of the Blaeu 1656 map).

33 For example, CA M1/867–872, 1780s.

34 For example, CA M1/335 of 1700; CA M2/16 of 1732 and CA M1/273, late seventeenth-century map of interior.

35 See Add MS 15,738.7, Dupre Eberard, 1720 (British Library) and CA M2/14, 1731.

36 Table Bay MLC 0002003, Van Keulen the elder, Amsterdam 1722, c.12.f.3, British Library, London.

37 Inset of Table Bay, B. Lakeman, Amsterdam n.d., maps *67,235(1), British Library.

38 CA M2/8, 1753(?). This becomes more common after 1780.

39 National Library of South Africa, Cape Town, KCB.CT, 1748; Gordon Panorama, CA M1/1106–7, 1777.

40 M. Foucault, *Discipline and Punish*, London, Tavistock, 1977.

41 CA M3/340, 1700; National Library of South Africa, Cape Town, KCB.CT, 1748.

42 See CA M2/14, 1731, and CA M3/5, 1731.

43 Apart from the general lack of detail before 1780, maps of Robben Island show a progression in hill-sign development that follows Denis Wood's analysis quite closely. See D. Wood, *The Power of Maps*, New York, Guilford Press, 1992.

44 U.A. Seeman, 'Coastal fortifications at the Cape Peninsula 1781–1829', unpublished paper, 7 December 1996.

45 CA M288, 1798.

46 Penn, 'Robben Island 1488–1805', in Deacon (ed.) *The Island*, p. 32.

47 CA M288, 1798.

48 H.J. Deacon, 'The British prison on Robben Island 1800–1896', in Deacon (ed.) *The Island*, p. 37.

49 Penn, 'Robben Island 1488–1805', in *ibid.*, p. 20.

50 1803 plans, CA M1/1138–9.

51 Penn, 'Robben Island 1488–1805', in Deacon (ed.) *The Island*, p. 21.

52 CA M3/19, 1796.

53 Penn, 'Robben Island 1488–1805', in Deacon (ed.) *The Island*, p. 32.

54 Plan of village, CA CO 4372, 1846; CA M3/35 or M3/558, 1870 and CA M3/1807, 1890; CA M4/1548, n.d.

55 Maps are less numerous than before, until mapmaking boomed in the 1890s. One of the few good maps is M3/35 or M3/558, wrongly dated as 1858–60 as it shows the lighthouse, built in 1863–4. Originally surveyed in 1858, it was updated and republished in 1870.

56 Compare the French map of 1824 (maps 147.e.12(1), British Library) with the British maps of Owen and Belcher (originals of 1849 and 1827 combined in a map of 1857) maps SEC.II. (1920), British Library.

57 Plan of village, CA CO 4372, 1846; CA CO 729, 1858.

58 Trigonometrical Survey of Robben Island, 1933, Trigonometrical Survey Office, Cape Town.

59 Cricket ground and tennis court are prominently marked on the 1905 map, CA M4/77.

60 H.J. Deacon, 'Remembering tragedy, constructing modernity', in C. Coetzee and S. Nuttall (eds) *Negotiating the Past*, Oxford, Oxford University Press, 1998, pp. 161–79.

61 H.J. Deacon, 'Madness, race and moral treatment at Robben Island lunatic asylum, 1846–1910', *History of Psychiatry*, 1996, vol. vii, pp. 287–97.

62 D. van Zyl Smit, 'Public policy and the punishment of crime in a divided society', *Crime and Social Justice*, 1985, vol. 21–2, pp. 146–62.

63 S. Swartz, 'The black insane at the Cape, 1891–1920', *Journal of Southern African Studies*, 1995, vol. 21 no. 3, p. 412.

64 Deacon, 'Racial segregation'.
65 Photographs of staff life, Cape Archives, Cape Town and the Robben Island Collection (Elsa Witt), MSC 35, National Library of South Africa.
66 See interviews with World War II veterans in Memories Project collection, Robben Island Museum University of the Western Cape Mayibuye Archive (RIM UWC MA), Cape Town.
67 Interviews with former Robben Island residents, Memories Project collection, RIM UWC MA; and the Robben Island Collection (Elsa Witt), MSC 35, National Library of South Africa.
68 M. Weideman, 'Robben Island: coastal defence, 1931–1960', unpublished MA thesis, University of the Witwatersrand, 1998.
69 *Ibid.*
70 We are, however, fortunate to have memoirs and interviews with ex-political prisoners. Some of these are referred to in subsequent footnotes.
71 I. Luden interview, 2001, Memories Project collection, RIM UWC MA.
72 Robben Island Register for 1960, RIM UWC MA.
73 CA M1/1166, 1784; aerial photograph of Robben Island, 1985, Trigonometrical Survey Office, Cape Town.
74 J. Pratt, this volume.
75 Ex-political prisoner E. Mzamo, personal communication, 2001, remembers the old jail on Robben Island (1960–3) being fenced in. The fences and dog runs of the maximum-security prison still stand today.
76 R. Wilcox, G. Shezi and V. Mcongo, Memories Project Reference Group meeting, Cape Town, March 2001.
77 N. Alexander, *Robben Island Prison Dossier 1964–1974*, Cape Town, UCT Press, 1994, p. 13.
78 N. Mandela, *Long Walk to Freedom*, Randburg, Macdonald Purnell, 1994, pp. 330–2, 372. Also on this issue see M. Dingake, *My Fight against Apartheid*, London, Kliptown Books, 1987, p. 150
79 Robben Island Museum Site Register Database.
80 C. Smith, *Robben Island*, Cape Town, Struik and Mayibuye Books, 1997 has quite a lot of material on this issue.
81 W. Bissell, 'Conservation and the colonial past', in D.M. Anderson and R. Rathbone (eds) *Africa's Urban Past*, Oxford, J. Currey, 2000, p. 246.

11 Legal geographies of Aboriginal segregation in British Columbia

The making and unmaking of the Songhees reserve, 1850–1911

Renisa Mawani

From the mid nineteenth century onward, with the rise of modern-day capitalism and colonial and imperial domination, social relations all over the world became more formally spatialised.[1] During this period, European authorities in metropole and colony established distinct and separate racialised spaces for the middle and working classes and for whites and Natives. Scholars have well documented these processes in geographical locales all over the world, revealing the ways in which spatial strategies of exclusion including racial segregation and containment figured prominently in European colonial and imperial projects.[2] Yet much of this literature has emphasised the role of exclusionary processes in colonial protectorates, where European expansion was aimed at the acquisition of resources and the exploitation of labour as opposed to large-scale and long-term white settlement. Keeping in mind that colonisation was uneven, differentiated, and complex around the globe, and thus cannot be uncritically dichotomised into 'dependant' versus 'settler colonies',[3] it remains important to explore how racial segregation figured in the making of 'white settler societies' like Canada, where colonisation went far beyond the appropriation of resources and labour, and was ultimately about European control over land.[4]

The purpose of this chapter is to explore the linkages between practices of isolation and exclusion, the formation of racialised identities, and the role of law in these processes. Focused specifically on late nineteenth- and early twentieth-century Victoria, British Columbia (BC), I use this context to examine how the forced confinement of Aboriginal peoples on to legally mandated reserves figured in the making of a mythical white settler society.[5] In particular, I ask how distinctions between 'coloniser' and 'colonised' were spatially articulated and legally sanctioned. In other words, how did the coercive displacement of Native communities on to reserves enable local authorities and white colonists to physically construct and symbolically envision BC as a European settlement colony? How was the forced and systematic confinement of Aboriginal peoples even possible in light of the liberal values of justice, fairness and civility that were thought to differentiate Europeans from Natives?

The late nineteenth and early twentieth century marked a formative period in Canada's provincial and national history. In various parts of the country, authorities were deliberately trying to construct a new and racialised identity. In BC, colonial élites endeavoured to reinvent the region from a transient and rough fur trade settlement into a stable and permanent white settler colony.[6] Here, as in other places around the world, early European colonisers largely viewed themselves as a 'superior race', surrounded by 'savage Indians' in a rugged, rough and sparsely populated territory. But in a racially mixed society like BC, where Native peoples outnumbered non-Natives until the late nineteenth century,[7] distinctions between civility and savagery were often unstable and insecure and thus inspired diligent and close management. Notwithstanding the multiple and overlapping racial projects under way in BC at the time, Native peoples became a salient racialised reference point through which Europeans constituted their own material and metaphorical visions of white superiority.[8] But in this transient society, and in a period when control over land and constructions of whiteness remained precarious, this large Aboriginal presence needed to be contained across a secure and steady boundary, eventually to be eradicated through policies of assimilation.[9]

Although colonisation took many forms in BC and Canada, the seizure of Native land was the cornerstone of conquest and white settlement.[10] As was the case elsewhere, colonial power in Canada's West was determined by who occupied, managed and controlled the physical space.[11] The forcible dispossession of indigenous peoples was often violent in various places including the United States and Australia.[12] In BC and in other parts of the country, land was not commonly appropriated through military warfare, but rather was commissioned through the rule of law. In many regions across the country, treaties were signed and agreements reached (often without the consent of Aboriginal peoples). Yet it is precisely this appearance of colonial integrity and lawfulness that has made it increasingly difficult to grasp the violence, illegality and enduring legacy of colonialism in Canada.[13]

Although contestations over land were deeply rooted in politics and economy, colonialism also operated through a range of cultural practices. As Edward Said reminds us, struggles over land are 'not only about soldiers and cannons but also about ideas, forms, about images, and imaginings'.[14] In Victoria, for instance, contentions over place did indeed reflect concerns about identity. Racialised constructions of self and 'other' laid the groundwork for the foundations of imperialism and the power relations that underpinned it. Colonial authorities in the newly formed city attempted to map these identities spatially by shifting the real and metaphorical boundaries between Europeans and indigenous peoples, particularly the Songhees. Located across from 'settler Victoria', the Songhees reserve became the focal point of territorial struggles between white colonists, government authorities and the Native community who had long resided in the area. While these conflicts were undeniably to do with place, *how* racial exclusion was enforced became crucial to constructions of white subjectivity.

Over the course of the late nineteenth and early twentieth centuries, European authorities and colonists aimed repeatedly to evict the city's indigenous inhabitants in order to secure territorial control over a region that was becoming increasingly valuable. However, the Songhees were not driven out by military force. Rather, colonial authorities endeavoured to dispossess them with great care and trepidation, often debating the fairness and legality of the proposed displacement strategies. While efforts to remove the Aboriginal community began in the 1850s, it was not until nearly sixty years later that Euro-Canadians saw the question as finally settled, when the reserve was (re)located outside the city limits.

This chapter charts the making and unmaking of the Songhees reserve. In the first part of the paper, I contextualise my analysis through a brief history of the making of a white Victoria. Here, I show how early European colonists encouraged and relied on the coercive exclusion and regulation of Aboriginal populations in efforts to establish a Euro-Canadian presence in the region. In the following section, I explore these practices more closely through the Songhees reserve. Specifically, I examine the ways in which the Songhees and their territory were invented in the white imagination. By constructing the reserve as a 'racial slum' – a place in need of cleansing and purification – I argue that government authorities already rationalised the forced removal and relocation of the area's Aboriginal residents. In the final section, I explore this eviction more closely. Here, I suggest that by relying on the rule of law, colonial authorities aimed to erase their own complicity in the dispossession of Aboriginal peoples across the country. And by constructing themselves as law-abiding, it seems that the colonisers were ostensibly preoccupied with creating a *specific* type of community and place-identity in Victoria, one which reflected the liberal ideals of justice and civility that were thought to be integral to whiteness.

The making of a white Victoria

In colonial societies, argues David Goldberg, racial categories were also spatial categories.[15] In the initial colonial encounter, colonisers claimed their racial superiority by naming the land as their own, a process entailing the dispossession of indigenous communities that was then rationalised through fictitious ideas about 'virgin land'.[16] Following these early stages of colonisation, Goldberg claims that European élites continued to enforce ideas of racial difference by spatially excluding the colonised from the colonisers. He explains this process as follows: 'Colonial administration required the bureaucratic rationalization of city space. This entailed that as urbanization of the colonized accelerated, so the more urgently were those thus racialized forced to occupy a space apart from their European(ized) masters.'[17]

The practices that Goldberg describes above are evident in the nineteenth- and early twentieth-century colonial initiatives aimed at making Victoria into a white space. Despite the longstanding presence of Native peoples in the region, there is little doubt that early European colonists and colonial authorities endeavoured to rationalise 'the city space' by constituting Victoria as racially homogeneous. Throughout Canada, this process began with the displacement of indigenous peoples on to reserves, a history too complex to detail here.[18] Briefly, in efforts to legitimise their claims to 'empty land', early Europeans endeavoured to remove Native peoples forcefully from the landscape, placing them on to legally designated spaces outside white areas. But unlike other regions in Canada, the provincial and federal governments did not push BC Natives on to a few major reserves. In most cases, Aboriginal communities were allowed to remain where they were, meaning that the total amount of reserve land on the West Coast was fragmented and paltry. The largest reserves were on the mainland in the farming and ranching regions of the Okanagan, whereas the smallest were on Vancouver Island, including the areas surrounding Victoria.[19]

The beginnings of Victoria can be traced to 1843, when the Hudson's Bay Company (HBC) secured a trading post and fort along the shores of Victoria Harbour. Formal colonial authority was not established in the region until 1849, at which point Vancouver Island was named a colony. During this early period, fur-traders and indigenous peoples lived together in a racially mixed and transient society.[20] Colonial administrators paid little attention to racial distinctions, as permanent settlement on the West Coast had not been envisioned by either the British or the HBC. It was not until the mid nineteenth century – with the discovery of gold on the mainland – that thousands of miners arrived on Vancouver Island, making permanent European settlement in the region a more viable possibility.

The Gold Rush had a particularly transformative effect on the soon-to-be city of Victoria. Although Vancouver Island was initially colonised by only 450 whites, a number that increased to 774 in 1855,[21] the 1858 Gold Rush brought thousands of gold-seekers – mainly white Americans, but also blacks and Chinese – to both the Island and the mainland. This mass and sudden increase in population shaped the destiny of the soon-to-be province, shifting it from a fur-trade society into small colonies of non-Native settlement.[22] The discovery of gold also influenced the colony's political culture. By 1858, the role of the HBC had declined significantly and the British government was finally compelled to assume responsibility for a region that they had successfully ignored in the past.[23] Fearing disorder with the jump in population, the British Colonial Office created a separate colony on the mainland and appointed James Douglas, the Governor of Vancouver Island, to become the Governor of the new mainland colony as well.[24] In 1866 the two colonies were united under the name of British Columbia, and in 1871 BC was joined to the rest of Canada through confederation.

The newly arrived colonists were particularly concerned about Victoria's Native presence. Because Vancouver Island continued to be inhabited by a large Aboriginal population, European dominance in Victoria and elsewhere remained tenuous.[25] The Gold Rush exacerbated growing tensions between Europeans and indigenous peoples. The exponential growth in the non-Native population resulted in many conflicts between Aboriginal and non-Aboriginal people, most of which had to do with land.[26] Because reserve boundaries were not clearly laid out, gold seekers and settlers sometimes successfully made claims to resources found on indigenous territories and in some cases to the land itself.[27] As white settlements like Victoria increased in size, racial and spatial distinctions between Natives and whites became increasingly imperative. In efforts to assert their dominance, colonists used a variety of strategies – including liquor laws, for example[28] – to evict Native peoples from white areas and from land deemed valuable for future settlement.

Despite efforts to push Aboriginal peoples away from Europeans and into racialised spaces, racial and spatial purity in Victoria remained illusive. Although racialised borders were sometimes carefully policed, the boundaries that separated reserves and white spaces remained porous and permeable. Just as indigenous peoples continued to frequent white spaces, white men often found their way on to Native territories.[29] But while colonial authorities and settlers were largely unsuccessful in operationalising their visions of racial and spatial exclusivity, Aboriginal peoples increasingly found themselves at the receiving end of segregationist laws and policies aimed at evicting them from the emerging white settlement.

Because Aboriginal peoples did not adhere to reserve boundaries and in many cases were not formally required to,[30] colonial authorities relied on elaborate rationales to legitimate their efforts to expunge the indigenous presence from Victoria. Racialised anxieties about disease and contagion, alongside fears of sexual immorality and excess, illegal liquor consumption and prostitution were evoked in different ways and at distinct moments, underscoring the need to evict Native peoples from much-sought-after valuable land. These concerns can be traced as far back as 1855, when settlers began complaining to the colonial government about the Indians from the northern coast who often camped in town. By 1859, European objections to the Native presence were becoming louder, prompting the Victoria Grand Jury to recommend that indigenous peoples who lived in or frequented the city should be removed altogether. In 1860, these directions led the colonial government to enact a coercive policy compelling Aboriginal men, and later women, to leave the city at night.[31] This ruling, combined with growing concerns about miscegenation, prompted local police officers to identify Native women as the problem. Although this policy was initially aimed at men only, it was indigenous women who were more often arrested and charged, for nothing other than being on the streets at night.[32]

Efforts to enforce racial categories spatially and to evict Native peoples from Victoria were frequently rationalised through racialised concerns about liquor and prostitution. For many Europeans, the presence of Aboriginal peoples in the city was seen to be 'an evil upon two grounds – moral and sanitary'.[33] In particular, anxieties about liquor and prostitution fuelled fears of immorality and lack of hygiene, in the process legitimising dominant constructions of Native peoples as corrupt and sexually depraved. Many missionaries, for example, blamed the close proximity between whites and Indians as the cause of both illegal liquor sales and of prostitution, and proposed racial segregation as the most desirable solution. As one source insisted: 'Being removed a distance from the city,' the Indians 'would spend less upon intoxicating drinks, would as a consequence have more to trade with, and … would advance materially and in sobriety and industry.'[34] In other words, the containment of Native peoples was not only needed for the future well-being of the city's white population, but was also necessary for promoting the civility of Aboriginal peoples.

For many Euro-Canadians, prostitution was a corollary of the illegal liquor market. In efforts to obtain alcohol, authorities alleged that Native women sold sexual services or were sold by relatives to unscrupulous white men. Government and religious authorities assumed that prostitution was rampant in cities. Newspaper headlines and reports documenting 'the alleged traffic in young girls by Indians'[35] reinforced these ideas even further. Writing about the prevalence of prostitution in New Westminster, one source insisted, there is 'not a corner of the city where these dens of putrid filth and infamy are not in sight'.[36] Not surprisingly, efforts to enforce racial separation in white cities including Victoria were also motivated by and legitimised through concerns about the uncontained and highly visible sex trade.

In light of these pervasive fears about prostitution, it is hardly surprising that segregationist policies in early Victoria came down most heavily on indigenous women. Throughout colonial societies, Native women were commonly characterised through racialised narratives of sexual excess and prostitution.[37] From the mid nineteenth century onward, local police used fears of prostitution to expel Native women from the city limits. Indigenous women suspected of working as prostitutes often ended up in Victoria's police court, charged with petty offences including drunk and disorderly conduct. Higher courts also charged some women with prostitution-related offences.[38] In many cases, Native women successfully convicted of selling sex were banished from the city and forced to return to their reserves.[39] On northern Vancouver Island, some Indian Agents attempted to enforce their own methods of segregation by instituting an informal pass system aimed only at Indian women.[40]

There is little doubt that the colonial government and early white settlers were endeavouring to invent Victoria as a white settler city. Strategies of racial containment played a vital role in these early visions of city-making and in the assertion of white superiority. While practices of segregation were directed at all indigenous peoples, Victoria authorities became particularly preoccupied with the Songhees, a community that had long established their presence in the area. As the city expanded and as the surrounding land became materially valuable and symbolically important, officials deployed a number of techniques to evict them. It is to the making and unmaking of the Songhees reserve that I now turn.

Creating the urban reserve

By the 1850s, colonial administrators and white colonists began expressing their anxieties about the Coast Salish community – named by settlers as the Songhees but known among Native peoples as the Lekwammen. Since the first European settlement had been established by the Hudson's Bay Company in what is now Victoria, the Songhees occupied the entire south-east part of Vancouver Island. Their primary village was located in Cadboro Bay, an area just east of Victoria that was soon to become a white upper-class residential neighbourhood. In need of this land, the colonial government sought to evict the Songhees from this vast and valuable territory, instead displacing the community into one contained and much smaller place. In 1850, Governor James Douglas, on behalf of the colonial government, accomplished this goal by moving the Songhees to a new reserve.

The reserve plot was 119 acres in size and was located on Victoria's inner harbour, directly opposite Fort Victoria and joined to the city by a bridge.

From the time the Songhees were relocated, their new reserve proved to be problematic for colonial élites and white residents alike. Both colonists and local authorities complained that the Indians resided too closely to the city and were a menace to civility and racial purity. That they were on a reserve separated from Victoria by a body of water and a bridge proved insufficient for both parties. Under pressure from the city's white residents local authorities launched a series of elaborate evictions to rid Victoria of the Songhees – a sixty-year process that eventually expanded to include the province and the Dominion. These exclusionary practices were undoubtedly underpinned by the colonial government's growing material interests in the appropriation of land. However, as I suggest in this section, the displacement of the Songhees was also fuelled by the desire to build a white settler society, one which was contingent upon the enforced expulsion of the region's Native inhabitants.

The Songhees reserve was constituted through a long and complicated history of colonial displacement and dispossession.[41] Briefly, the reserve was legally created through one of several treaties initiated and signed between Native peoples and Governor James Douglas. In what is now known as Canada, Aboriginal land title was recognised to some degree through the Royal Proclamation of 1763. This legislation extended British sovereignty and protection over Native peoples, acknowledging that the indigenous inhabitants continued to own the land they used and occupied.[42] In the prairies and in what is now Ontario, these rights were realised and eventually extinguished through the signing of treaties. On the West Coast, however, Aboriginal land title was only formally recognised in a few instances. To elaborate, Douglas acknowledged Native ownership over land on only a small portion of Vancouver Island. Specifically, he signed fourteen treaties with various Nations between 1850 and 1854. Eleven of these agreements were made with Native peoples who resided near Fort Victoria (including the Songhees), two were signed at Fort Rupert, and another in Nanaimo.[43]

Douglas did not only affirm but also extinguished Aboriginal title through these fourteen treaties. In addition to the financial compensation the respective indigenous communities received for surrendering their territories, many were relocated to new areas, often physically and discursively cordoned off from white settlements. In exchange for their territorial rights, the Songhees were moved to the inner harbour where they remained for over half a century. Despite the presence of a legal agreement that set out the parameters of the Songhees reserve, their ownership was constantly challenged by white settlers, as well as by local, provincial and federal authorities. Although Douglas and the colonial government were the ones who agreed to relocate the Songhees community to this area, Aboriginal control over land remained ambiguous and uncertain. From the 1860s onward, as the white population grew and the city of Victoria was incorporated, the Songhees territory became increasingly valuable. This growing desire for land, and the forgetting of indigenous peoples that accompanied this appropriation, prompted governmental efforts aimed at reterritorialising the reserve.

European uneasiness about the Songhees can be dated to the 1850s, soon after their relocation. From the outset, the reserve was constructed both by early settlers and by authorities as an affront to imperialism, white civility and respectability, racialised ideas that were materially inscribed into space. The local press played a pivotal role in fuelling these discourses of racial degeneracy. Sensationalist accounts about conflicts between white settlers and Native peoples reinforced views that inter-racial contact was at best undesirable and at worst dangerous to Europeans. In 1858, for example, the *Gazette* chronicled a disturbance on the Songhees reserve. The commotion allegedly 'created considerable excitement at the time, and seemed to threaten a collision between the whites and red-skins'. It was reported that the Indians were 'armed and painted as if for war', and that one of the Indians had been found with a rifle. When the police attempted to arrest him, the *Gazette* insisted, the 'Indians raised their war cry, rescued their comrade, and wrestled the rifle from the hands of the officer'.[44] For the newspaper and its readers, this was evidence enough that because of their 'barbaric' customs and predisposition to violence, the Songhees could not live peacefully near 'civilised' white areas.

Through stories such as these, local newspapers (re)constituted and reinforced derogatory images of the Songhees reserve and its inhabitants. The reserve came to signify a perilous zone, a place of racial disorder where 'savage' Indians practised their 'uncivilised' customs, a space where whites could never be safe. The mere physicality of the area also symbolised racial degeneracy. As spatial theorists remind us, undesirable places are located across real and metaphorical boundaries.[45] The Songhees reserve was placed across both. While geographically separated by a body of water, the reserve was connected to settler Victoria by a bridge, a liminal space or no-man's land that physically distinguished 'savage' from 'citizen' (see Figure 11.1).

The bridge did not only serve as a metaphorical border between white and Native, but during times of racial crisis and uncertainty also became a material marker. Specifically, it enabled local authorities to divide society by enforcing racial and spatial differences. In 1861, when the local police issued orders aimed at driving Aboriginal peoples out of the city, Victoria's Native inhabitants – regardless of language and nation – were forced across the bridge on to the Songhees territory. Any indigenous person found on the 'wrong side of the bridge' after 10 p.m. was to be searched and detained unless they provided adequate proof as to why they were frequenting the white quarters.[46] But by pushing *all* Native peoples across the bridge, local authorities were not only enforcing a system of apartheid but were constructing an observable and concrete reality. Through colonial policies including segregation, the reserve *became* a place of racial disorder, overcrowding and degeneracy, and a justified object of colonial governance.

These discursive constructions were as much about the colonised as they were about the colonisers. Over the sixty years that the Songhees resided across the harbour, the reserve and the bodies that inhabited it were layered with different meanings, but ones that continuously marked their degeneracy. While the reserve came to symbolise a space of disorder and decay, images that later justified the displacement and dispossession of the Songhees, at other times this space was constituted as an exoticised and fetishised symbol of Indian culture, one which also

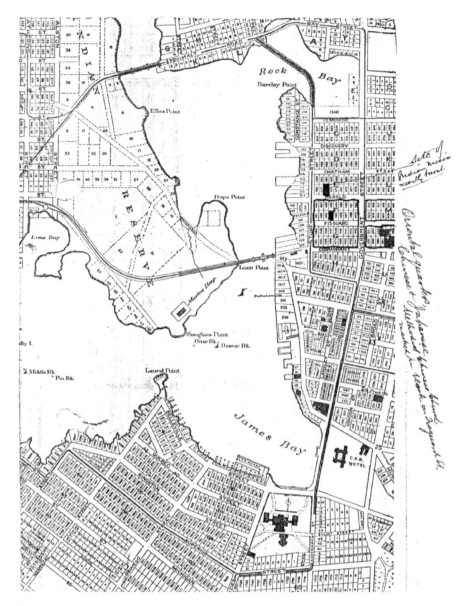

Figure 11.1 Map of Victoria Harbour, *c.*1907, showing the Songhees reserve connected by bridge to 'white' Victoria

Source: United Church of Canada/Victoria University Archives, Toronto. A.E. Roberts to Sutherland (30 June 1907), Sutherland Papers, From Mission to Partnership Collection, photograph 93.049P/620

Note: The sites of the Indian Mission and the Methodist Chinese Church are marked in black enabled European onlookers to know their own superiority. In a 1910 article, the *Victoria Daily Colonist* described the Songhees reserve as 'a showplace for visitors':

> Set along the waterfront, bordered by a fringe of dugouts and Indian craft of every description, the first row or two of community houses afforded the tourist a real taste of Indian life within a stone's throw of the steamer docks. *It was like a perpetual section of a world's fair* and its interest to the new comers and itinerant cheechakos was never failing.[47]

Spaces are not 'fixed, dead, or undialectical', as Edward Soja explains, but, on the contrary, have an important relationship with the people seen as interior and exterior to that space.[48] Conflicting colonial narratives of the Songhees as both 'savages' and 'imperial specimens' enabled colonial authorities to constitute their own subjectivities as civilised and superior. Thus, at a time when Victoria's citizens were still creating their own civic identity and imaginings of subjectivity, the Songhees and their reserve signified the antithesis of whiteness and came to symbolise everything that Europeans were not.

It is important to note that these imaginings of the Songhees and their reserve had material consequences. Ultimately, the creation of racial and spatial difference justified daily colonial interventions, legitimised technologies of segregation, and finally led to the forced removal of the Songhees. As Victoria became more and more attractive to Euro-Canadians and the city's population and land values increased, white colonists became preoccupied with moving the Songhees as far away as possible. These concerns began brewing as early as 1859,[49] but became more and more intense as the city grew larger. In 1862, when smallpox broke out in the city, authorities attempted to evict the Songhees by burning their homes.[50] Notwithstanding their treaty with the colonial government, fears of widespread contagion prompted some authorities to try to move the community to the San Juan Islands, and thus outside the Canadian border.[51] Although these and other coercive efforts worked to reduce their numbers, the Songhees continued to maintain their presence in Victoria for several more decades.

The general consensus among Victoria's local authorities and white residents was that the Songhees reserve was 'a disgrace to the government, a scandal to religion and an offence to our boasted civilization'.[52] Yet there was little agreement, particularly among colonial officials, as to how their removal should be initiated. Despite numerous suggestions and repeated attempts to evict the Songhees, their displacement from Victoria was obstructed by a number of inter-governmental conflicts. For one, there were fundamental disagreements as to who really owned the land, the province or the federal government. Not surprisingly, but importantly, there was no discussion here about indigenous peoples as the rightful owners.

Efforts to evict the Songhees were also hampered by growing concerns about law and justice. Whereas the ultimate objective was to seize their territory, colonial authorities continually debated the legality of the process, questioning whether this eviction was lawful, just or fair. Although the forced removal of a people from their territory is always violent and oppressive, these debates and negotiations tell us a great deal about *how* government officials used the law to envision and constitute their own whiteness and civility. Colonial efforts to construct Victoria as a white settler society were not simply endeavoured through the forced removal of the Songhees, but ironically, through their *lawful* exclusion, a point I develop in the next section.

Displacements and evictions

From the time the Songhees were relocated to Victoria Harbour, several attempts were made to eradicate their presence. Initially, these strategies began at the local level and were brought forth by the city and then the province. The city had repeatedly raised the issue, but it was not until 1869 that the Legislative Council of Vancouver Island initiated a more formal request for their ejection. The Council questioned Governor Douglas as to whether or not the Songhees could be removed from their reserve, explaining that 'the residence of the Indians on this reserve' has 'become obnoxious to the inhabitants of Victoria'. In addition, the Council added that Victoria 'had become a town of considerable importance and the land included in the reserve' had greatly 'increased in value'.[53]

To their dismay however, Douglas denied their request, declaring 'it would be unjust and impolite to remove the Indians'. In the interests of cultivating the city, he assured the Council that he would rent out portions of the reserve, and would apply 'whatever revenue might be obtained from this source to the benefit of the Indians … and particularly to the improvement of their social and moral condition'.[54] Such concerns with justice and fairness were not Douglas' alone, but permeated many subsequent inter-governmental discussions about the Songhees question.

In 1873, the Department of Indian Affairs stepped in. On advice from Ottawa, I.W. Powell, BC's Superintendent of Indian Affairs, attempted to deal with the Songhees problem. After a careful investigation, he recommended that the government purchase an island twenty miles from Victoria that would be a suitable location for the indigenous community. This proposal was endorsed by all levels of government including the city, province and Dominion. However, the Songhees refused to relocate[55] and officials agreed that it would be illegal and unjust to force them out. In 1881, the issue was brought forth again. This time, the Songhees agreed to move, but only if they could return to their original village in Cadboro Bay. This suggestion posed two difficulties for government officials. First, authorities could not agree on the selling price of the current reserve, and second, the prospective territory had already been colonised by Euro-Canadians and was 'now a charming suburb of the city'.[56]

Despite continuous pressure from white residents and local authorities including the Legislative Council, it was not until the turn of the century that a government initiative was finally agreed upon. While local authorities had tried to evict the Songhees in a number of different ways, by the dawn of the twentieth century the issue had become a far more serious matter, one that was to be debated in the House of Commons. In 1899, Victoria's white citizens once again lamented that the Songhees reserve was too close to the city. Echoing earlier complaints, the

Speaker of the House explained that the 'people of Victoria are very anxious to have these Indians removed, as they are a menace to the town in many ways'.[57] The Minister of the Interior clarified that the matter had been brought before his attention two years prior. He added that it was not only local whites who desired that the Songhees be relocated, but now 'the authorities of the city, and the authorities of the province'[58] were also exerting pressure on the federal government.

Several members of the House alleged that the displacement of the Songhees would no longer be an issue as the land was only 'inhabited by a small number' of Indians who continue to 'stick to their reserve'. These notions of emptiness were reminiscent of early colonial encounters, once again legitimising government initiatives to erase the Songhees. Because there were believed to be so few living on the reserve, officials alleged that relocation would cause little or no trouble.[59] Despite these assurances, authorities did indeed experience difficulties in evicting the Songhees. From the 1850s onwards the community had displayed its strength by resisting the various strategies of displacement that Euro-Canadians invoked against them. As Jane Jacobs explains, the 'colonised engage not only in resistance but also in complicity, conciliation, even blithe disregard'.[60] That the Songhees continued to live across the harbour irrespective of efforts to remove them is illustrative of Jacobs' point. However, these negotiations were also hampered by other factors, including inter-government disagreements and liberal qualms about law and justice.

Many of the contentions surrounding the removal of the Songhees were due to jurisdictional disputes between the federal and provincial governments. In particular, the two levels disagreed over who should financially benefit from the sale of land. But while they attempted to work this out, pressure from white settlers and local authorities continued to increase. Local residents were becoming more and more frustrated with the lack of action taken in the matter and especially with the jurisdictional battles between the federal and provincial governments. As one source explained:

> Every man in Victoria wants to see the Indians removed. Whether the land goes to the Dominion or to the province, is a matter of very little consequence to them. As long as the land can be made available for railway purposes or some other purpose.[61]

The city was equally dissatisfied with the provincial and federal government's lack of progress. In 1899, city officials proposed that they would remove the Songhees at their own expense. According to the *Victoria Colonist*, the city had agreed to 'assume the expense and take the property', as they recognised that the 'investment would be a good one, and the sale of lots would at a very early day reimburse the city for the outlay and yield a handsome profit'.[62] Despite their zeal, however, the city was trumped by provincial and federal interests.

The growing value of the Songhees territory made their removal both urgent and imminent. A Member of the House reminded the Minister of the Interior that when the reserve was allocated by Douglas and the colonial government, 'it was of very little value'. He pointed out that it is now exceedingly valuable, and the rise in value is not due to anything the Indians have done but to the way in which the inhabitants and ratepayers of the city, right opposite the reservation, have built up the town.[63]

Despite the government's social, political and financial interests in evicting the Songhees, federal authorities recalled that a treaty had been signed and that the 'Indians have the right to stay on the reservation, and nobody else can have any right to it as long as they stay there'.[64] This legal question settled the issue for the time being, as the Songhees, who had been propositioned on several occasions, were dissatisfied with the offers and were not planning to leave any time soon.

Only one year later, in 1900, concerns about the Songhees and the fate of Victoria were brought once again before the House of Commons. This time, the Department of Indian Affairs had received numerous complaints from white settlers living in Lime Bay who objected to the location of the Songhees burial ground. The 'cemetery in question', explained one official, 'is situated at a point at the entrance of Lime Bay, and the houses of the city of Victoria are across the bay, at least one hundred yards distant'.[65] Although the graves were on the other side of the harbour, opposite white Victoria and separated by water, the white residents argued that this was not far enough. In fact, many insisted that the graves were 'too close' to their homes and for sanitary reasons needed to be moved from the city limits as soon as possible.

After his investigation of the matter, Superintendent Powell reported that the cemetery was not as close to Victoria as the residents had claimed. In addition, he observed that the 'grounds are tidy and well kept and could hardly be considered in the light of a nuisance'.[66] Since it was too expensive, not to mention undesirable, for the Songhees to bury their dead in the public cemetery, the Superintendent concluded that he 'was not willing to take any steps at that time to prevent the Songhees Indians from interring their dead in their own burying ground'.[67]

In 1901, the matter was once more deliberated in the House of Commons. This time, however, the federal government began to bend. James Dunsmuir, the Premier of BC, had already met with the Attorney General and, together with the Minister of the Interior, finally reached what they deemed to be a satisfactory agreement. The BC government made the proposal to the Superintendent of Indian Affairs, arguing that if the Native community were allowed to remain in Victoria, their presence would be detrimental to the burgeoning white population. Consequently, they began taking steps to move the Songhees 'on a reserve at a distance from the city'.[68]

On 4 April 1911, the Songhees' land was transferred to the province. In keeping with their desire to uphold their liberal ideals of law and justice, the province was determined to elicit agreement from the Songhees that their relocation was both just and fair. Each family was compensated 10,000 dollars and paid for any improvements they had made on their existing reserve. In addition, they were moved to what several sources described was a 'beautiful reserve', west of the city in Esquimalt, an area known to locals as 'Maplebank'.[69] Despite the fact that the reserve across the harbour had been the birthplace for many members of the Songhees community, the *Victoria Daily Colonist* alleged that the Songhees were quite content with the agreement. The 'leave taking by the Songhees of their home and that of their fathers was marked by dignity, good feeling and restraint', wrote the newspaper; both men and women 'donned their best apparel and entered quietly and cordially into the ceremonies' (see Figure 11.2).[70]

These lengthy and protracted negotiations between the province and the Songhees cannot be interpreted as consensual, nor can the outcome be seen as an agreement between equals. Rather, many scholars have reminded us that a legal framework premised on European concepts of justice, fairness and equality is deeply racialised, and cannot serve the basis for developing a more equitable relationship between coloniser and colonised.[71] However, these inter-governmental debates provide us with a window through which to observe the ways in which colonial authorities constructed and understood themselves through these processes. Because they adhered to legal doctrines and did not violently force out the Songhees with soldiers and guns, authorities attempted to erase their own complicity in colonisation by creating their own subjectivities as virtuous, moral and law-abiding.

Ultimately, the removal of the Songhees was not constituted as in the interests of the state alone. Rather, some government authorities, including BC's Premier, rationalised their eviction as a necessary step in civilising the Natives. Mr Ditchburn, the Inspector of Indian Agencies, predicted that with 10,000 dollars and a 'beautiful [new] reserve', the people of the Songhees tribe could now live

Figure 11.2 Songhees people, in 'their best apparel', 'taking leave of their home' in 1911

Source: British Columbia Archives, E–00251: 'Victoria, ceremony attending transfer of Songhees, April 4th, 1911', accession number 193501–001

in increasing happiness, prosperity, and comfort. They would be able to make for themselves nice homes ... and would be in a position to maintain themselves in a manner commanding the respect of all, and without recourse to the old methods of fishing or hunting as a means of livelihood.[72]

In the end, colonial administrators understood the enforced expulsion of the Songhees as consensual, contractual and legal.

Conclusion

The title of David Sibley's book *Geographies of Exclusion*[73] nicely summarises the processes I have described in this chapter. I have argued throughout that the making of Victoria as a white space was asserted through the racial presence, exclusion and legal containment of Aboriginal peoples. During this period, Euro-Canadian colonists envisioned their own subjectivities and their civic imaginings against the bodies and spaces of the city's indigenous inhabitants. But in a period when Native peoples outnumbered Europeans and when control over land was not yet secure, the region's large Aboriginal presence needed to be contained across a physical boundary. Yet how was the forced exclusion and confinement of Native communities even possible in light of the liberal values of fairness and rationality that were assumed to differentiate coloniser from colonised? As the Songhees case illustrates, this contradiction was reconciled through the legitimacy of law.

Rather than violently drive out the Natives through military might, colonial élites relied on equally oppressive legal strategies through which they forced the Songhees to vacate their land and relocate to a reserve further away from Victoria. By evoking the rule of law, authorities aimed to erase the violence of this displacement, insisting that it was not only consensual but also in the best interests of the Songhees community. In the process, colonial officials were able to constitute their own subjectivities by upholding the ideals of justice and equity that were assumed to be integral to whiteness. But it is important to remember that despite the 'civility' of this process, legal geographies of Aboriginal segregation dispossessed peoples like the Songhees from their ancestral territories, destroyed traditional ways of living, and forced indigenous communities into an enduring and ongoing condition of social, economic and political marginality in Canada.

Acknowledgements

I would like to thank the participants of the Isolation Symposium held in June 2001 at the Centre of Criminology, University of Toronto, for their valuable feedback. In particular, I would like to extend my deepest gratitude to Alison Bashford and Carolyn Strange for their helpful comments on various drafts.

Notes

1 See N. Al Sayyad (ed.) *Forms of Dominance: On the Architecture and Urbanism of the Colonial Enterprise*, New York, Ashgate Publishing, 1992; K.J. Anderson, *Vancouver's Chinatown: Racial Discourse in Canada, 1885–1980*, Montreal and Kingston, McGill-Queen's University Press, 1991; A. McClintock, *Imperial Leather: Race, Gender, and the Colonial Contest*, New York, Routledge, 1995.

2 Al Sayyad (ed.) *Forms of Dominance*; Anderson, *Vancouver's Chinatown*; McClintock, *Imperial Leather*. See also A. Bashford, 'Quarantine and the imagining of the Australian nation', *Health*, 1998, vol. 2, no. 4, pp. 387–402; A.L. Stoler, 'Making empire respectable: the politics of race and sexual morality in twentieth century colonial cultures,' in A. McClintock, A. Mufti and E. Shohat (eds) *Dangerous Liaisons: Gender, Nation, and Postcolonial Perspectives*, Minneapolis and London, University of Minnesota Press, 1997, p. 351.

3 For a useful distinction between protectorates or dependant colonies and colonies of settlement, see C. Hall, 'Colonizers in Britain and the Empire in the nineteenth and twentieth centuries', in C. Hall (ed.) *Cultures of Empire: A Reader*, New York, Routledge, 2000, p. 7.

4 Many scholars working in the Australian context have examined how spatial strategies of separation have informed imaginary national formations. See, for example, A. Bashford, 'Quarantine and the imagining of the Australian nation'; J.M. Jacobs, *Edge of Empire: Postcolonialism and the City*, London, Routledge, 1996, especially chapters 5 and 6. In Canada, however, this type of analysis has been slow to catch on. For some notable and more recent exceptions, see K.J. Anderson, *Vancouver's Chinatown*; A. Perry, *On the Edge of Empire: Gender, Race, and the Making of British Columbia, 1849–1871*, Toronto, University of Toronto Press, 2001; S.H. Razack (ed.) *Race, Space, and the Law: (Un)Mapping a White Settler Society*, Toronto, Between the Lines, 2002.

5 On the white settler myth, see D. Stasiulis and R. Jhappan, 'The fractious politics of a settler society: Canada', in D. Stasiulis and N. Yuval-Davis (eds) *Unsettling Settler Societies: Articulations of Gender, Race, Ethnicity, and Class*, London, Sage, 1995, pp. 95–131.

6 See Perry, *On the Edge of Empire*.

7 According to the 1880 census, Aboriginal peoples still made up the majority of the province's population, but by 1891 they constituted less than one third. See R. Fisher, *Contact and Conflict: Indian–European Relations in British Columbia, 1774–1890*, Vancouver, University of British Columbia Press, 1977, p. 201.

8 R. Mawani, 'The "savage Indian" and the "foreign plague": mapping racial categories and legal geographies of race in British Columbia, 1871–1925', unpublished doctoral dissertation, Centre of Criminology, University of Toronto, 2001.

9 J.L. Tobias, 'Protection, civilization, assimilation: an outline history of Canada's Indian policy', in J.R. Miller (ed.) *Sweet Promises: A Reader on Indian–White Relations in Canada*, Toronto, University of Toronto Press, 1991, pp. 127–44.

10 On this general point, see E. Said, *Culture and Imperialism*, New York, Vintage Books, 1993.

11 C. Harris, *The Resettlement of British Columbia: Essays on Colonialism and Geographical Change*, Vancouver, University of British Columbia Press, 1997, especially p. xii.

12 W. Churchill, *Since Predator Came: Notes from the Struggle for American Indian Liberation*, Littleton, Colorado, Aigis, 1995. On Australia see Jacobs, *The Edge of Empire*, p. 107.

13 These legacies are illustrated in the legal initiatives made by the Gitskaan and Wet'suwet'en to reclaim their land. See D. Culhane, *The Pleasure of the Crown: Anthropology, Law, and First Nations*, Burnaby, Talonbooks, 1998.

14 Said, *Culture and Imperialism*, p. 7.

15 D.T. Goldberg, *Racist Culture: Philosophy and the Politics of Meaning*, Oxford, Blackwell, 1993, p. 187.

16 McClintock, *Imperial Leather*, p. 5.

17 Goldberg, *Racist Culture*, p. 187.

18 See K. Brealey, 'Travels from Point Ellice: Peter O'Reilly and the Indian Reserve system in British Columbia', *BC Studies*, 1997/8, vol. 115/16, pp. 181–236; P. Tennant, *Aboriginal Peoples and Politics: The Indian Land Question in British Columbia*, Vancouver, University of British Columbia Press, 1990.

19 H.J.M. Johnston, 'Native people, settlers, and sojourners, 1871–1916,' in H.J.M. Johnston (ed.) *The Pacific Province: A History of British Columbia*, Vancouver, Douglas and McIntyre, 1996, p. 172.

20 Perry, *On the Edge of Empire*.

21 Perry, *On the Edge of Empire*, p. 13. I have taken this number from Perry, who is drawing from W.K. Lamb, 'The census of Vancouver Island, 1855', *British Columbia Historical Quarterly*, 1940, vol. 4, no. 1, pp. 51–8. On this point, see also Tennant, *Aboriginal Peoples and Politics*, p. 3.

22 Jean Barman, *The West Beyond the West: A History of British Columbia*, revised edition, Toronto, University of Toronto Press, 1996, p. 71.

23 Barman, *The West Beyond the West*, p. 71.

24 J.I. Little, 'The foundations of government', in H.J.M. Johnson (ed.) *The Pacific Province*.

25 As late as 1881, the Native population constituted half of the entire population of BC. In 1891 this number dropped to one quarter; in 1901 one seventh; and in 1911, Aboriginal people made up one eighteenth of BC's entire population. See J.D. Belshaw, 'Provincial politics, 1871–1916', in H.J.M. Johnson (ed.) *The Pacific Province*, p. 167.

26 Fisher, *Contact and Conflict*, p. 102.

27 'British Columbia Indians', *House of Commons Debates*, Session 1899, vol. 49, pp. 5703–4.

28 On the policing of liquor, see Mawani, 'The "savage Indian" and the "foreign plague"', pp. 312–22.

29 There is evidence for this in liquor convictions, as many white men were arrested for selling liquor to Indians or for being in possession of alcohol on an Indian reserve. Mawani, 'The "savage Indian" and the "foreign plague"'.

30 At various points, missionaries and Indian Agents often encouraged Native men in particular to leave the reserve to be employed in canneries and on hop fields. Mawani, 'The "savage Indian" and the "foreign plague"', chapter 4.

31 For a discussion of this policy see Perry, *On the Edge of Empire*, p. 113.

32 Perry, *On the Edge of Empire*, p. 113.

33 'The Indian question again', *British Columbian*, 3 May 1862, p. 2.

34 'The Indian question again', *British Columbian*, 19 December 1871, p. 3.

35 J. Fulton to Attorney General, 22 January 1906. British Columbia Archives and Records Service [hereinafter BCARS], GR–0429, box 13, file 1.

36 'The Indian question again', *British Columbian*, 3 May 1862, p. 2.

37 See K. Ballhatchet, *Race, Sex, and Class under the Raj: Imperial Attitudes and Policies and their Critics*, New York, St. Martin's Press; on this point in the Canadian prairies, see also S. Carter, 'Categories and terrains of exclusion: constructing the "Indian woman" in the early settlement era in western Canada', in J. Parr and M. Rosenfeld (eds) *Gender and History in Canada*, Toronto, University of Toronto Press, 1996.

38 Perry, *On the Edge of Empire*, p. 110.

39 Mawani, 'The "savage Indian" and the "foreign plague"', especially note 76. See also Carter, 'Categories and terrains of exclusion'.

40 Mawani, 'The "savage Indian" and the "foreign plague"', pp. 175–84.

41 For a discussion of Aboriginal land claims in BC, see R. Fisher, *Contact and Conflict*.

42 Tennant, *Aboriginal Peoples and Politics*, p. 11.

43 Fisher, *Contact and Conflict*, p. 66.

44 *Gazette*, 12 October 1858, p. 2.

45 See, for example, S.H. Razack, 'Race, space, and prostitution: the making of the bourgeois subject', *Canadian Journal of Women and the Law*, 1998, vol. 14, no. 1, pp. 338–76.
46 Perry, *On the Edge of Empire*, p. 113.
47 'Songhees Indians agree to move', *Victoria Daily Colonist*, 6 November 1910, p. 1 (my emphasis).
48 E. Soja, *Postmodern Geographies: The Reassertion of Space in Critical Social Theory*, New York, Routledge, 1989, p. 7.
49 Perry, *On the Edge of Empire*, p. 114.
50 Perry, *On the Edge of Empire*, p. 115.
51 Perry, *On the Edge of Empire*, p. 114, especially note 79.
52 This quote is taken from Perry who is citing an article from the *British Colonist*, 7 September 1868. Perry, *On the Edge of Empire*, note 92.
53 'More documents found on Songhees reserve', *Victoria Daily Colonist*, 17 June 1909, p. 2. In this article, the *Colonist* reprinted a letter from Joseph Trutch to the Colonial Secretary, dated 30 December 1869.
54 'More documents found on Songhees reserve', p. 2.
55 'Songhees Indians agree to move', p. 2.
56 'Songhees Indians agree to move', p. 2.
57 *House of Commons Debates*, Session 1899, vol. 49, 22 June 1899, p. 5705.
58 *House of Commons Debates*, Session 1899, p. 5705.
59 *House of Commons Debates*, Session 1899, p. 5705.
60 Jacobs, *The Edge of Empire*, p. 15.
61 *House of Commons Debates*, Session 1899, p. 5705.
62 'The Songish [sic] reservation', *Victoria Daily Colonist*, 12 December 1899, p. 4.
63 *House of Commons Debates*, Session 1899, p. 5708.
64 *House of Commons Debates*, Session 1899, p. 5708.
65 *House of Commons Debates*, Session 1900, vol. 52, 4 June 1900, p. 6625.
66 *House of Commons Debates*, Session 1900, p. 6625.
67 *House of Commons Debates*, Session 1900, p. 6625.
68 *House of Commons Debates*, Session 1901, vol. 1, 10 April 1901, p. 2774.
69 'Agreement is concluded', *Victoria Daily Colonist*, 25 October 1910, p. 1.
70 'Historic event on reserve', *Victoria Daily Colonist*, 5 April 1911, p. 1.
71 P. Monture-Angus, *Journeying Forward: Dreaming First Nations Independence*, Halifax, Fernwood Publishing, 1999, pp. 30–1; S.H. Razack, 'Introduction', in special issue of *Canadian Journal of Law and Society*, 2000, vol. 15, no. 2, pp. 7–8.
72 'Historic event on reserve', p. 15.
73 D. Sibley, *Geographies of Exclusion*, New York, Routledge, 1995.

12 Palestinian refugee camps

Reinscribing and contesting memory and space

Randa Farah

Space is fundamental in any form of communal life; space is fundamental in any exercise of power.[1]

This chapter examines the Palestinian refugee camp as a site that functions as an exclusionary place, even when the inhabitants are not always strictly confined within the legal boundaries of their camps. Based on extended research and fieldwork in al-Baq'a Palestinian refugee camp in Jordan,[2] the study will delineate the imprints and reinscriptions of colluding and contesting actors, most notably the refugees, who have challenged their exile for over half a century, transforming its exclusionary and marginal existence into an arena of political and social struggle to reproduce, sometimes against insurmountable difficulties, a Palestinian identity. Land, exile and the dream of return, or the contestation over the Homeland as land and history/memory, are the key elements around which the struggle pivots.

In international law refugees are defined as individuals and communities who through fear of persecution have fled their country of origin and crossed into the territory of another sovereign state seeking asylum. In Palestine, however, refugees seek repatriation and not resettlement in host societies. Moreover, their uprooting in 1948 entailed clearing the land for a new Jewish settler community. The settlers did not intend to live in Palestine as part of the larger Arab society; rather, they embarked on a demographic war to alter the balance in favour of the Jews and to wipe out the geographical and historical sites of a Palestinian existence that attests to their national past. In addition, the Zionist movement, which emerged in Europe in the late nineteenth and early twentieth centuries and organised the Jewish immigration to Palestine, had a political objective: that of establishing a Jewish state.[3] As a result the political nexus and geo-political boundaries in the region changed radically.

In the discourse of humanitarian agencies the terms 'refuge' and 'asylum' signal protection. The refugee camp is intended as a temporary sanctuary that facilitates the provision of basic needs until refugees are either permanently resettled or can return to their country of origin. In reality, however, many refugee camps are vulnerable to human rights violations that render them into enclosures of repression, isolation and discrimination. More dramatic has been the vulnerability of camp-dwelling refugees to armed assaults resulting in death, disease, hunger and, in some cases, ethnic cleansing.[4]

Several authors charge that the international community, through relief organisations, has produced the concept of the 'refugee'[5] and innovated the refugee camp to monitor and control a population perceived outside the order and borders of the nation-state.[6] According to this view, refugee camps are sites that mark their inhabitants as different and potentially dangerous. In almost all refugee camps, methods of control, monitoring and management are applied and range from direct state coercion to seemingly benign and liberal forms of legal exclusion.[7] Humanitarian discourses obscure the political and historical dimension of most refugee populations' displacement. Media images of death, disease and poverty signal that they are a people 'in need', but also a potential destabilising element to nation-states predicated on notions of citizenship and territorial sovereignty.

In recent years, host states have become less amenable to refugee flows escaping armed conflicts and natural disasters. In fact, state borders have become more rigid and hostile to refugees in both the North and the South, with the concomitant result of a shift in the way the United Nations High Commissioner on Refugees (UNHCR) is dealing with refugees. In previous decades, the UNHCR favoured resettlement of refugees seeking asylum in host countries; by the late twentieth century, its emphasis had shifted to repatriation to country of origin. Relatedly, many refugee camps are treated by host governments as elements that may 'contaminate' society and are therefore isolated near state borders and away from populated areas to ensure minimum contact with the local population. It is also important to note here that repatriation, as one of UNHCR's durable solutions for refugees, is theoretically premised on individual *free choice*, which represents an important principle in refugee law. Yet this has not always been the case. For example, when refugees were involuntarily repatriated to Rwanda from camps in Tanzania in 1996, despite fears of persecution.[8]

Palestinian refugees confront a double form of isolation: the prohibition of return or repatriation by the Israeli state and the disappearance of their Homeland and landscape as they knew it. In addition, the Zionist colonisation of Palestine and the establishment of the Israeli state in 1948 led to the fragmentation of the Palestinian nation as a continuous and contiguous geographic, civil and political society. Today, most of the Palestinian refugees live within Palestine/Israel and in Jordan, Lebanon and Syria. Others are scattered in the Middle East and the rest of the world.

It is not surprising, then, that in exile the refugee camp became the spatial symbol of struggle 'against forgetting' and for the maintenance and reproduction of Palestinian identity. Yet the camps are also sites of struggle against social, political and economic marginalisation by Arab host-states, which fear their presence as a destabilising and revolutionary force in the region. Throughout the last half-century, Arab governments with few exceptions have treated camps and their inhabitants with caution, and in some cases have used violence and coercion in order to exercise their political control.

Historical context

Palestinian refugees are the living witnesses of *al-Nakbah*, literally meaning 'the Catastrophe', the term Palestinians use to describe the 1947–8 war. During and consequent to the war, over 750,000 Palestinians were displaced from their homes, villages and towns. Depopulation was accompanied by the destruction of some 530 Palestinian villages.[9] Movable and immovable assets of the local population were seized by the nascent Israeli state and distributed to Jewish settlers.[10]

On 15 May 1948, the Zionist dream of creating a state for the Jews was fulfilled. For the Zionist leaders, this achievement was viewed as the solution to rising anti-Semitism in Europe. However, the Zionist dream turned into the Palestinian nightmare: their dispossession and protracted exile. Today, there are over 5 million Palestinian refugees – the largest refugee population in the world, constituting nearly one third of the global refugee population in the year 2001.[11] Their predicament, spanning over half a century, is one of the longest-standing in contemporary history.

Upon their displacement in 1948 and after their repeated but failed attempts to return, the United Nations, following a recommendation from the Economic Survey Mission, established the United Nations Relief and Works Agency (UNRWA) on 8 December 1949 under UNGA Resolution 302 (IV), to provide humanitarian assistance exclusively to Palestinian refugees. It is important to mention that the word 'Works' in the Agency's name reflects one of its objectives envisaged for refugees in the early 1950s by Western powers, namely the absorption of refugees through large-scale economic projects. This scheme of integrating refugees failed, mainly due to the resistance of refugees and their insistence on their right to return as declared in UN General Assembly Resolution 194 (III) in 1948.[12]

Today, the Agency administers fifty-nine refugee camps, most of which were established as a result of *al-Nakbah*. Seven were erected following the second major war in 1967 to provide refuge to approximately 350,000 displaced Palestinians, over half of them uprooted for the second time as a result of Israel's occupation of the West Bank and Gaza as well as other Arab territories in Syria and Egypt. UNRWA camps are spread out in the West Bank, Gaza, Lebanon, Syria and Jordan. There are over 3.7 million refugees registered with the Agency (approximately 2 million are unregistered). A third of the total registered population lives in camps.[13] Generally, the inhabitants of camps represent the poorer segments of Palestinian society, who once belonged to the destroyed villages and upon which Jewish settlements and neighbourhoods were established. The Israeli Jewish names for these settlements mockingly mimic the old Arabic village names.[14]

It is impossible here to catalogue the status of refugee camps in the various host countries; however, it is important to point out for the purpose of this chapter that most refugees living in camps in the Middle East are not legally prohibited by UNRWA or by state laws from relocating outside, with the exception of Lebanon, where in 2002 the policies of the Lebanese government make it virtually impossible for a Palestinian to do so. However, the histories and ethnographies of camp boundaries and the movement across these liminal zones are significant in documenting the history of the relationship between the host state, the host society at large and the refugees.

Lebanon is a good example of a country where refugee camps today are strictly monitored by the state security services. In fact, one of the Lebanese authority's responsibilities is to ensure that refugees do not carry building materials to improve their shelters destroyed during the war. However, the conditions for camp-dwelling refugees were different in the 1960s and 1970s, when they had relative autonomy, especially following the signing of the Cairo Agreement in 1969, between the Palestine Liberation Organisation (PLO) and the Lebanese government. The Cairo Agreement, which was abrogated in 1987 by the Lebanese Chamber of Deputies (and a decision that was confirmed by the Lebanese President a month later), had granted the PLO relative freedom to manage the camps and the right to 'work, residence and movement'.[15]

Following their displacement in 1948 and 1967, and upon registering with UNRWA, refugees were granted a fixed area of 96 square metres for each family, upon which they could erect their tent even when they did not legally own the land. To be eligible for UNRWA's various services, refugees obtained an identification card or the 'Relief Card'. Due to the economic and social vulnerability wrought upon them by uprooting and dispossession, refugees became a source of cheap labour in host societies, providing skilled and unskilled day labour and seasonal work.[16] The camp boundaries in all host states were delineated and have been fixed since their establishment, a move that has led to severe overcrowding in camps today. In the first few years a passer-by could observe from a distance the camp with its bounded space filled with tents. Today, tents have been replaced with more durable materials and the boundaries of camps are porous and ambiguous; for outsiders it is difficult to differentiate them from other poor urban areas in the region. The dramatic increase in population since their establishment resulted in a 'spill-over' of many refugees outside the camps, many of them choosing to live in their vicinity. This was facilitated by the fact that there is no law that prohibits refugees from living outside the camps. Yet those who end up leaving the camp are households that can afford to do so.

Notwithstanding this freedom in residence, most refugees remain within the camp, where housing was provided without charge as part of humanitarian aid. In addition, village, family and neighbourly social networks provide a source of significant support for refugees, especially for women. Remaining in the camp has emerged as a form of political resistance against integration in the host society – a symbol of their insistence on repatriation to their original villages and homes.

Jordan is an interesting case as the only host state willing to provide most Palestinian refugees with citizenship. Nevertheless, in practice such citizenship has failed to guarantee equal rights or to prevent discrimination based on national origin. Historically, the relations between Jordan and the Palestinians fluctuated, and refugees' sense of belonging has varied by class, social and legal status and history of displacement.[17] However, the ethnic boundaries along a Jordanian/Palestinian divide solidified in the early 1970s following the armed clashes between the Jordanian army and the Palestinian Resistance Movement (PRM). During that period and ever since, camps have been closely observed, and during crisis the Jordanian army and police often surround camps to ensure that the 'intransigent' elements are controlled, not infrequently through imprisonment. As an example, during the second major Palestinian uprising in the West Bank and Gaza, which erupted in September 2000 and became known as *al-Aqsa Intifada*, refugees in Jordan were prohibited from demonstrating outside the confines of camp boundaries and were strictly monitored. Both the Jordanian army and police have arrested and/or interrogated Palestinians suspected of supporting wider efforts to establish Palestinian statehood.

Within the occupied territories and especially in Gaza, Israel has systematically encroached on refugee camps and violated its space, although refugee camps are considered United Nations installations and are technically inviolable and protected. In Gaza, where over 75 per cent of the population live in refugee camps, the situation is worse.[18] Movement has been severely obstructed by the Israeli army through closures, curfews, check-points and trenches, and the whole of the Gaza Strip is isolated by an electric fence. A double isolation in Gaza manifests the colonial structure mapped out on to camps and territories.

Following the outbreak of *al-Aqsa Intifada*, refugee camps and other UNRWA installations once again became prime targets of armed Israeli assaults. On 24 March 2002, UNRWA's Commissioner General, Peter Hansen, stated that despite complaints about its aggression against UNRWA facilities, Israel persists in destroying refugee homes and UNRWA buildings without an explanation or apology.[19] This assault on UNRWA installations did not spare a pilot project and the only centre in Gaza for the visually impaired. Again, on 12 March 2002, Israeli armed units entered the Amari refugee camp in the Ramallah-al-Bireh area. The Israeli soldiers dug trenches around the camp, followed by a house-to-house search campaign. The same kind of violation of this place of asylum or refuge has been conducted in most refugee camps in the Palestinian territories.[20]

Al-Baq'a refugee camp in Jordan

In Jordan, refugee camps are paradoxically sites of inclusion and exclusion. Although most refugees hold Jordanian passports, they still fall under the jurisdiction of the United Nations Relief and Works Agency, the mandate of which states that humanitarian aid will continue to be provided to Palestinian refugees until a political solution has been reached. Thus, refugee camps are simultaneously international and national spaces, in which various political agendas are played out in opposition.

As a site of contestation, al-Baq'a camp reveals the multiple and sometimes conflicting reinscriptions over the meaning and memory of the space. There are three major actors constantly reinscribing the meaning of exclusion in the camp: the Jordanian state; the UNRWA; and the refugees themselves. The reinscriptions of the Jordanian State are obvious and inescapable. The camp, which lies 20 km north-west of Amman, the capital of Jordan, is not easily discernible to a visitor passing on the main road from the capital to Jarash; yet for the local inhabitants the boundaries, as well as the presence of the state and its hegemony, are clear. In addition to a Jordanian flag that flutters alongside the UN flag, there is a police centre, secret service and Jordanian civil defence. There are also banks, a post office and two government secondary schools. State control is also achieved through the Camp Services Committee, whose members are appointed by the Department of Palestinian Affairs (DPA), which falls under the aegis of the Ministry of Foreign Affairs.

Jordanian authorities ensure that any 'outsiders' who wish to visit the camp must acquire permission from the DPA, where they are questioned about the reason for the visit. If the visitor, tourist or journalist is carrying a camera, the visit permit becomes even more difficult. The visitor is usually accompanied by a member of the Camp Services Committee and is taken around on a 'tour'. In this scenario, the refugee camp is transformed into an 'exhibit', and particular 'refugee' sites are designated for show. This accompanied tour of outsiders asserts that refugees exist in a particular place, even though official Jordanian maps do not chart the camps. In addition, the regulation of visitors ensures that refugee voices are silenced as most fear government agents and are unwilling to express their views publicly. Moreover, this control over 'outsiders' entering the camp re-establishes the power of the state within the camp boundaries.

The Jordanian state is keen to maintain the representation of the camp as a '*Jordanian* place for *refuge*', while repressing the Palestinian identity. For official state visitors the camp is represented as a 'humanitarian space', where people in need of assistance live. In this context, Jordan wishes to emphasise to foreign delegates (especially those representing donor countries) that refugees are a financial and material burden on Jordan. As to its internal policy, the Jordanian government treats the camp as a 'Jordanian place'. The fact that most of the refugees carry a Jordanian passport classifies them as 'refugee–citizens', a dual and paradoxical status. Refugees are expected to carry out their responsibilities as Jordanian citizens – that is, to be loyal to the state. However, refugees carry their UNRWA registration cards, which places them under the mandate of an international body as a *de facto* stateless population. Consequently, that inhabitants are allowed to exist both as *refugees* (in its humanitarian sense) and as *Jordanian* citizens, but are prohibited from freely expressing their Palestinian national belonging, reflects state policies and control.

The second authority shaping the camp differently – into a 'place for refugees' – is the UNRWA. As a bureaucracy whose top officials and management staff are linked to the powers that fund it, the Agency has to represent and reproduce the Palestinian as a 'refugee in need' in order to mobilise for funds and justify its expenditures. In al-Baq'a, the Agency installations include a main office that manages and coordinates the various activities. There are UNRWA schools, several health centres and clinics, including mother and child healthcare, family planning and a rehabilitation centre. Through these institutions the UNRWA's various services reflect the segmentation of society according to modernist visions of society and Western approaches to education, health and family.[21]

UNRWA's work in refugee camps (shelter, healthcare) is similar to the services provided by a welfare state. Within these territorialised domains (camp boundaries),[22] however, 'refuge' and 'welfare state' converge. Viewed from this perspective, UNRWA represents a state for the stateless within a nation-state – Jordan – the UN blue flag symbolising its supra-national dimension. As Nader, a man in his late forties, recalls, refugees regarded the Agency as a 'government':

> When an UNRWA official used to knock at someone's door, it was like the government had arrived. The role of UNRWA was basic, substituting for a government ... I don't know if you heard the saying (in the 1950s among Palestinian refugees), which says: 'We only have God and the Ration Card!'[23]

Consequently, while the inhabitants resist the Jordanian state's reinscription of the camp as a 'Jordanian place for refugees', another struggle exists between the inhabitants who reinscribe the camp as a place of political exile and UNRWA's attempt at reproducing the camp as simply a humanitarian space. It follows that the main contradiction between refugees and UNRWA is based on the objectives and the historical genesis of the Agency and the refugees. UNRWA's history of itself begins *after* 1948: for refugees the 'beginning' is their lives in their original village *before* their Catastrophe. Thus, 1948 is the demarcating line that radically ruptures the natural flow of historical time for refugees. The Agency's memory of itself and of refugees begins in tents and camps. For refugees they have history and politics, whereas UNRWA has its bureaucracy and 'beneficiaries'.

For UNRWA the camp is a *humanitarian* place *for refugees*, while for Palestinians it is a place of exile, which they have reinscribed as Palestinian. The inhabitants of the camp do not regard themselves as 'beneficiaries of humanitarian aid' nor as Jordanians, because the camp is foremost a Palestinian place. For the refugees, their identity as Palestinian was to be asserted by navigating through multiple layers and frameworks of existing identity references, while simultaneously reproducing new frameworks and nodes of references drawn from the present and the surrounding milieux. These identities include the land (village) of origin, clan, Palestinian and/or Arab nationalism, Islam, Jordanian citizenship and their refugee 'international' status. However, it is important to point out that identities are not necessarily contradictory: for example, a sense of belonging to Palestine, the Arab Nation and Islam can co-exist harmoniously.

Given this, the territorial boundary of the camp becomes a significant, if not the only, marker for delineating 'us' and 'them'. In other words, the camp has become a signifier of their identity, an appropriation of the place of enclosure. The physical boundaries are reconstructed and drawn upon to map out difference and 'otherness'. As indicated in earlier sections, the process of uprooting Palestinians from their homes and land was accompanied by a negation of their history and culture in Palestinian territory. Consequently, foremost in the Palestinian project is the re-territorialisation of their history as Palestinian, and the re-historicising of their territory.

In exile, camps have come to symbolise such re-territorialisation as they have been reinscribed as Palestinian and as temporary substitutes of the village of origin and Homeland.

The camp as a temporary place

Abu Basil, a man over 70 years old, describes the camp as a temporary place for the duration of exile, where homes are 'borrowed' from the Jordanians; the inhabitants' status (and not their identity) is that of refugees until they return:

> Those to whom this country belongs are Jordanians. We do not have a country, we do not have land or anything, we are here like merchants, we sell and buy, we are close together as you may see … We are living in these houses as borrowed homes. Maybe Jordan after one year or four years will tell us, go back from where you came.[24]

When the camp was first established, the inhabitants attempted to bring to the camp the ways of the village, their familiar practices and daily tasks. As photographs and interviews show and after the tents began to be replaced with barracks, almost all the shelters had small gardens – at least while space allowed – tended by women who used the produce for home consumption. In addition, women tended poultry, also a familiar task, while some raised pigeons and rabbits on roofs of shelters. The increasingly cramped spaces in camps have eliminated almost all possibility of resorting to the production of food at home, and refugees have thus been forced to turn to the market for ready-made food and basic commodities.

The small shelters or housing units are 'refugee units', or what I call 'hesitant structures', that speak of a long state of temporality. In the mid 1990s the landscape was one of densely packed shelters. Corrugated metal sheets held down with stones and old tyres were used as roofs. The refugee barracks, also called 'units', looked rather shabby and incomplete, needing a wall, railings for steps, or a paint job (see Figure 12.1).

In addition to economic imperatives, there is another reason why almost all housing units are half-finished. Most of the first generation of refugees living in camps have refused to invest in anything durable and permanent because they hoped they would return and because such improvements to shelters would signify acquiescence to integration. While I was conducting fieldwork, almost without exception men, women and children pointed out that their parents/ grandparents had not wanted to improve on the housing unit at all, since they held firmly to the belief that they would return. As Aida said:

> No one at the time used concrete for their shelters … they used to say this is not our Homeland, we should not build here … My maternal uncles … used to tell my father 'Abu Mahmoud, why don't you buy?' He used to say 'NO! If we do not return today, we will tomorrow'. My father, until he

Figure 12.1 al Baq'a refugee camp, spring 1995

Source: Author's photo

Note Zinc roofs are held down by stones and old tyres

passed away in the 1980s, believed we shall return. He didn't even want to build a ceiling with cement, he kept saying we shall return, but we didn't![25]

However, in more recent years renovations and new structures have become more noticeable. Unlike the first generation of refugees who viewed 'permanent-looking' housing as a sign of forfeiting their political right of return, the younger generations have driven a wedge between their political stance (which has been radicalised due to their marginalisation in the Oslo peace process and later its total collapse) and their desire to improve their living conditions. Sa'eed, a young man in his early thirties, explains that, until the mid-1970s,

People viewed the liberation of Palestine as a strategic objective, and most still believed that tomorrow [soon] they will be able to return. When the Revolution left [the expulsion of the Palestine Liberation Organisation from Jordan], a process of change in consciousness began, beginning in 1971 to develop and improve oneself, conditions and life. For example, suppose Palestine will return next week; then it is okay for my children to sleep as the water is leaking or that they sleep on the ground … But today, even if he [any Palestinian in the camp] builds a second floor, he does not think of it in terms of integration and stability any more. Even if he builds a house and leaves the camp, to them it is not stability. There is a reality that imposes itself. Take a household of a married couple who have seven or eight children, and the children, they got married, where are they going to live? Should he set up a tent and say, 'I want to go back to Palestine?'[26]

In the 1990s, the real-estate market in the camp was active. Housing units were being sold, bought and rented, despite the fact that such activities were infringements on building regulations. As one resident said, such transactions are *illegal* but they are *legitimate*. Thus, the inhabitants created their own parallel real-estate market and set regulations for legitimate transactions, or a parallel legal system. However, material investment within the camp continues to be a source of anxiety, and many refugees worry that they may be relocated forcibly yet again. Rumours that often circulate among the inhabitants regarding the possibility of being removed or relocated to another area are taken very seriously. The history of successive forced displacement and relocation, a precarious political situation, deteriorating economic conditions and the status of camps as temporary spaces are factors that force refugee households to develop flexible livelihood strategies, which marginally enhance feelings of economic and political insecurity.

Territorial fragments in exile

Inside the shelters, the items and artefacts that decorate the walls include Palestinian maps, flags and embroidery, and pictures of martyrs (the local and cultural term used to describe those killed by the Israeli military). Diplomas and certificates, Islamic verses and sometimes pictures of important leaders adorn the walls. What is important to highlight is that these items reflect central symbols of the Palestinian predicament and also signal the political and ideological transformations that have occurred in refugee camps over the past few decades.

The Palestinian flag, prior to the initiation of the Oslo negotiations in 1993, was an important symbol in Palestinian political culture. Inside the occupied territories, a person would be imprisoned for possessing it, drawing it or hanging it in public places. Even in Jordan, during periods of political repression (the 1970s and 1980s), boasting of a Palestinian flag would have exposed the person to interrogation and harassment. Nevertheless, the Palestinian flag, embroidered, made of cloth or painted, decorates most of the shelters in the camp (see Figure 12.2).

As for the Palestinian map, it is a document verifying historical claims over a territory. As a pre 1948 map it does not show Israel or the new Israeli sites that followed its creation. For refugees, what is even more significant about the pre 1948 map is the fact that it features the names of their original villages. The maps produced after the creation of the state of Israel expunged these villages of origin, since they have been literally wiped off 'the face of geography' in subsequent mapping. The significance of the map as a constant reminder of home

Figure 12.2 Grandmothers care for young children

Source: Author's photo

Note: The wall decoration features the word 'Jerusalem' embroidered in the colours of the Palestinian flag

and homeland was stark for a young woman in her late teens. Nadia pointed out that her father uses the map as if his original village still exists. In her view he has never recovered from the shock of expulsion:

> I will tell you something: we are from Iraq al-Manshiyya [a village in Palestine destroyed and depopulated during the 1948 war]. My sister married someone from Summayl, also in the district of Hebron; between them and us there is probably only one village, if only I could show it to you on the map. Imagine, we are neighbours and live in the same camp; when they came to ask for my sister's hand, my parents measured it by the distance on the map of Palestine. My father said, 'Summayl is close to Iraq al-Manshiyya, which means they are not "strangers" [*ghuraba*]' – they knew they were not far from each other. If the village was far, he would have refused. I'll tell you why: not because of anything, but in his mind the visits will be close to each other. Imagine, my father believes that we will return someday and when we return, it would be easy then to visit his daughter in Summayl, which will be close to Iraq al-Manshiyya – imagine![27]

In most of the refugee houses, there are pictures of martyrs. It is usually a father, husband, son or a relative who was killed in an armed conflict. The martyr (or *shaheed* in Arabic) elicits feelings of sorrow, but in Palestinian society and culture such individuals also spur public acknowledgement of the suffering and sacrifice through the struggle for the liberation of Palestine. This is not unlike the concept of the patriotic soldiers who died for the 'Nation' in Europe, and who are lauded for their heroism and self-sacrifice and allocated particular sites for public commemoration. In the Palestinian case, names and pictures of martyrs fill both public space (wall graffiti) and the private enclaves of households.

Diplomas and certificates are a source of utmost pride and are similarly hung on shelter walls. Following the uprooting, education became an important coping strategy. Education became the means through which Palestinians hoped they could deliver themselves economically and politically. Generally, the eldest child (usually a male) was entrusted with the redemption of 'home' (economically) and 'Homeland' (politically). Thus, certificates and diplomas decorate most of the shelters, one more reinscription that defies their 'refugee' status. More importantly, diplomas and pride in work counter the general view in Jordanian society that refugee camps are sources of social problems, and they also challenge the stereotypical images of refugees as people in need and a 'burden' on society.

While there is a bricolage of artefacts reflecting the various ideologies, political and social discourses over time, Islamic symbols became more prevalent in Koranic verses, usually set against a black background and elaborately framed, are hung on the walls of most shelters. It is not unusual to find an Islamic verse alongside the pre 1948 map of Palestine. For Palestinian refugees it is a framework for the revival of their dream of return and a disavowal of the concrete political processes in which they have been marginalised.[28] The Holy Koran and cassettes with religious sermons, books on Islam and exegesis have all significantly infused refugees' political culture. In general, this trend reflects the need of the population in the region and especially the Palestinians to reassert their identity in the face of increasing Western and imperial domination, reflected in political, economic, cultural and military encroachment in the Middle East and North Africa, as is the case in other parts of the world today.

One of the most moving moments for visitors in refugee camps occurs when hosts retrieve land documents attesting to their ownership of land and homes, and/or the keys to their houses, rusted with the passage of time, but protected as one would a treasure. These are presented as the ultimate symbols of authentic belonging to Palestine and the consequent dispossession. Yet, for refugees, no matter how many documents they possess, proof of ownership means little for the occupiers or the international community. Nevertheless, refugees hold on to these, as part of a larger counter-narrative to their Exile and in the hope that some day 'historical justice' will reign, a concept that is frequently used in refugee narratives.

By the 1990s few women, especially young women, continued to wear the Palestinian dress or 'Western' clothes. Palestinian peasant women in their villages of origin wore *al-thowb* (the Arabic name for the long (usually black) dress embroidered with different colours, predominantly red). The patterns of the embroidery identified the woman's village and district of origin. The conditions of displacement led to two interesting developments regarding Palestinian dress: first, it was appropriated by the nationalist movement and became a symbol of Palestinian land, origin and rural culture. Many Palestinian artists, for example, symbolised Palestine as the 'motherland' through the image of a Palestinian peasant woman wearing her embroidered dress. Second, the urban élite appropriated the Palestinian *tatreez* or embroidery, including organisations interested in preserving Palestinian culture. Several training centres and workshops were set up to produce Palestinian embroidered artefacts, transforming these into commercial items identified as part of the Palestinian 'cultural heritage'. When I visited the women's union in the camp in 1998, a woman in her early seventies was wearing the Palestinian dress, as most women of her age do. She commented that 'buying off' the Palestinian dresses by tourists and outside organisations was 'a conspiracy by the enemy, so that nothing remains to remind us of the Homeland'. Arguing with her daughter about the peasant dress, Imm Yousef, who lives in the camp, insists:

Imm Yousef [the mother]:	I am not going to listen to you; I am going to embroider one for you. The dress keeps on reminding us of the smell of the land [that is, the Homeland].
Nahed [daughter]:	This is all nonsense. It is power [what Palestinians need is power]. It is nonsense. It does not depend on the dress [meaning, to maintain the Palestinian dress as a symbol is useless and will not bring Palestine back, it is force and power that will make the difference].[29]

The above-mentioned generational debate manifests the changing ways that Palestinians are reinscribing their exile, the older generation insisting that the old dress represents a Palestinian fragment, while younger generations prefer wearing the 'Islamic dress'. Some women have chosen to wear what they refer to as the Islamic dress out of personal choice and religious faith. Others wear what they call 'modern clothes', make-up and so on, but ensure that their hair is covered. For some women there is social and family pressure to cover up, while others wear it because it is the 'fashion', implying that the traditional dress is for 'older women'. A primary reason for the spread of the Islamic dress beyond the ideological and social causes is that it is economical. Most refugee women can no longer afford the expensive thread and material or the long hours required to produce the Palestinian peasant dress (see Figure 12.3). Finally, the Islamic attire allows women to move more freely in overcrowded camps, where the social environment is conservative, and to obtain family support to enrol in universities or to work.

More broadly, the significance of the Palestinian traditional dress symbolises the various struggles among Palestinians, particularly in camps, over issues of identity and political ideologies. The traditional embroidered Palestinian dress was a way to assert a Palestinian identity and to differentiate Palestinians from Jordanians. Today's Islamic dress simultaneously highlights the popular support for Islamic organisations and is a way to diffuse Palestinian identity in Jordanian

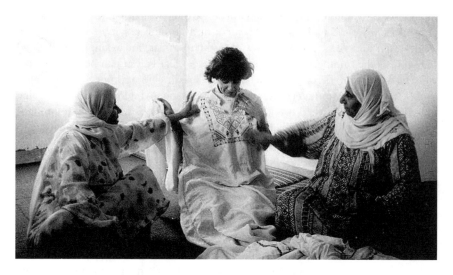

Figure 12.3 Women of the camp proudly show the author a Palestinian embroidered dress
from the district of Tulkarem in the West Bank

Source: Author's photo

society as a whole, in order to have access to employment and minimise possibilities of discrimination, drawing upon the larger Islamic identity in the region.

A final way in which the space is reinscribed by refugees is through graffiti and commercial signs, both of which maintain a tradition of village associations and naming. Graffiti writings on street walls and on buildings such as schools and local community centres signal the highly politicised environment. Virtually all graffiti relate to Palestinian history and current events, including dissent against collaboration and against the Oslo Agreements. Large signs and names of shops, retail stores and centres also assert Palestinian identity. Many of these are named after the Palestinian original village or the name of the clan, such as al-Ajjouri or al-Falouji shops (that is, the shop belonging to a person from the villages of Ajjour and al-Falouja respectively). There are also shops called Filasteen (Palestine), al-Quds (Jerusalem), al-Karameh (the name of a battle and a refugee camp), al-Awdah (the Return) and al-Sanabel (*sanabel* means 'wheat', representing the image of Palestine as a rural society). Besides the names of shops, there are numerous village associations carrying the name of Palestinian villages: for example, al-Sama'nah, al-Dawaymeh and al-Faloujah, Sidna Ali and Bayt Jiz. The names of areas within the camp similarly refer to Palestinian districts or important events in their history, such as al-Quds (Jerusalem) and al-Khalil (Hebron).

Conclusion

In light of the current political context, with both the *Intifada* and the recent Israeli incursion, the boundaries around Palestinian refugee camps have become increasingly solid and clear. In 2002, Israeli tanks rumbled through narrow refugee alleyways, destroying flimsy shelters and violating the concept of the camp as a sanctuary. The refugee camps of Sabra and Shatila in Lebanon, the sites of massacres and war crimes during the protracted war (1975–90), have now been juxtaposed with Jineen, the refugee camp in the West Bank, heavily bombarded and bulldozed by the Israeli army. Jineen has now been integrated into the political culture as the symbol of Palestinian heroism; in fact, newborn Palestinians and Arabs are being named after the camp – 'Jineen'. In this political context, the struggle over the meaning and existence of 'camps' has re-emerged. The Israelis, many Arab governments and the international community would like to see an end to refugee camps and the 'refugee problem'. In contrast, refugees believe that they constitute the central issue in the Palestinian national question. For them the camps symbolise their right of return to their land.[30]

Camp-dwelling refugees have appropriated their enclosed spaces, lacking in political, legal and social freedom, and transformed them into powerful political symbols of resilience and identity. Refugees reinforce the political boundaries around their camps whenever attempts are made to dismantle them, as these attempts have historically signified plans of integration and not repatriation. In a manner of speaking, the camp for refugees functions both as a symbol and as a 'territorial fragment of Palestine in exile', the direct link between the refugee and her or his original village. As Hanan, born in the late 1970s in al-Baq'a camp, defiantly expressed it in 1995:

> You know it is not that the camp is a substitute or will make up for Palestine, but the word *Mukhayyam* [camp], means *takhyeem* [camping], which means that one day we will destroy the tents and return, we shall return. Can you imagine, there are plans to erase the word 'camp'? We suffer in the camp, but suffering moulds the human being.[31]

The international community established camps exclusively for Palestinian refugees, with the hope that this would facilitate the delivery of basic needs until a political solution was reached. Dominant powers (mainly Israel and its supporters in the West) hoped that Palestinians would be integrated over time in the various surrounding countries and their right of return would no longer be an issue. Indeed, over time refugees living in camps made a qualitative leap in terms of education and were able to contribute to household income and social and economic upward mobility. Most of the refugee camps today look like urban slum areas as the tents have disappeared. For an outsider, the boundary is a mirage and refugee camps are sometimes invisible.

For Palestinians, however the camp boundaries and the social, political and physical space within are real and crucial for the nation. Indeed, one of the main reasons why the Oslo framework for peace failed is because it marginalised refugees. In this political landscape, the refugee camp is the potent symbol of a struggle that has lasted over half a century. Without confronting the issue and referring back to international legitimacy and principles, the inhabitants will continue to map out their memory and identity on its space and within its boundaries. Over half a century, camp inhabitants have reappropriated the practice of 'exclusion' in their political struggle for the right to return to their homes and Homeland.

Notes

1 From an interview conducted by Paul Rabinow with Michael Foucault and translated by Christian Hubert; P. Rabinow (ed.) *The Foucault Reader*, New York, Pantheon Books, 1984, p. 252.
2 This paper is based on my PhD thesis, 'Popular memory and reconstructions of Palestinian identity, al-Baq'a refugee camp, Jordan', submitted to the Anthropology Department at the University of Toronto, 1999.
3 The idea of the Jewish state was outlined as far back as 1986 by Theordor Herzl, known as the father of Zionism, in his book *Der Judenstaat* (The Jewish State), which he wrote in German. The translated text may be viewed at http://www.us-israel.org/jsource/Zionism/herzl2.html. On this topic also see G. Shafir, 'Zionism and colonialism, a comparative approach', in I. Pappe (ed.) *The Israel Palestine Question, Rewriting Histories*, London, Routledge, 1999.
4 Human Rights Watch and UNHCR reports on camp refugees note that camps on the Thai–Burmese border and the refugee camps in West Timor have experienced ethnic cleansing. The same situation has been reported in Zaire (Rwandan army Hutu camps) and in European refugee camps.
5 R. Zetter, 'Labelling refugees: forming and transforming an identity', *Journal of Refugee Studies*, 1972, vol. 4, no. 1, p. 41.
6 L. Malkki, 'National geographic: the rooting of peoples and the territorialisation of national identity among scholars and refugees', *Cultural Anthropology*, 1992, vol. 7, pp. 24–44.
7 See this volume Chapter 1, 'Introduction', for an elaboration of this point.
8 For a detailed account on the erosion of refugee protection, see B.S. Chimni, 'Globalization, humanitarianism and the erosion of refugee protection', *Journal of Refugee Studies*, vol. 13, no. 3, pp. 243–64.
9 S. Abu-Sitte, *The Palestinian Nakba 1948*, London, The Palestine Return Centre, 1997, pp. 1–4.
10 W. Khalidi (ed.) *All That Remain: The Palestinian Villages Occupied and Depopulated by Israel in 1948*, White Plains, Institute of Palestine Studies, 1992, pp. xxxi–xxxii.
11 G. Boling, 'Palestinian refugees and the right of return: an international law analysis', *BADIL Brief Nos 1 and 8*, Bethlehem, BADIL Resource Centre for Palestinian Residency and Refugee Rights (UNHCR 2001).
12 On the role of UNRWA and large-scale economic projects see B.N. Schiff, *Refugees Unto The Third Generation: UN Aid to Palestinians*, New York, Syracuse University Press, 1995.
13 The source for the figures cited and more details on Palestinian refugees may be obtained from www.unrwa.org and www.badil.org.
14 Khalidi, *All That Remain*, p. xxxii. The village of Saris, which belongs to the district of Jerusalem, for example, became the Jewish settlement of Shoresh. Khalidi writes (p. xxxii):

> A dozen [villages] or so, though depopulated, were spared or suffered only minor damage. The rest were either totally destroyed or virtually so. They have literally been wiped off the face of the earth. The sites of their destroyed homesteads and graveyards, as well as their orchards, threshing floors, wells, livestock, and grazing grounds were all parcelled out among Jewish colonies that had been their neighbours or among new ones established afterwards on the erstwhile

village lands. The Hebrew names of these latter have replaced their Arabic predecessors, sometimes faintly and mockingly echoing them.

15 L. Takkenberg, *The Status of Palestinian Refugees in International Law*, Reeks Recht En Samenleving, 1997, pp. 145–6.
16 S. Farsoun and C. Zacharia, *Palestine and the Palestinians*, Oxford, Westview Press, 1977, pp. 146–7.
17 L. Brand, 'Palestinians and Jordanians: a crisis of identity', *Journal of Palestine Studies*, 1995, vol. xxiv, no. 4, pp. 46–72.
18 See the official website of the United Nations Relief and Works Agency (UNRWA) at http://www.un.org/unrwa/refugees/gaza.html. On the Israeli incursions refer to: http://www.palestinechronicle.com/index.php?topic=PINA&page=17
19 25 March 2002 Palestine Media Centre (PMC) http://www.palestine-pmc.com
20 http://www.un.org/unrwa/news/releases/index.html. See the following titles: Israel assault on refugee camps imposes heavy costs on UNRWA, Gaza, 21 March 2002; Director of UNRWA Operations in West Bank expresses deep concern at the use of the United Nations school in Tulkarem to detain Palestinians, Jerusalem, 9 March 2002.
21 Based on author's fieldwork in the camp in the late 1990s.
22 Some of UNRWA's installations, such as technical schools, may be found beyond camp boundaries, and many refugees who moved out of camps, especially those living in their vicinity, make use of the various services provided by the Agency whether inside or outside camps.
23 Nader, interviewed by the author in 1999, Amman.
24 Abu Basil, a refugee in his seventies, living in al-Baq'a camp in Jordan. Interviewed by the author in 1997.
25 Aida, a woman in her late thirties, interviewed in the mid 1990s by the author during fieldwork in the refugee camp.
26 Sa'eed, a man in his mid thirties when interviewed by the author in the mid 1990s. He lived with his parents in a room built on top of the original shelter with his wife and children.
27 Nadia was 18 years old when interviewed by the author in the camp in 1997.
28 The Oslo Agreement, signed between Israel and the Palestinians, and subsequent agreements to end the conflict have marginalised refugees uprooted in 1948 and living in host countries.
29 The conversation was recorded by the author during fieldwork in the camp in the late 1990s.
30 Farah, 'Popular memory'.
31 Hanan, a woman in her late teens when interviewed by the author in the camp in 1995.

13 'This is not a place for civilised people'

Isolation, enforced education and resistance among Spanish Gypsies[1]

Paloma Gay y Blasco

In the mid 1980s the local authorities in Madrid kick-started a massive campaign to solve once and for all 'the Gypsy issue' (*la cuestión Gitana*). There were at least 15,000 Gitanos (Spanish Gypsies) in the city, the majority concentrated in huge Gitano-only shanty-towns or in very deprived council accommodation built during the Francoist period. There, large families lived in poverty, crammed into *chabolas* or 'cardboard houses' without running water or electricity, precariously earning their subsistence in the informal sector of the economy or, in some much publicised cases, through drug-dealing or theft. The Gitanos had become intimately associated in the non-Gypsy popular imagination with these areas, and people and places together were being increasingly criminalised in media and governmental discourses: shanty-towns like La Celsa or El Pozo del Tío Raimundo were portrayed as urban black holes where lice-ridden children ran around naked and drug addicts went shopping for their daily doses. They were also described as massive eyesores in the modernising capital, perched on the edges of Madrid, the first view of the city that tourists arriving by road or railway confronted. These shanty-towns had to be eradicated and their population had to be dealt with, brought into line with the rest of European Spain.

In 1986 the national and regional governments teamed up with the mayor's office to do away with the shanty-towns and to assimilate their inhabitants into the dominant population. They commissioned a complete census and assessment of the shack-dwelling Gitanos of Madrid. Those who were classified as most reluctant or least able to live among and as the non-Gypsies were to be housed in special accommodation – purpose-built, isolated housing estates. Once there, they were to be subjected to intensive social work and compulsory re-education schemes. When their re-education was complete and they were ready to take their proper place in society, the official line went, some of these Gitanos would be resettled among the non-Gypsies. Others were to remain indefinitely in their *Viviendas de Tipología Especial* (Special Type Houses), because these were said to fit perfectly their economic needs and cultural idiosyncrasies. Among these were not only Gitanos particularly resistant to giving up their way of life, but also scrap dealers and fruit vendors who needed space for their produce and could not so easily be accommodated in standard high-rise blocks of flats.

Jarana – the housing estate that is the focus of this chapter – was designed as one such area of special accommodation, a Special Colony for Marginal Population (*Colonia Especial para Población Marginal*). It was built in the suburban wastelands to the south of the city, and was in effect a liminal zone in both spatial and temporal terms, physically isolated so as to provide the adequate environment to help the Gitanos out of their poverty and marginality – or, as a local social worker said to me, 'to cure them of their backwardness and childishness'. When I began my field-work in Jarana in 1992, eighty Gitano and mixed families from all over Madrid had been living there for three years. Most were very poor and earned a meagre living through the street-selling of fruit, vegetables and textiles, through scrap dealing, or by searching at the municipal rubbish dump. Many had to attend compulsory re-education classes at the local social work centre. Then, in 1995, the priorities of the local government changed, and resources were diverted away from this estate. Although the social workers have long left and the classrooms are closed, the Gitanos who were resettled in Jarana in 1989 have been living there for over ten years. There is no prospect that housing for them will be made available anywhere else. Indeed, since then new estates not unlike Jarana have cropped up throughout the southern periphery of Madrid. As recently as 2000, Gitanos were being evicted from their shacks and resettled in purpose-built, isolated housing estates. Best known among these are Valdemingómez, located next door to one of the largest rubbish dumps in Madrid; La Celsa, beside a major sewage filtering plant; and Torregrosa, on a traffic island in a confluence of superhighways.[2]

In this chapter I examine the rationale behind the construction of Special Colonies like Jarana, and what it tells us about the ways in which, in late twentieth- and early twenty-first-century Spain, the state deals with its largest indigenous ethnic minority. However, rather than taking the state as a homogeneous, unified and depersonalised category, as an anthropologist my interest lies with the indi-vidual social workers, politicians and bureaucrats that design and implement state policies, and with their perspectives and worldviews. Theirs is just one of the many standpoints on the Gitanos and their place within Spain. As elsewhere in Europe, Gypsies appear in Spanish public debate as the 'other' against which competing projects of society and nation are constituted,[3] and the teachers and social workers who implemented public policy in Jarana were careful to position themselves oppositionally *vis-à-vis* discourses that they described as openly racist and discrimi-natory. By contrast, they presented their own role as that of benevolent and patient caretakers.[4] And yet, this benevolence included full support for the notion that forceful physical isolation in what can well be described as Gitano ghettos is the best policy to solve the Gitanos' radical marginalisation by the rest of Spaniards.

The social workers, teachers and policy-makers whom I met during my field-work described the spatial isolation of the Gitanos as a tool to achieve their integration into society. As I explain at length below, the concept of *integración* appears again and again in official documents and in minutes of meetings at the Social Work Centre in Jarana, and is a key organisational metaphor in the world-views of these 'benevolent' non-Gypsies. And yet, as Samers has graphically pointed out in his analysis of 'social exclusion' and minorities in the European

Union, 'integration' involves the perpetuation as well as the novel creation of hier-archies and inequalities, because 'integrating "into something" ... implies some stable form of society where hegemonic cultures are not contested by the political, economic, social and cultural participation of "ethnic minorities" themselves'.[5] Indeed, in their attempts at sustaining the homogeneity and moral righteousness of the dominant society, the policy-makers and social workers whose views I outline below went as far as to deny the Gitanos any cultural distinctiveness at all: the Gitanos were just the poorest and most morally defective of the poor. Their integra-tion was halted because, as the social workers of Jarana told me again and again, 'they do not want to integrate'.

The temporal dimension of the notion of integration as used in Jarana is particularly significant for understanding its paradoxical intertwining with the practices of state-dictated isolation and ghettoisation. In estates like Jarana, the orthodoxy goes, isolation is realised in the present so that integration can take place in the future. And, while the foundations for integration are being laid, the sensibilities of the non-Gypsies are being spared. For another key concern of the policy-makers who designed Jarana – albeit a much less pub-licised one – was the reluctance on the part of non-Gypsies to have Gypsies living in their midst. As Sibley describes, referring to Kristeva's work, there are 'others' who are 'introjected as bad objects, that is, they enter the psyche as objects which cause unease and discomfort'.[6] Gypsies are a striking example of this. Social and spatial distancing of the kind discussed in this article and this volume more widely need to be conceptualised with the awareness of this kind of 'abject difference' in mind. The repugnance that social workers, teachers, policy-makers and other non-Gypsies feel when faced with Gypsies and their way of life is verbalised and rationalised through what Wacquant calls 'the trope of disor-ganisation': in descriptions of Jarana and its inhabitants, as in the representations of the ghetto that Wacquant analyses, we come face to face with 'a place of disorder and lack, a repository of concentrated unruliness, deviance, anomie and atomisation, replete with behaviours said to offend common precepts of morality and propriety'.[7]

But what about the perspectives of the Gitanos themselves? By considering their 'work of collective self-production'[8] I elucidate how, in the midst of these pressures, they manage to exert control over their lives and to reproduce a mean-ingful and coherently shared Gypsy identity and life-style. The title phrase of the chapter – 'This is not a place for civilised people' – provides a good starting point for this analysis. I heard it first from an elderly Gitano man who was enumerating in disgust the worst features of Jarana – its isolation, the poor quality of its materials, and the lack of basic services like public phones or bus connections. He knew well that the social workers and bureaucrats who had designed the estate and resettled him and his family shared his opinion of the neighbourhood: to them, Jarana was what a dysfunctional group not only needed but deserved, rather than a place where they themselves might live. And yet, the old man knew himself privileged for being a Gitano and was sure of his moral superiority over the non-Gypsies whose whims he had to deal with every day. In spite of having ended up in Jarana, it was he, and not the social workers and bureaucrats, who was truly civilised and who knew how to live a proper, decent, human life.

Isolation in context

Ethnographic and historical records reveal ample evidence that, even if they see themselves as different from the non-Gypsies that surround them, Gypsies throughout Europe also define themselves by connection to national territories and national populations.[9] It is also clear, however, that such self-definitions are most often contested or denied by the non-Gypsies and that European states have again and again undermined any links that Gypsies might have to the people and physical and social landscape around them – take, for example, the post-socialist Czech and Slovak reshuffling of Roma and refusal to grant them citizenship. This undermining by the dominant groups of any right the Gypsies – as Gypsies – might have to be symbolically and historically attached to the land of the state is significant for understanding both their trajectory through the early modern period – when land was redefined as national territory through narratives of history – and their present position at a time when such narratives are being rewritten.

There is strong evidence that anti-Gypsy and anti-Traveller discourses gain in strength through the growth of nationalism, when '[t]he very idea of a people conjure[s] up images of a national community with a strong territorial identity, linked to the national territory by a "blood and soil" nationalism'.[10] By the same token, control over Gypsies has repeatedly been made into an index of overall state control in totalitarian contexts – such as socialist Eastern Europe[11] or Francoist Spain[12] – or of state competence and reliability in democratic regimes – such as Britain in the 1970s[13] and Spain throughout the 1980s and 1990s. Across all these situations, isolating the Gypsies, while ensuring that their hold over the places where they are made to live remains precarious, has been a favoured and widespread strategy. Moreover, policies seemingly aimed at assimilating the Gypsies into the dominant population have simultaneously reinforced and reproduced their poverty and marginality. This has been the case in Spain where discourses on Gypsyness have, since the early fifteenth century and up to the present, revolved around two competing yet deeply intertwined drives: towards the Gypsies' assimilation, and towards their complete excision from the body of the nation. Spatial isolation has repeatedly been constructed as equally essential to both processes and has in fact often helped make them indistinguishable.

In twentieth-century Spain, control of the Gitanos by the state was enabled by the concentration of Gitano and non-Gypsy rural migrants in urban peripheries during the late post-war economic expansion, by the determination of the Francoist dictatorship to demonstrate its grip over all those who threatened it and, more recently, by the democratic consolidation of the welfare state. It was when the dictatorship's hold over the nation began to weaken in the late 1960s and early 1970s that the repression of the Gitanos by the state grew stronger and better organised: Gitanos were repeatedly forcefully removed to ever more peripheral and deprived areas, and massive raids of Gitano shanty-towns followed such events as anti-Francoist demonstrations or terrorist attacks.[14] Since the advent of democracy such punitive assaults no longer take place and, throughout the 1980s, 1990s and early 2000s, policies regarding the Gitanos have instead been justified by appeals to anti-exclusionary discourses and to the responsibilities of the welfare state towards the poorest people of the nation. And yet, under a liberal constitutional monarchy, the Gitanos have continued to be settled and resettled according to the whims of the administration, most often in out-of-sight, deprived and under-developed zones: isolation has remained at the core of the treatment they have received and are receiving more than twenty-five years after the end of the dictatorship.

Isolation 'to aid assimilation': social work discourses and the paradoxes of exclusion

Madrid has been a primary focus for the implementation of the post-dictatorship isolationist policies and for the elaboration of the social work theories that justify them. In 1986 the Consorcio para el Realojamiento de la Poblacion Marginada (Consortium for the Resettlement of the Marginal Population) was constituted through an agreement between the local and central governments, with a remit that combined rehousing programmes and social work invigilation and intervention. That year, the Consorcio carried out a census that reported 1,894 Gitano families living in shanty-towns throughout the city. Proposals were then made to resettle 684 of these – the only ones who were deemed to have a sufficiently high level of 'cultural development' – among the non-Gypsies in the kind of high-rise flats that are the norm for the working- and middle-classes throughout urban Spain. Those who failed to meet these standards – 1,210 families – were to receive permanent or temporary accommodation in purpose-built, isolated housing estates. At best, these new estates were constructed in the vicinity of peripheral low working-class neighbourhoods, in many cases in the face of widespread protests on the part of local non-Gypsy inhabitants. More often, they were built at a distance from the nearest inhabited areas, lacking access to many basic public facilities and in urban spaces previously qualified as non-inhabitable. While some of these estates were made of two-storey terraced houses, others consisted merely of *sanquis* or metal pre-fabs with minimal insulation against the scorching summers and the freezing, windy winters of Madrid. Always the resettlements were compulsory and were justified by appeals to the illegal status of the Gitanos' current housing, its infra-human quality, and its role in perpetuating their exclusion from the rest of Spanish society.[15]

Jarana is representative of these Gitano estates – the so-called Special Settlements or Poblados Especiales. It was built in stark physical isolation, one and a half kilometres away from the area of Villaverde Alto where the nearest public facilities and shops are located. To the visitor, Villaverde appears as a thriving urban environment, with blocks of flats, leafy streets, a bustling market, bars, schools and an underground station. Jarana, by contrast, consists of three rows of low, dirty-looking, cream-coloured houses sticking out of the skyline in the middle of the suburban no-man's land. There are also a handful of sickly looking trees, and a social work centre and a kindergarten guarded by heavily grilled windows and doors. Cursory inspection reveals the cheapness of the materials used to build the estate: huge cracks threaten to bring down many walls, the street lamps are broken, and potholes and missing slabs dot almost every square metre of pavement. Although by 1992 Jarana had been inhabited for three years a public telephone had been installed only a few weeks before I arrived, and it was only well into my research that one of the municipal bus lines began to stop within walking distance. Today these remain the only public facilities: the estate lacks even a post box, and mail takes much longer to reach there than the nearest houses in Villaverde.

Why spend public funds in building estates like Jarana? Paradoxically, isolation was and is today presented in social work and public policy discourses as a tool to fight the Gitanos' marginality and exclusion from the benefits of non-Gypsy society. In the words of a senior civil servant, people living in so-called *areas de infra-vivienda* (infra-housing areas) such as Gitano shanty-towns 'harbour the highest indices of typically urban pathologies and psychological imbalances'.[16] These groups, the social workers and policy-makers argue, face very real problems and need urgent help. But they cannot be resettled amid the rest of the population because of their 'idiosyncrasies'. Isabel, a social worker from Jarana, told me that most of the people of the estate would not know how to live in standard accommodation. 'Understandably', she added, their potential neighbours would not relish the prospect of having Gypsies in their midst. These stereotypes permeate official texts and internal unofficial documents relating to the resettlements, on which the likely reaction of the non-Gypsies already living in the areas selected often appears as a major concern, as does the idea that many Gitano families lack the habits of hygiene, respect for the shared public environment, disposition to pay bills, and so on, necessary to live among the non-Gypsies. These 'particularities', as the social workers call them, are therefore said to need correcting – and hence also careful monitoring – before the Gitanos are ready to move in among the non-Gypsies. Concentration in places removed from the rest of the city is designed to avoid hurting the sensibilities of the non-Gypsies as well as to facilitate the Gitanos' re-education and eventual integration into Spanish society. State-planned ghettos like Jarana then receive the official name of 'Housing for Social Integration' (*Vivienda de Integración Social*).

According to the policy-makers, the complex situation of the shack-dwelling Gitanos demands an *intervencion integral* or holistic intervention, combining improvements in health, employment, housing, schooling, social services, infrastructures, environment and so on.[17] In practice, however, state initiatives are always aimed at triggering a transformation in the Gitanos' attitudes rather than in the attitudes of the society at large. It is the Gitanos who have to be 'helped to achieve their social promotion and cultural development'[18] and who therefore have to be made the targets of intense social work. 'Holistic intervention' is thus translated into programmes for the assessment of the Gitanos' 'cultural level' and then for the re-education of the most 'maladapted'. For instance, the 1986 allocation of flats – that is, 'normal housing' (*viviendas normalizadas*) – to Gitano families, or else of houses or pre-fabs in purpose-built Gitano estates by the Consorcio, was premised on very detailed evaluations of their level of 'social promotion and cultural development' as well as of their capacity for 'adaptability' to a new environment. Detailed information was collected on each family regarding their 'habits of hygiene', their mode of earning a livelihood and income levels, how long they had been in their present accommodation and where they had lived before, their type of medical cover, whether they were likely to pay their bills, whether the children attended school and how often, whether the adults knew how to read and write, and whether there were any particular personal problems in the family – such as wife-battering or drug-addiction. It was only the families who ranked highest and who did not need ground-floor space to keep scrap metal who were allocated flats. In effect, this most often meant those families with the largest and most stable incomes, and in particular those who earned their living in the formal, rather than the informal, economy. To places like Jarana went not only scrap collectors, but also many who were simply thought not to be ready to live among the non-Gypsies. Once in Jarana, their re-education was to begin.

The Gitanos in the social work imagination

The social work carried out in isolated housing estates such as Jarana is therefore particularly thorough and, indeed, such estates are almost always designed around a social work centre. During my fieldwork in 1992 and 1993 there were six full-time social workers in Jarana: approximately one per thirty inhabitants, a disproportionately high rate by comparison to the non-Gypsy population. Moreover, participation in re-education programmes is repeatedly made into a prerequisite for Gitano access to new housing – a powerful tool in the hands of the authorities, given that the evictions that precede the resettlements are almost always compulsory. Physical isolation in housing purpose-built for Gitanos and re-education are therefore closely intertwined, and the expected combination of their effects is conveyed by phrases such as *Vivienda de Integración Social* (Housing for Social Integration) or *Programa Para el Realojamiento y Accion Social Integral* (Programme for Resettlement and Holistic Social Work), the name given to the 1986 plans for Gitano resettlement in Madrid.

The creation of ghettos like Jarana responds to a deliberate plan and a clearly articulated vision of what the Gitanos are like and how they must be treated. Like the Hungarian Rom among whom Michael Stewart worked, the Gitanos of Jarana 'were deemed by their social superiors to be too stupid and uncivilised to have a culture at all'.[19] 'These Gitanos have no culture other than their musical tradition,' Juan, a social worker, explained: 'They are indistinguishable from the most deprived and problematic of the urban poor.' 'These Gitanos,' Ernesto, a teacher for adults, added, 'are not true Gitanos. They are not nomadic, they have lost all the features that made their ancestors Gitano.' The people of Jarana, both told me, are *incultos* – a blanket term used by these non-Gypsies to imply not only lack of formal education but also of manners and know-how, as well as a basic inability to behave in a moral and civilised manner. They and their colleagues also described the Gitanos as children (*son como niños*) – and particularly difficult children at that: noisy, unruly, disruptive, hard to bend, resistant to adapt to norms and regulations. This childishness, they argued, is thoroughly institutionalised and hence essential to the Gitanos' collective character – together with their *incultura*, it is the most distinctive of their traits as a people. As Teresa, a teacher at the kindergarten, put it: 'They marry so young, they have no time to grow up before they pass on their immaturity to their offspring. As a people, they are chronically immature.'

As problematic, semi-delinquent children – 'the children of an adult society'[20] – and as a-cultural adults, the Gitanos' minds were not portrayed as blank slates but rather as slates full of indecipherable, meaningless scribble. This had to be erased and substituted by meaningful writing. Hence, the disruptive and anti-social habits of the Gitanos had to be eradicated, and they had to be taught basic skills – not just literacy and numeracy, but general hygiene, family health and respect for the public environment, as well as how to pay bills and how to deal with the bureaucracy. Any notion that the Gitanos might have their own elaborate and meaningful cleanliness rules, their own sophisticated conceptualisations of the human body, and their own rational relationship to the urban environment, was dismissed by the non-Gypsies who worked in Jarana. In the same way, they also ignored the fact that the Gitanos' particular way of dealing with the non-Gypsies and, in particular, with the representatives of the state, has emerged throughout five hundred years of persecution and marginalisation and has been functional in enabling the Gitanos to survive as a group in the midst of an aggressive non-Gypsy society.

Nonetheless, the Consorcio described its main objective in the following terms: 'to incorporate this (marginal) population into the structures of the dominant society, attempting to give them ... all the mechanisms that would favour such *integration without the loss of their idiosyncrasy as ethnic minority*'.[21] In practice, efforts were made to preserve the Gitanos' quaintness rather than their distinctiveness: the Gitanos were encouraged to develop an unobtrusive and almost decorative Gitano identity, the kind of identity that San Román has described in the following terms:

> One option is to reduce the Gitano identity to the minimum necessary cultural support, to the cultural support that is indispensable in order to symbolise an ethnic identity. Put simply, this means not to practice the Gitano culture, the Gitano social organisation, the Gitano strategies and moral codes, whilst retaining the odd Gitano trait as a symbolic support of identity. In this way, Gypsyness becomes militancy, while the cultural content, the cast-aside and forgotten culture, is enthroned as myth.[22]

Thus, guitar lessons and dance competitions were set up at the social work centre 'because of the Gitanos' natural talent for music' – and the few elderly who had lived as nomadic basket-makers were asked to set up basketry workshops, 'to pass on their knowledge to the youth'. Similarly, promises by the government to devote funds to enhancing the non-Gypsies' understanding and appreciation of the Gitano culture are invariably translated into programmes for the dissemination of Gitano music, dance and story-telling – folklore rather than culture in a holistic sense.

In fact, transforming and educating the Gitanos was seen as a mission by everyone who worked in Jarana, whether in charge of the adult education lessons or not, and every interaction between Gitanos and non-Gypsies was constructed by the latter as a potentially educational encounter. The teachers at the kindergarten, for example, were particularly concerned with the perceived inability on the part of Gitano parents to adhere to a timetable and to respect the rules of time-keeping. Hence, if a Gitano mother was late one morning delivering her child to the kindergarten, the child would in all likelihood not be accepted on the grounds that the mother had to be taught to be punctual. Or else, as I repeatedly witnessed, the child would be taken in, but at the cost to the mother of a heavy lecture on 'your [the Gitanos'] constant lateness'. Similarly, the people of Jarana had to pay a small amount as rent for their houses: although the quantity was purely nominal any Gitanos who fell behind in their payments were threatened with eviction. The purpose of the rent, as described to me by Esteban, the head of the social work unit, was not to obtain an income – any gain was offset by the administrative expenses involved – but to teach the Gitanos essential skills that would facilitate their integration into non-Gypsy society.

Social workers and teachers attempted to impart these skills at literacy classes and workshops: driving lessons for the illiterate, hairdressing for young unmarried women, plumbing for young men and so on. They also organised talks on family planning, health and education. The actual knowledge delivered and acquired at these workshops was extremely limited, and they were envisioned by the social workers as arenas where the Gitanos – a captive audience – could be provoked into questioning their values and life-style. The Gitanos themselves described the lessons as a waste of time, and said they attended only because of the financial reward that came to them in the form of the Ingreso Madrileño de Integración (Madrid Income for Integration) or IMI. This was a system set up in 1990 by the Comunidad Autónoma (Regional Government) of Madrid whereby an individual, as representative of a family, signed a contract agreeing to a series of demands and in return received a significant monthly financial package from the state. During 1991 forty-two Gitano families of Jarana received this income, and at one time or another most of the Gitanos of the neighbourhood had access to it. The recipients committed themselves to keep the children clean, send them to school daily, attend particular lessons at the social assistance centre and pay the house bills regularly. In return they received from 7,000 to 57,000 pesetas every month, depending on the number of dependants and their declared income. If they failed to fulfil any of these conditions they lost their IMI. One of the main tasks of the social workers was to monitor the Gitanos' response to the IMI and report it to the relevant authorities.

Invigilation of the Gitanos was therefore essential to the role of the social workers. As representatives of the Consorcio they monitored the payment of rent and bills and the allocation of the houses, arranged medical cover for the people of the neighbourhood, helped them in their dealings with the police and the bureaucracy of the state, and facilitated and monitored the children's attendance to the local schools – not an easy task, given the protests of non-Gypsy parents and the reluctance of the schools authorities. In their files they kept extremely detailed information on all aspects of the Gitanos' lives.

Gitano redefinitions

The Gitanos of Jarana did not differentiate between the initiatives and schemes of the social workers and the openly racist and aggressive attitudes of many non-Gypsies – such as those who demonstrate against Gitano children being admitted into non-Gypsy schools, or who refuse Gitanos entry into non-Gypsy establishments like bars or restaurants. Instead, they saw themselves as inhabiting a world of enemies. Like Gypsies throughout Europe they rejected and inverted the negative images endorsed by the members of the dominant society, and premised their identity as Gitanos on the assertion that it is they who conform to the highest ideals of morality. Throughout my time in Jarana my Gitano friends constantly reminded me of the endless deficiencies of the non-Gypsies: they neglect their children – the orphanages are full – despise their elders – the old people's homes are also full – and kill each other through terrorism and war; their women are all whores on the lookout for sex, and their men are all weaklings. Life among the non-Gypsies is meaningless, they believed, because it is not governed by the good, beautiful moral norms that make it worth living. This inversion of dominant values and stereotypes has historically been essential in enabling the Gitanos to survive as a group in the midst of an aggressive non-Gypsy society.

In the eyes of the people of Jarana, the non-Gypsies lack 'knowledge' of what is right and wrong, and this basic and overwhelming moral deficiency puts them outside the bounds of proper humanity. This turns them into a resource to be wisely and skilfully manipulated and utilised. Their very lack of 'knowledge' (*conocimiento*) of what is right and wrong makes this relatively easy – if you are a Gitano 'who knows' (*que sabe*). Even Gitano children can get the upper hand with a non-Gypsy, and demonstrating the stupidity of the social workers – and the anthropologist! – was one of their main sources of fun on rainy afternoons during my time in the neighbourhood. At the social work centre, a bunch of 6- and 7-year-olds would sneak into one of the offices and use one of the two phone lines to ring the other. Invariably, time after time, day after day, the social worker in charge would leave the task at hand to answer the phone – to the delight of the Gitano children.

Meanwhile, their parents would spend the afternoon in the classrooms, learning macramé or how to read and write. At the classes that I attended, the women of Jarana would knowingly parody every non-Gypsy stereotype of Gitano behaviour: they would be noisy, aggressive and disrespectful to the teacher; they would shout, swear, refuse to engage with the task at hand, pretend that they were more ignorant than they were, tell the most unlikely stories. Out of their performance of Gypsyness – otherwise a wasted afternoon – they would get a financial reward. Attending the lessons was really no different from scavenging at the rubbish dump, calling for scrap, selling at a market stall, or begging in the streets of Madrid – all economic activities that relied on the gullibility of non-Gypsies. If the burden of attending the classes became too heavy, or if a more lucrative way of spending the time presented itself, the Gitanas would drop out and lose their right to the IMI. In the Gitanos' eyes, the social workers and bureaucrats who had engineered their resettlement to Jarana and who had control over so many areas of their lives were just some of the many non-Gypsies who, if skilfully managed, would do or get things for the Gypsies and get nothing in return. These were pejoratively called *machacas* – 'grinders'. As Barbara, a Gitano woman in her twenties, explained: 'Ha! That's what they are here for, isn't it? Let them do things, let them give things.'

Even being 'dumped' in Jarana could be reconceptualised and invested with a new Gitano meaning. Whereas the non-Gypsy teachers and social workers portrayed shanty-towns and housing estates like Jarana as part and parcel of the essence of Gypsyness, the Gitanos themselves described it as a mere accident or coincidence. They went to great lengths strongly to downplay their ties to unrelated Gitano neighbours, and to emphasise instead their links to kin *outside* the estate. In the process, they rejected Jarana as a source of personal or shared Gitano identity. It was links to kin – which transcended the physical boundaries imposed by non-Gypsy policies – that were elaborated as the sources of individual and communal identity, as well as of practical and emotional support. Indeed, like other Gitanos throughout Spain, the people of Jarana were fragmented into *razas*: groups of patrilineally related men with their wives and children who often feud with each other and who solve conflicts through the separation in space of the parties. As I have described at length elsewhere,[23] people belonging to different patrigroups avoid contact with each other in everyday life, and make tangible the kinship-based segregation of the Gitano community through their use of space.

The estate consists of four rows of twenty terraced houses along three streets. The social workers in charge of the resettlement in 1989 decided to respect the Gitanos' wishes, and so patrilineally related men, together with their wives and children, tend to occupy adjacent houses. Patrigroups assert their exclusive control over a section of the neighbourhood by demarcating as theirs the space – pavement and open field – immediately in front of their houses. Those Gitanos who earn their living as scrap collectors, for example, place their scrap metal on the pavement outside their houses, rather than inside their yards. Many Gitanos stretch lines for hanging clothes to dry between two trees in the same space. Householders take care of or neglect the trees and ornamental bushes that are planted outside their respective doors. Many have fenced off a section of the pavement: some Gitanos park their cars there, others have planted vegetables and herbs. Every Gitano in the neighbourhood is acutely aware of which area belongs to whom. When going shopping in Villaverde, for example, or to the Evangelical church, the Gitanos avoid walking past the houses of non-kin, even if that means making long detours. Unrelated next-door neighbours taking the sun by their doorsteps on a spring afternoon will not even acknowledge each other. And, similarly, children play with their siblings and cousins, rarely with non-kin, and always in the section of the neighbourhood where their relatives live. No one takes care of the communal areas – the small plaza at the core of the estate, or the area surrounding the kindergarten and the social work centre.

By the same token, people from the same *raza* who have been resettled by the social services in different areas of Madrid and even beyond strive to visit and support each other both politically – in feuds or minor conflicts among Gitanos – and economically. Although estates like Jarana are often dominated by the strongest – most numerous – patrigroup, and come to be seen as an area under their control, for the Gitanos it is *raza* affiliation rather than residence that defines the place that a person occupies within a social, political and moral universe divided first between Gitanos and non-Gypsies, and second, among Gitano patrigroups. Indeed, after a feud patrigroups sometimes have to flee the houses that they have been allocated by the social services – something that creates serious problems for institutions like the Consorcio.

This is a way of organising political and sociable relations proper to the Gitano way of life that the people of Jarana have brought with them to the estate, and that they have managed to perpetuate in the face of the forceful concentration of multiple patrigroups. It is these political fragmentations, as well as divisions based on economic success and status, that the non-Gypsies remain ignorant about and that the Gitanos elaborate. By emphasising the divisions among the people who live in Jarana, and their allegiances to others elsewhere, the Gitanos claim for themselves sources of identity that defy the definitions of the non-Gypsies. In the eyes of the Gitanos, Gypsyness is about how you live, not about where: 'what's important is to do things well, as must be – wherever you happen to be. You can do that anywhere, even here.'

To the non-Gypsy definitions the people of Jarana thus oppose their own redefinitions, their own meaningful interpretations of reality. However, and as the account above illustrates, these are to a large extent precarious. To this day, the Gitanos' very sense of self, both as individuals and as a group, remains grounded on their marginality at the hands of the non-Gypsy majority.

Concluding thoughts

State-directed measures for managing Gypsies and Gypsy-like populations have repeatedly taken on strongly racist undertones, and have most often been analysed in relation to the emergence and consolidation of the nation-state. Elaborating on an often-stated point, MacLaughlin explains how

> anti-Gypsy racism is neither an epiphenomenal diversion from more hegemonic forms of racism, nor an inchoate expression of a more general social prejudice. In its modern phase it emerged as part of a post-Enlightenment nation-building discourse on development which sought to encourage progress while simultaneously marginalising and dealing with nomadic groups both in the colonies and in European nation-states.[24]

In this chapter I have taken this insight as my starting point: still haunted by the spectre of the Francoist dictatorship, needing to prove itself as competent, modern and deserving of the label 'European', the Spanish nation-state is in many ways not very different from the consolidating nation-states that MacLaughlin and others discuss. And yet, my aim has also been to move beyond this kind of large-scale historical analysis and to investigate the precise, day-to-day workings of the democratic Spanish state. To this end, I have concentrated on the voices, worldviews and actions of some of the individuals who make up its visible arm – in this case, the social workers, teachers, politicians and bureaucrats of Jarana. They described Jarana and other Gitano housing estates in Madrid and elsewhere in Spain as spaces for care and benign reform, perfectly suited to the Gitanos who inhabit them and built with their needs, perspectives and demands in mind. From the ethnographic account above, however, it is clear that the Housing for Social Integration is a punitive institution where a racially defined group is forcefully concentrated, removed from sight and subjected to re-education schemes that are premised on the firm belief of its moral inferiority. Moreover, by reinforcing and re-creating the Gitanos' isolation and peripherality to Spanish society, these policies also reproduce the very conditions on which the Gypsyness they want to eradicate depends in order to exist. These policies thus achieve the opposite of what their practitioners so vocally strive for: the perpetuation of a distinctive, resistant and defiant Gitano life-style rooted in the Gitanos' poverty and marginality.

Notes

1 This article is based on a year of full-time anthropological participant observation carried out during 1992 and 1993, and on subsequent yearly shorter fieldtrips. All quotes from informants in the article were obtained in the course of informal conversations while sharing the daily life of the people of the estate. At the request of my informants, and following the ethical guidelines of the American Anthropological Association and the Association of Social Anthropologists of the Commonwealth, I have used pseudonyms to refer to the inhabitants and social workers of the estate and also to refer to the estate itself. Fieldwork was supported by New Hall, Cambridge.

2 J.M.M. Terrén, 'Urbanismo marginal para marginados', *Boletín Ciudades Para un Futuro Más Sostenible*, 1998, vol. 4 (http://habitat.aq.upm.es/boletin/n4).

3 C. Clark and E. Campbell, ' "Gypsy invasion": a critical analysis of newspaper reaction to Czech and Slovak Romani asylum seekers in Britain, 1997', *Romani Studies*, 2000, vol. 5, no. 10, pp. 23–47.

4 M.L. López Varas and G.F. Pato, *Margen y Periferia: Representaciones Ideológicas de los Conflictos Urbanos entre Payos y Gitanos*, Madrid, Asociación Secretariado General Gitano, 1995.

5 M. Samers, 'Immigration, "ethnic minorities", and "social exclusion" in the European Union: a critical perspective', *Geoforum*, 1998, vol. 29, no. 2, pp. 123–44, p. 129.

6 D. Sibley, 'The problematic nature of exclusion', *Geoforum*, 1998, vol. 29, no. 2, pp. 119–21, p. 119.

7 L.J.D. Wacquant, 'Three pernicious premises in the study of the American ghetto', *International Journal of Urban and Regional Research*, 1997, vol. 21, no. 2, pp. 341–53, p. 345.

8 *Ibid.*, p. 347.

9 A. Bancroft, 'Gypsies to the camps! Exclusion and marginalisation of Roma in the Czech Republic', *Sociological Research Online*, 1999, vol. 4, no. 3, available at http://www.socresonline.org.uk/4/3/bancroft.html; C. Pasqualino, 'Naissance d'un peuple: les forgerons-chanteurs d'Andalousie', *Social Anthropology*, 1997, vol. 5, pp. 117–95.

10 J. MacLaughlin, 'The political geography of anti-traveller racism in Ireland: the politics of exclusion and the geography of closure', *Political Geography*, 1998, vol. 17, no. 4, pp. 417–35, p. 423.

11 M. Stewart, *The Time of the Gypsies*, Boulder, Co., Westview Press, 1997.

12 T. San Román, *La Diferencia Inquietant: Velles e Noves Strategies dels Gitanos*, Barcelona, Alta Fulla, 1994.

13 J. Okely, *The Traveller Gypsies*, Cambridge, Cambridge University Press, 1983.

14 EEPG (Equipo de Estudios Presencia Gitana), *Los Gitanos Ante la Ley y la Adminstración*, Madrid, Presencia Gitana, 1991, p. 25; T. San Román, 'Reflexiones sobre marginación y racismo', in T. San Román (ed.) *Entre la Marginación y el Racismo: Reflexiones Sobre la Vida de los Gitanos*, Madrid, Alianza, 1986, p. 211.

15 J.M.M. Terrén, *ibid.*

16 M.P. Muñoz, 'El acceso a la vivienda como condicionante de la exclusión social', *Comité Habitat II Hoja Informativa: Día Mundial del Habitat, Point*, 1999, vol. 1, no. 12 (http://habitat.aq.upm.es/ch/g014.html#P7).

17 *Ibid., Point*, vol. 1, no. 18.

18 Consorcio para el realojamiento de la poblacion marginada de Madrid, 'Programa de Realojamiento y Accion Social Integral', 1986 (internal document).

19 M. Stewart, *ibid.*, p. 2.

20 J.L. Anta Félez, *Dónde la Pobreza es Marginación: un Análisis entre Gitanos*, Barcelona, Editorial Humanidades, 1994, p. 90.

21 Consorcio para el Realojamiento de la Poblacion Marginada de Madrid, *ibid.*, p. 4.

22 T. San Román, *ibid.*, 1986.

23 P. Gay y Blasco, *Gypsies in Madrid: Sex, Gender and the Performance of Identity*, Oxford, Berg, 1999; P. Gay y Blasco, 'The politics of evangelism: hierarchy, masculinity and religious conversion among Gitanos', *Romani Studies*, 2000, vol. 10, no. 1, pp. 1–22.

24 J. MacLaughlin, *ibid.*, p. 418. Original emphases removed.

14 Epilogue

Carolyn Strange

Trajectories: histories and futures of isolation

What does the history of isolation have to say about the possible futures of exclusionary practices? Astronomical leaps in prison inmate counts across the Western world signal that democratic nations, particularly those with marked class stratification and low rates of citizen involvement in governance, find confinement a necessary and politically palatable strategy for dealing with criminals. The emergence of 'truth in sentencing' laws and the widening scope of mandatory imprisonment statutes have undermined the proportionality principle, consigning minor offenders to serve lengthy prison terms alongside violent criminals. The recent recourse to indeterminate sentencing of 'dangerous offenders' is also based on this justification of detention in which 'prevention' and 'punishment' become disturbingly unclear.[1] What is 'protective custody' and what is 'preventive detention'? The inseparability and the recurrent intertwining of 'prevention', 'punishment' and 'protection' reveals the historic connection between all of these state-endorsed practices in modernity, as well as between the populations rendered into 'problems'. The persistence of these connections into the present day indicates the pressing political need to analyse confinement practices with respect to one another.

As the deinstitutionalisation of mentally ill people continues, and as social welfare programmes fold under cost-cutting regimes, the prison has become the catch-all institution for the vulnerable and marginalised – perhaps a postmodern coda to the premodern 'Great Confinement'.[2] At the same time, people who have committed no criminal offence are subjected increasingly to prison-like detention. In Australia, for example, refugee claimants are incarcerated within barbed-wired detention centres run by private US-based correctional enterprises.[3] It would seem that such signs point to isolation as a literal growth industry, as many countries, abandoning the ethos of state welfarism, are contracting out their carceral means of managing the dangerous and undesirable to the lowest bidders.

Yet innovations in surveillance technology and treatment techniques have simultaneously made it possible to curtail freedom without the necessity of physical detention. The portable isolation booth for tuberculosis carriers is one example. A small plastic tent, mounted on patients' own bodies, provides a translucent protective barrier between the diseased and the healthy. Like the tent, the electronic bracelet for non-institutionalised offenders controls without walls. By emitting an electronic signal, the device transmits data on the wearer's location. Providing a kind of far-sighted panoptic eye, the bracelets allow unseen observers to track wearers' compliance with sentencing provisions or probation orders. As ageing nineteenth-century prisons, asylums and hospitals become more costly to operate, and as governments balk at ballooning social welfare budgets, technological and pharmacological alternatives to spatial isolation are becoming strategies of choice.

At the same time, public space is scrutinised to an unprecedented degree, as closed-circuit cameras, linked to a myriad of monitoring stations, gather data on passers-by.[4] Through these new technologies public space is fractured into a jumble of criss-crossing no-go zones.[5] The contested boundaries of Indian reservations remain, but they have been joined more recently by other invisible boundaries that are policed to restrict the free movement of 'suspicious' people.[6] Now it is the rich, secluded behind the perimeters of their 'gated communities', who erect walls of their own making to create exclusionary pockets of privilege. As a recent advertisement for an expensive condominium complex proudly purrs, 'so inclusive ... so exclusive'.

Our imaginations are anchored in our historical experiences, and we are consequently prone to project in terms of what has passed. The essays in this collection cover the types of institutions and exclusionary practices that characterised the nineteenth and twentieth centuries. But there is mounting evidence that a new political and cultural era is developing, influenced by the thawing of the Cold War, the rise of globalism and the imperatives of the 'risk' society. Just as modern forms and rationales of confinement differed from premodern techniques of exclusion, so future modes and justifications of exclusion may change in ways that are difficult to imagine at the beginning of the twenty-first century.[7] Optimists predict that 'the less necessary confinement becomes from a purely technical point of view (that is, without loss of effectiveness), the more we seem to be ready to define its use as an offence to human dignity'.[8] Troublingly, this projection may prove to be wishful thinking. As Pratt has written:

> If we are now prepared to ignore the political and cultural stigma that these powers bear as a result of their ancestry in Nazi Germany and Soviet Russia, then we are also able to live with the consequences of so doing: massive increases in the prison populations.[9]

Our historical imagination has clearly inspired the recrudescence of antiquated penal practices, such as chain gangs and publicly witnessed executions, as well as the re-emergence of detention of the infected.[10] Given the plasticity of rationales for exclusion, and considering the trans-historical tendency of Western and colonial cultures to exclude deviant individuals and denigrated peoples by force, it is difficult to imagine that isolation will become a thing of the past.

Notes

1 M. Brown and J. Pratt (eds) *Dangerous Offenders: Punishment and Social Order*, London, Routledge, 2001.

2 N. Christie, *Crime Control as Industry: Towards GULAGS, Western Style*, London, Routledge, 2001; L. Snider, 'Understanding the second great confinement', *Queen's Quarterly*, 1998, vol. 105, no. 1, pp. 29–46.

3 A. Bashford and C. Strange, 'Asylum-seekers and national histories of detention', *Australian Journal of Politics and History*, 2002, vol. 48, no. 4, pp. 509–27.

4 W.G. Staples, *Everyday Surveillance: Vigilance and Visibility in Postmodern Life*, Lanham, Ma., Rowman and Littlefield, 2000.

5 T.P.R. Caldeira, *City of Walls: Crime, Segregation, and Citizenship in São Paulo*, Berkeley, University of California Press, 2000.

6 M. Cross and M. Keith (eds) *Racism, the City and the State*, New York, Routledge, 1993.

7 R. Bergalli and C. Sumner (eds) *Social Control and Political Order: European Perspectives at the End of the Century*, London, Sage, 1997.

8 S. Scheerer, 'Beyond confinement? Notes on the history and possible future of solitary confinement in Germany', in N. Frinzsch and R. Jütte (eds) *Institutions of Confinement: Hospitals, Asylums, and Prisons in Western Europe and North America*, Cambridge, Cambridge University Press, 1996, pp. 349–61, 361.

9 J. Pratt, 'Dangerousness and modern society', in M. Brown and J. Pratt (eds) *Dangerous Offenders: Punishment and Social Order*, London, Routledge, 2001, p. 47. See also W.A. Gamson, 'Hiroshima, the Holocaust and the politics of exclusion', *American Sociological Review*, 1995, vol. 60, no. 1, pp. 1–20.

10 J. Pratt, 'The return of the Wheelbarrow Men; or the arrival of postmodern penality?' *British Journal of Criminology*, 2000, vol. 40, pp. 127–45; R. Coker, *From Chaos to Coercion: Detention and the Control of Tuberculosis*, New York, St Martin's Press, 2000.

Index

Aboriginal peoples: British Columbia
176–8, 187; confinement on legally
mandated reserves 173–4, 177;
dispossession of in Australia 89; part-
recognition of land title in Canada 179,
see also Songhees
Aborigines Protection Act (1897) 90
Aden: convict settlement 40
adultery: and divorce in Argentina 120,
122, 124
Africa 104, 155; colonial hospitals 89;
colonial outposts of containment 5;
early maps 156; high incidence of
stigmatised disease 108, 109, *see also*
North Africa; Rwanda; South Africa
African National Congress (ANC) 154
African-Americans: and hip-hop 11, 61
Afrikaners 166; Great Trek 168–9
Aggarwal, S.N. 48–9, 51
AIDS *see* HIV/AIDS
Alberdi, Juan Bautista *see* Bautista Alberdi,
Juan
alcoholics 144
Alipur Jail, Calcutta 43, 44
American revolution 3
Americans: and hip-hop 61, *see also* United
States of America
Andaman Islands: British transportation of
Indian convicts to 14, 40–1, 44–5,
47–50; location over 'black water' 10,
40; nationalist discourses 47, 49; and
the post-colonial gaze 50–1; as
symbolic of anti-colonialist struggle 40,
50, *see also* Cellular Jail, Port Blair
Anderson, Clare 10
Anderson, Warwick 104, 114–15
anthropology and anthropologists:
approaches to isolation and exclusion 1;
ideas on subjectivities 12, 14; mapping

of people's histories 46; nineteenth-
century interest in Andaman Islands 44
anti-capitalism: dead prez 64
anti-colonialism: story-telling 46; symbolic
space of Andaman Islands 40, 47, 50
anti-exclusionary discourses: and policies
towards Gitanos 212
anti-Semitism 193
apartheid: key role of Robben Island 10, 15,
153–4, 155, 167–8, 168, 169, *see also* Jim
Crow laws
Arabs: governments' views on refugee
camps 192, 205; of Palestine 191
architecture: Australian peculiarities 140;
colonial asylums 92–4; early nineteenth-
century prisons 24–30, 31, 32–3; early
twentieth-century penal institutions
33–4; and isolation 2, 10, 16; postwar
prisons 35–6; and spaces 57
Argentina: houses of deposit 9, 119–30
armed forces: homosexuality 78–9, *see also*
military
Armley Prison, Leeds 31, 36
Asia: colonial outposts for problem
populations 5; high incidence of
stigmatised disease 108, 109
Asian-Americans: and hip-hop 61
asylum: as term 191; violation of 195
asylum seekers: UN's shifting policies 192
asylums 2, 8, 41; architecture and location
11, 89, 92–4; in British India 89–90,
101; and change to therapeutic
rationale 7; and fears of contagion of
madness 12; identities of the
'dangerous' 13; increasing cost of 223;
as institution of isolation 89, 90, 92, 94,
98–101; management of colonial
institutions 89, 94–8; in modern period
4; as refuge and gaol 16; Robben Island